fb

a soul's journey

scott wells

This is a work of fiction. Names, characters, businesses, places, events and incidents are either the products of the author's imagination or used in a fictitious manner. Any resemblance to actual persons, living or dead, or actual events is purely coincidental.

Printed in the United States of America

First Printing, 2017

ISBN 978-0-692-97830-6

Book cover design and layout by, Ellie Bockert Augsburger of Creative Digital Studios. www.CreativeDigitalStudios.com

Cover design features:
Team: © Kimberly Reinick / Adobe Stock
American Football Field: © Danny Hooks / Adobe Stock

Special thanks to:

Guy and Sharon, my wonderful editors at PaperTrue

Ellie Augsburger, my amazing graphic designer
at Creative Digital Studios

My friends and family for their encouragement and support

PARENTAL ADVISORY

THIS BOOK CONTAINS GRAPHIC SEXUAL CONTENT INVOLVING ADOLESCENT BOYS: BOTH AMONGST EACH OTHER AND WITH ADULT WOMEN

chapter one

Today marked the fourth day of summer football camp for us boys at Putnam Middle School, home of the Panthers. Football was such a celebrated sport in our town that it drew a ginormous amount of seventh and eighth grade Putnam students, myself included, to the intense four-week training program - almost a hundred of us this year. Those who showed up got for themselves a real advantage at the tryouts in the fall. In fact, if a kid hadn't been to camp, he'd have a hard time securing a precious A-Team spot, especially if he was just a seventh grader, like myself.

We were all eating lunch in the cafeteria, cooling down after having spent the morning running drills in the hot sun. Most of the kids ate with their own sub-team, a group of about twenty-five boys led by a team captain. These captains were always star eighth grade players who had been chosen the previous season by the coaches.

As is the tradition, on the second day of camp, the captains chose two boys as squad leaders of about twelve kids; they were almost always the two best eighth graders. Although, in my case, our captain had chosen a seventh grader, my blond-haired twelve-year-old friend, Jack Murphy, aka The Shield. Even though he wasn't the most powerful defensive player around, Jack could

somehow manage to stop even the strongest kid, whether on offense or defense.

A loud blare from the speaker signaled the end of our half-hour break. It wasn't enough time to dry off our sweat, but it was certainly more than enough to fill the cafeteria with its stench – all hundred boys' worth of stench.

"Let's get going, Warriors," Jack hollered. He thought taking the team name, something our captain had come up with, built team spirit. Jack and fullback Travis Bower, the other squad leader, were in charge while our team captain met the coaches.

"Hit the restroom first if you need to," Jack said, almost as an announcement, "We'll meet out on our field." He stood up from his seat and stretched, his chest and biceps bulging. Since we weren't scheduled to practice in full gear until tomorrow, many of us spent the day bare-chested, with our practice tees either dangling from our shoulders or lying in our laps while we ate.

Jack swung his gray practice shirt over his shoulder, and the rest of us stood up and followed suit. Most of our squad headed outside, with the remaining few of us, including Jack and myself, using the restroom. On our way out, we ran into a few boys from the Jets sub-team, including Ty Green, a seventh grade safety and probably my best friend. He had a small nose with a scar running down its right side, a deep gash that he had gotten from a hard hit in a match last year. As usual, he had his brown hair cut to a near buzz. Dirt covered his body.

"Gonna pound you into the ground at today's scrimmage, Scott," jeered Ty, all the onions from lunch reeking out of his mouth. Today marked the first scrimmage that we were to have, after three days of just practicing drills.

"Hey, easy there onion-breath, we don't even know if our teams will be paired up together," I bit back, waving my hand over my mouth. A few of the boys grinned.

Ty took a quick sniff of my armpit, fanning it with one hand and pinching his nose with the other. "Oh, we will, B.O. Boy," Ty quipped back. A few boys let out some "oohs" at Ty's comeback.

"He got ya there, Scott," chuckled Ryder Banks, a freckled, red-haired tight end on my squad. When this eighth grader opened his mouth, the small gaps between his front teeth became really noticeable, as did his northern accent. Ty wasn't smelling any better, neither was Ryder, or any of the other boys for that matter.

"Like any of *you* guys can talk," I said. "Besides," I continued, smelling my own armpit and noticing the strong odor, "I smell like a real boy, Ty."

I found another kid on our squad, Austin Miller, a seventh grade center, smelling his armpit as well. "Yeah, me too," he pointed out.

From around the corner, a group of girls from the volleyball team passed by us. "Boys are *so* gross," cringed one to her clique.

"And they *all* smell bad," said another, flinching as she looked at our group. I recognized her from last year, sixth grade – Stephanie Williams. We had a few classes together. She had gotten taller in the last few months, and chest'ed nicely, too. Her light, auburn hair was still stopped at the shoulders, just where it was at before summer, and I noticed for the first time how her small nose looked almost exactly like Ty's. Her cringe dissolved as she glanced at me.

She then looked at her friends and continued, "My brother comes home from football practice and usually doesn't even shower... He's so gross!"

"Ew!" recoiled two of the other girls.

3

Another girl, this one tall and thin, and one I didn't know, shrugged. "I think your brother is kind of cute."

She had long, brown hair, with fringes that almost touched the frames of her glasses.

"Ew!" Stephanie repeated, looking at her. "And I hate to tell you this, Jean, but he's only interested in football. I don't think he's ever even talked to a girl except me."

Jack motioned for us to get going, but I refused to pass up this chance to talk to them – I probably wasn't going to see another girl I knew for weeks.

"Hey, Stephanie," I called out, making her and a few others stop.

When they turned around, I continued, "Who's your brother?"

"Calvin" she answered.

"Calvin Williams?" Ty asked, snapping his fingers in recognition.

The girl nodded.

"And you're Stephanie, his little sister," Ty said, looking as though he had just solved a puzzle.

I raised my eyebrows in disbelief. Calvin had small, almost slanted green eyes with long eyebrows and short, messy black hair; not to mention an even smaller nose than Ty's. He also had a dark, big triangle-shaped birthmark on the bottom-left side of his cheek, which distinguished him amongst the team. With the exception of the same eyebrows, he and his sister couldn't look any more different.

"Little? Umm... Only by *one* year. You know him?"

All of us boys nodded.

"Yeah, we all do," Ryder was the one to respond. "He's one of our team captains now."

"That's what he told us last year," Stephanie replied, brushing away a lock of hair from her eyes, "That his coach had chosen him."

"And he automatically makes the A-Team," Ty added, the hint of jealousy clear in his voice.

Ryder picked up on Ty's envy. "He's earned it, Ty. He's probably our best player."

Ty grunted, but it was Jack who actually voiced his disdain, "Yeah, whatever."

"Going by what I've seen so far, you aren't so bad yourself, Jack," said Ryder, turning now to our squad leader, "but Calvin's got a whole year on you."

Jack folded his arms. "I wasn't thinking about *me*," he grumbled. He was probably talking about our team captain – Billy Thompson, the boy he looked up to the most.

"So, do you have a birthmark as well, Stephanie?" I asked.

Stephanie squinted, "Birthmark?"

I told her how her brother's stood out.

"Oh. No, that's uniquely my brother's."

Then, she pointed at my bare chest. "Anyway, why are you boys practicing without shirts on? Where's your equipment?"

"We don't start with full pads until tomorrow," I explained, rubbing a bruise on my arm, "Didn't your brother tell you that?"

She shook her head. "No. I figured he left his equipment here at school. He can be so forgetful. So, you guys are running around in just shorts and shoes?"

"Well, until our scrimmage starts later," I replied. "It's cooler without a shirt."

Jaden Ludge, another friend of mine and a fellow seventh grade squad member, flexed his muscles, jumping at the

opportunity to show off. "So," he asked, "Like what you see?" That made us boys laugh, but his boldness impressed me.

Jean pointed at Jack and said, "His muscles got yours beat by a long shot."

"Hey!" Jaden exclaimed, grinding his teeth, while Jack blushed and rubbed the back of his neck. The rest of us burst out laughing at Jaden.

Jaden folded his arms and frowned at us, then looked over at Jean.

"What are you girls doing here anyway?" he asked.

"It's volleyball camp, Jaden," Jean replied, shaking her head in annoyance. "You boys don't own this school, y'know."

"We football players certainly do," Ryder replied, pointing at all of us.

"That's right," Ty affirmed, making Jean roll her eyes.

"Calvin certainly acts like he does," Stephanie began, "and all the adults that run this school seem to agree. The boys get four weeks of football, but we're stuck with just a week of only half a day of camp for volleyball. Plus, they get catered meals."

"That is *so* not fair!" replied another girl. The smallest among her friends, she wore glasses like Jean, except that they were thicker. She had a nice face, though, and freckles to go with them. I think her name was Tina Pinchin. I had seen her several times the previous year, carrying an oboe to school.

Jean pushed her glasses up to the bridge of her nose and said, "Maybe we should just join the football team and show these boys a thing or two, yes girls?"

"Ew, gross!" squirmed Stephanie, her face scrunched at the other girl.

"Football's for boys only!" Jaden declared, fisting his hands, and shaking them vigorously near his chest. The rest of us football players nodded.

"Yeah, football's a boys' sport," I said.

"A manly sport," added Ty.

"Wow, you guys sure get threatened easily," Jean chuckled, shaking her head. I couldn't understand what she meant by that.

Stephanie asked, "What girl would really want to be around all you sweaty, stinky boys?"

"Not anyone I know of," replied Tina. "Jean just want to be close to Calvin, and that's about it."

"Ew!" Stephanie scrunched her face again.

"I do not, Tina!" Jean exclaimed, "I was only kidding!"

"Uh-huh," Tina replied, her voice dripping with sarcasm. Then, she glared at Stephanie. "And don't 'ew' at me! Even *you* like *that* smelly boy!" she said, pointing at me all of a sudden.

My face flushed so fast that I had to I turn my head away. All the other boys ooed and burst out laughing, this time at my expense.

"Jean!" Stephanie shouted, turning away from my direction.

"Scott," Jean said, and I looked at her, "She really does."

It was difficult to not break into a stupid grin. Stephanie told Jean to shut up and stormed off, the other girls cackling as they followed her. When they were a few more yards away, Stephanie gave a quick glance in my direction. I winked back, folding my arms to make my biceps bulge. She then turned her head back, but before that, I could have sworn I saw a smile on her face, a faint one, but a smile nonetheless.

"Oooo..." Jaden began in a sing-song voice, "Scottie's got a hottie!" The other boys chorused along with him. I felt my face turn warm.

7

Ty slapped my back, saying, "Football players get all the girls, man!"

Jack pointed toward a boy on our field; he was waving frantically at us and yelling through his cupped hands. It was our team captain, Billy Thompson, Jack's idol. Billy was a muscular eighth grade linebacker with a great tan. I had heard that he'd moved here from the West Coast last fall, missing training camp, but he impressed the coaches enough at the tryouts to be immediately put on the A-Team. The talent Billy displayed on the field was enough for Jack, and most of us sixth grade players, to watch all the A games last year. Jack studied every move Billy made and practiced them at our youth games.

"Billy's gonna blow a gasket if we don't hurry," Jack said as Billy's waving grew more frantic.

"Who cares?" spat Ryder. His sudden bad attitude toward our team captain caught me by surprise.

Jack ignored him, "Let's get going."

Ty's squad split from ours. We headed toward our team's spot on the field, where Billy was waiting, arms crossed and eyes narrowed, as we approached. Billy charged at us, yelling at Jack in his prepubescent voice, "You're supposed to be in charge of your squad, Murphy! You're *late*! You'd rather talk with a bunch of girls than play football?"

Jack's face fell at being yelled at by his hero, but he stood eye to eye with Billy as he answered confidently, "No."

"Doesn't look like it yet to me. I want your entire squad to get down and give me thirty!"

Having played pee-wee and youth football for years, most of us were used to being yelled at, treated, and punished like soldiers. It was all part of being a disciplined football player; at least that's how the coaches saw it.

8

All the kids on our squad, except for Ryder, got down on the ground and began doing pushups.

"Don't make me regret making you squad leader, Murphy!" Billy snapped.

"Jesus, Billy!" came Ryder's voice, "This isn't the fucking army, man!"

I heard a few boys growl and mutter, "Shut the fuck up, Ryder."

The other boys were actually right in scowling at Ryder. What was Ryder's problem anyway? He should have known better than that – especially as a kid who had come to this camp the previous year. A team captain had the authority to deal out punishments for misbehavior; as did squad leaders.

I looked up at Billy, his mouth and eyes wide open in disbelief; but before he could say anything, Jack sprung up and got into Ryder's face, almost spitting as he yelled, "When you're finished with those pushups, Ryder, you can run ten laps around our field!"

Ryder's eyes widened. Billy folded his arms and closed his mouth, glaring at the disobedient kid.

"Unless you don't want to play in the scrimmage today..." Jack threatened.

Ryder opened his mouth to draw in a breath, all set to protest. His mouth, however, closed shut once Jack inched closer.

"You got something to say to me?" he snarled, pointing a finger right in Ryder's face. Ryder squinted his eyes at Jack, huffed for a second, then shook his head. Our squad leader pointed to the ground, "Then do your fucking pushups like a man."

Ryder got down on all fours. The rest of us, including Jack, finished our punishment, while Billy watched on. I did feel a pinch of guilt in the pit of my stomach for getting the other squad members in trouble; but talking to the girls sure made the pushups

worth it. Besides, with the rest of our summer to be spent on the gridiron, what were the chances we'd see them again until school started? Of course, I wasn't going to explain this rationale out loud – that would land me right next to Ryder on his laps.

When he finished, Jack thumbed Ryder over to the side of the field; he took off without a word.

"Us Warriors wear red, Murphy," Billy said, his anger seemingly subsided. Jack's additional punishment for Ryder had probably calmed him down. He continued, "After warmups, grab the red scrimmage vests and meet at the high school field. We're up against Holden's Jets."

Jack nodded. It hit me right then. We actually *were* going to play against Ty. I glanced over at the other side of our field, trying to spot his squad. As I scanned the field, I saw him and a few others running laps around the field, a good distance ahead of Ryder. It looked like they had angered Mason Holden, their captain, by turning up late as well.

Billy looked at Jack and cracked a smile, "Let's get going, Murphy... and beat the pants off Holden's team."

"Sure," grinned Jack.

Since the camp was split into four teams, we had two scrimmages going at once, at our school field and the other at the nearby high school.

For scrimmages without pads, tackles were two-hand touches. Most guys, which included me when I played defense, ended up using more of a push than a touch.

We lined up on the field, eyeing the guys on the other team and cracking our knuckles, while they responded in kind. Even though this was just a scrimmage without pads, I could feel the excitement and crackling energy amongst us. Billy took on his authoritative stance, sending a few eighth graders to play running backs for the

first half. I assumed my position as the backup linebacker with Jack. I put my hands on my thighs and got ready for the whistle. Once it blew, we darted forward like bullets.

After some running and huffing, I realized quick enough, I didn't have much to do on defense – Billy and The Shield barreled through the line almost at every play. Ryder too was sent in as a tight end; boy did his mood take an upswing when he started kicking dirt.

In the second half, I finally got to play halfback, my main position, and Ty wasted no time in covering me. I caught a few passes and managed to evade Ty not once, but twice, even making a twenty-yard gain. The second time, though, Mason tackled me, knocking me off my feet. Ty then got me three times in a row, but unfortunately for him – not to mention his team – he was called for a pass interference on the last one. It led us right into the winning touchdown on the next play. Poor Ty got an earful from Mason.

After the game, most of us took off our scrimmage jerseys and undershirts to cool off, then guzzled down Gatorades.

Billy slapped me on the shoulder. "Nice playing there, Weston," he said. He always called us by our last names, as if it was a custom of his. He began to wipe some sweat away from his forehead, but it didn't do him any good.

"You play a great offense... and not a bad defense either," came Billy's first ever praise of my skills.

"Thanks," I grinned. I too was dripping down from just about every pore. I, however, made no effort to wipe the sweat off. You're doomed to perspire as a football player.

Jack, who was standing next to me, finished his Gatorade, wiped his mouth, and patted me on the back.

"Told ya so, Billy," he said. Jack looked around at our team, all of us covered in dirt and drenched in sweat, "We have some really good players here."

Suddenly, I felt someone jump up on my back from behind. An aggressive cry hit my ears. "Gonna knock ya down, Scott!" came Ty's voice.

"Hey!" I shouted back, trying to retain my balance in vain. Ty was just too heavy. I decided to land on top of him, falling on my back.

"Oomph!" he cried, "Ugh! Get this stinky kid off me!" He let go, and I got up and pinned him to the ground. The other guys kept laughing.

I smirked at Ty; the strong odor from his armpits making me cough. "Talk about B.O., Ty," I said, in between dramatically exaggerated coughs. He sprang to his feet as soon as I got off him and started punching me playfully in the ribs, blocking me as I tried to return the favor.

"Since you guys won the first game, you'll be playing the Colts next, right?" Ty asked.

Billy nodded, "Williams' team, yeah."

Jack joined in, "They beat Damian Jackson's Rams twenty to zip."

"Yeah, I heard it was a slaughter," Billy added.

"I guess that means my team's playing Damian's," Ty said, wiping his face with his towel, "Calvin's team is mostly eighth graders, aren't they?"

"Sixty–forty, actually," Billy corrected, "But they're all pretty tough."

"Hey, so are we," Jack said, with me adding, "Yeah!"

This made our team captain grin. "I know," he said, "But I'm just saying – be prepared. I know Calvin... He'll push his guys really hard, especially those on defense. Plus, he was an all-star quarterback in youth football. Don't take him lightly."

We cooled down inside for about twenty minutes, eating protein bars to fill ourselves. The last scrimmage started soon after. We Warriors found out quickly just how right Billy was. On offense, we hardly made any gains and gave up two touchdowns and a field goal. Calvin's guys evaded us like pros. Even with Billy playing quarterback, our offensive line couldn't stop their defense, so we runners kept getting creamed. Then, toward the end of the first half, we finally started making some headway - until the drive stalled at about the twenty-yard line. It was now fourth down, and Billy made the bold call to fake the field goal and pass to me instead. Everything worked perfectly. The ball landed right into my hands.

I made my way past the line of scrimmage... to the fifteen... to the ten.I saw a big defensive linesman, with thick brown hair and dirt smeared all over his face, barreling toward me from the side of the field. He reached me when I got to the five-yard line, and just as I started to leap past him, he thrust his hands out, hitting me with such brute force that a loud grunt escaped me, and I hit the ground hard on my side. Stars flooded my vision, the taste of blood in my mouth. A sharp wave of pain sprang through the whole of my right side, bolting all the way up to my head, making me yelp. I heard Coach Thimbleton's whistle, and when I managed to look up at my attacker, he glared down and walked away.

I was so fucking close to a touchdown, but this asshat had to put me through that unnecessary pain, causing me to just snap. I jumped up, and with all the force I had left in my legs, I leapt at him, grabbed him hard by the waist, and threw him to the ground – my actions greeted with shocked gasps from other kids.

13

"Ack!" he shouted, as he fell smack on his face, hitting a small rock. Blood poured out of his mouth. We were now even. Fall for fall, blood for blood. The whistle blew again, but I ignored it. "Why you little *fuck!*" the boy screamed, his voice as deep as a prepubescent boy's vocal cords could afford. He snarled, leapt up, and punched me right in the face. Another spike of pain. Another loud yelp. What followed was the feeling of my consciousness trickling away quickly; my eyes shut themselves, and I collapsed to the ground, on my back. The footsteps of my teammates rushing towards me was the last thing I heard before blackness consumed me.

chapter two

With a soft groan, I slowly opened my eyes, the impact from the punch still echoing through all my facial muscles. I placed a hand to my cheek, feeling a bandage attached to it. I then realized that I was lying in a bed in the nurse's office; and for some reason, I had been stripped right down to my cupped underwear. Puzzled, I looked around, searching for my clothes. Posters of good health tips covered the wall, and the smell of antiseptic was looming heavy in the air.

"Looks like you're awake now, Scott," came a sexy, young female voice.

I turned my head, and my eyes widened as they beheld, sitting at a computer, the most beautiful woman I'd ever seen in my life, outside of girly magazines that Ty had 'acquired' from his dad's closet. In fact, she was a splitting image of a model that Ty and I had become familiar with from the silky pages of those magazines.

She must have been in her twenties, and had tanned, silky smooth skin wrapping her thin curved frame. Her petite nose helped accentuate the soft features of her face. The long brunette strands of her hair cascaded all the way down to her back. I couldn't help but notice that not much effort had been put into hiding her large breasts underneath her white nurse's outfit. In

fact, her skirt barely reached her knees, allowing a full view of her long legs.

My heart began to race.

She smiled; the deep blue of her eyes mesmerizing.

"My name is Veronica," she said. "I'm the new nurse here." Perfect name for a perfect girl. "How are you feeling?"

I began to sit up, but she placed her hand on my chest, sending a jolt of excitement through me.

"Take it easy, sweetie," she said, "Just lie down for a few more minutes."

I obeyed.

"What's the last thing you remember?"

"Some kid punching me out after a play," I grunted.

"What about after that?"

"I woke up here."

"No dreams or anything?"

I shook my head. "No, just blackness."

Then, I asked, "How'd I get here? Where're the rest of my clothes?"

Veronica pointed to the edge of my bed, where my practice tee, socks, red mesh jersey, and shorts were lying limply. My socks and shirt were still soaking in my sweat. She had also placed my muddy cleats near the foot of the bed.

"You still haven't answered my question," she said.

"I'm... I'm still in a bit of pain," I replied, rubbing my cheek.

"Not feeling dizzy at all? No nausea or ringing in your ears?"

I shook my head and downplayed the pain. "No. My face just hurts a little."

She continued to smile at me. I repeated my question, "How did I get here?"

"Two of your teammates, Jack and Billy, brought you in here... with another one, Calvin, following. They were worried about you," she continued, "I checked your pulse, then tried waking you up with smelling salts. But when that didn't work, I told your teammates to just leave you here. I said that if you didn't wake up within about half an hour, I'd call an ambulance, otherwise once you woke up I'd call them to come get you."

"So, how long was I out?"

"Twenty minutes or so," the nurse replied, her eyes fixed unflinchingly on my body, "Wow, you are such a handsome boy."

"Is the game still going on?" I asked, ignoring her opinion on my body for the moment. If it was indeed on, I wanted to get even with that other kid, whoever he was, before anything else.

Veronica shrugged, "I don't know."

"I want to go back outside," I said, sitting up, "I want to play the rest of the game."

She pressed on my chest again, letting her finger gently rub my nipple. Her touch made me lie back down and relax, except for my dick, which started to get really hard.

"Just take it easy for now. I'll call Billy to come get you, but I told him that you should take the rest of the afternoon off to heal, and then see how you feel tomorrow."

"I feel fine *now*," I insisted, "And why did you take my shirt and shorts off?"

"Well, I have a confession to make," Veronica declared, as she gently brushed her finger against one of my nipples again.

My penis started to throb.

"I like strong, dirty young boys like you," she came dangerously close to me and whispered.

My eyes widened, and my mouth dropped opened. My brain wasn't convinced that what I had heard was right. I thought being knocked out for those twenty minutes was fucking with my head.

"Especially smelly football players," she went on to say, "That's why I'm a nurse at your camp."

"Huh?" was all I could respond with. Was she really coming on to me? A twelve-year-old kid? Terribly confused, I couldn't do anything beyond staring at her.

She moved one of my arms above my head, and then squeezed my bicep. "You have such strong twelve-year-old muscles, Scott, and such strong body odor to go with it. This room smells so great with all your sweat," she said. Then, she felt the bumps of my six-pack, running her fingers over them and up by my armpits.

"Um, Nurse?" I said, my nerves making my voice crack. This couldn't really be happening, could it? She got on the bed and laid herself next to me, deeply inhaling my body as she hugged me tight. Her strong, intoxicating perfume and lavender-scented skin made me close my eyes, I wanted to savor it.

"Boys make me feel safe," she said, "Their strong, masculine scent makes me feel like a woman. That's the good thing about boys your age. They don't care how they smell, do they? Your friends smell pretty bad too."

"Um... well... not when we're playing football." I stammered, not knowing what else to say. For months, I had fantasized about meeting a woman like this, wondering what it'd be like. But for it to actually happen – wait... was I really awake?

"Am I still dreaming?" I asked, "This can't be real."

She leaned in and gave my lips a wild suck, taking one of my hands and placing it over her breasts. Instinctively, I squeezed it.

Veronica moaned. "I want you to touch me with your dirty hands, Scott."

Holy shit! She removed her top, and then slowly, her bra, giving my eyes ample time to gorge on her figure. It was the first time I was in such close proximity to a woman's breasts. No way this was really happening.

She pressed my palm against her tits, tighter this time, making it easy for me to grab them harder. She moaned again and then put my fingers in her mouth, sucking them.

"They taste like dirt," she said, "We don't have much more time, and I want you to take me."

I blinked. "T... Take you? What... what do you mean?"

"While you were still unconscious, I looked at your penis."

My eyes widened. *"What?"*

"I had to look... just to see... I didn't do anything. You don't mind that I did that, do you?"

"Um..."

"You have a cute one, with hardly any pubic hair around it. Just how I like it."

Oh my God!

"I bet it isn't as limp now as it was when you were unconscious," she said, smiling teasingly while pointing to my crotch, "Now that you're awake, I want you inside me."

What? It was all happening so fast. My head began to race with all sorts of thoughts, all of which were still trying to convince me that this wasn't real, that I had to be dreaming, since women like Veronica didn't go for young boys. Plus, I had absolutely no idea what I was supposed to do.

"Please, Scott. I need a strong boy like you right now."

She lifted her nurse uniform up and slid down her panties, and my eyes were instantly drawn to her vagina, which only had a small tuft of hair around it. Suddenly, my thoughts stopped racing. I gulped, as if to swallow all my disbelief and nervousness. Fuck it.

"Didn't I make *you* happy?" I asked, my lips curving into a grin.

"Yes... yes, you did."

"You know," I said, "some girls passed by some of us boys earlier, and they were complaining about how bad we smelled."

"Most girls are like that," Veronica replied, tracing my chest muscles, down around my six-pack, "Some women are too. But not me. A strong, young boy's body odor is something to enjoy."

"Yeah, okay..." I said, trailing off as I didn't really understand that.

"But, it's time for me to get going." She stood up and walked over to her desk. I figured that meant it was time for me to go too. So, I sat up and reached for my clothes. Veronica turned around and pointed some kind of a canister at my face.

"What is that?" I asked, "Cologne or something?"

"I'll call Billy and tell him you're fine now. You just need to rest for a few more minutes."

"I'm not in the least tired," I said.

"Sweet boy dreams, Scott," Veronica said, spraying my face with some sweet-smelling gas.

A sudden urge to pass out came over me, with that slight pleasant sensation of just drifting away that I always get right when I'm about to fall asleep. My eyelids hung heavy, and I moaned a soft 'ahh...' as I began to fall. My eyes rolled back and shut. My head crashed down on my pillow, and I was out yet again.

chapter three

"Hey! Hey! Wake up, Scott!" came Jack's voice as I regained consciousness, "I thought the nurse said he had woken up!" His voice came in so loud and his smell was so strong, that I could tell, even in my dazed state, he was right next to me. Someone then began shaking my body – it must have been him.

"Well, she said he did, but also that he was going to rest until we got here," I heard Billy reply.

When I opened my eyes, Billy said, "Look, he's waking up now."

I rubbed my face and looked around. I was still lying in bed in the nurse's office, but this time, except for my cleats, I was fully clothed.

I sat up looking for Veronica, but she was nowhere in sight – just Billy and Jack, both still covered in dirt and sweat.

"Where's Nurse Veronica?" I asked.

They exchanged a confused look. Jack asked, "Who?"

"The nurse, dummy," I replied, giving him a glare.

"Was that her name?" Jack asked Billy. Our captain shrugged.

I threw up my arms. "You know, the really hot woman who was in here when you brought me in?"

Jack looked puzzled. "Dude, there was no hot woman here. Just the old lady." I frowned. Jack started to rub my hair. "I think Jimmy knocked the sense out of you, Scott."

Oh, so that was that kid's name. I guessed that I really did dream all that with Veronica. It was, it seemed, too good to be true. Although, it certainly *felt* real. Maybe, I had had a massive wet dream or something... I'd have to check my underwear.

I placed my hand to my cheek and felt a bandage. So, at least that part was real.

"Where's the nurse?" I asked.

Billy shrugged, "Don't know. She just called me and said you were waking up, so Jack and I came to get you."

He looked over at the table near my bed and took some pills and a glass of water from there. Handing them to me, he said, "She also told me to make sure you took these pain pills."

"So how long was I out?" I asked after washing down the medicine.

Jack said, "Thirty minutes maybe?"

"So the game must still be going on!" I exclaimed.

Billy grunted, "Scott..."

I jumped out of bed to get my cleats. But as soon as I got up, the pain made me wobble.

"Oh, no you don't!" Billy snapped as he and Jack stabilized me. "The nurse said not to allow you to play until at least tomorrow... and even if she hadn't, there's no way I'd let you after what you did to Casten."

"Casten?" I asked as Jack handed me my cleats. "Is that Jimmy's last name?"

Jack nodded in affirmation.

"You sure you can walk?" Billy asked after I had put on my cleats.

"Yeah, I just have a little bit of pain," I replied, downplaying it.

He stared at me for a few seconds. "A *little* bit. Right, Mr. Macho Man. You aren't playing the rest of the day. However, that doesn't mean you can't run laps for lying to me."

I grumbled, but Jack smiled for some reason.

We started to make our way out of the building, my two teammates walking beside me to make sure that I don't start to wobble again.

"What happened after I fell?" I asked.

"Everyone rushed over to you," Jack started to explain.

"We tried waking you up while you were lying on the field, but you didn't budge," Billy joined in.

"Your eyes were rolled back in your head... like this," Jack said, as he rolled his eyes back as far as he could. He then gave me a smile.

"Yeah, Jimmy really knocked you out cold," Billy said.

I growled, shaking my fist. "He wouldn't have if he hadn't pushed me to the ground so hard before that. I'm not so easily taken down."

Jack rubbed my hair. "Yeah, you're a tough one."

I puffed out my chest, "Damn right I am."

"And you got Jimmy pretty good with that tackle," he added.

Billy shot him a disapproving look.

"Where is that asshole?" I asked, fired up suddenly.

"Calvin's making him run laps and do crab crawls until the end of practice," Billy explained.

Fitting punishment. I knew Jimmy would be a wreck after that.

"Too bad you missed the ass reaming Calvin and Coach Thimbleton gave him," Jack added.

"He deserved it," said Billy, "Coach told him that if he punched someone like that again, he'd be booted out of camp and lose any chance of making the A-Team."

"Wow," I replied, feeling better that, if nothing else, at least he'd gotten into trouble.

Jack said, "I think he nearly cried." This bit of information brought me more satisfaction.

When we passed the restrooms, I excused myself and went into a stall. I held my underwear out to detect cum spots, but I didn't see any. I rubbed my penis and sniffed my hand, but sweat was all I could smell. I thought I detected another odor, but I wasn't sure... I was definitely not sure enough to chalk up the experience as anything but a dream.

I joined my friends again, and we headed outside.

"The guys will be happy to see you," Jack said.

As we approached the field, the guys on the sidelines began to clap and cheer. Once the current play was over, the others did, too – even the boys on the other team.

My squad ran up to me, and I received a lot of pats, shoulder shakes, and hair rubs. The combined stench of their sweat hit me, and when Jaden gave me a noogie, his body odor came on strong that it nearly made me cough. It was all just another reminder of how hard they had been working out here, and how much of the game I had missed.

"How ya feeling, Scott?" Jaden asked.

"Not bad," I replied, beaming with all the positive reception that I was at the receiving end of. Ryder pressed his hand against my bandages, which made me wince in pain. "Man, Jimmy really knocked you out flat, Scott," he exclaimed.

My mood soured. "Yeah, I *know*," I said, giving him a look of disdain.

His good nature soon faded away, and he folded his arms adding, "Can't say you didn't deserve it, though."

"Excuse me?" I shouted back.

"You picked a fight with one of the biggest kids on the team... practically threw him to the ground."

I couldn't believe he was saying this, and I raised my shoulders in frustration. "Didn't you see him push *me* to the ground before *that*, Ryder?"

"We *all* saw that bullshit, Scott. But, that's the point. Coach Thimbleton had blown the whistle already. Yer supposed to let him or your team captains handle shit like that."

Billy nodded in agreement, but some of the other kids shook their heads.

"No way, man," said my squadmate Austin Miller, pumping his fist. "If you don't put a stop to that, you'll be targeted *again*." He swept away his blond fringes from his eyes and wiped his palms on his shirt.

"Then you take it out on him during a play," Billy grunted, "And you keep at him until he hopefully learns his lesson. Besides, you have your teammates to back you up."

Austin let out a sigh.

"Look," Billy continued, "football's all about letting out your aggressions, but you have to know when."

I had to keep myself from rolling my eyes at getting lectured by him. I knew that stuff already.

"Yeah, well, if it's during a real game against some other school's kids, I can tell you the refs don't always call shit like that," Austin said.

"No shit?" Ryder asked in a high-pitched, sarcastic tone. Then, he looked at Billy and said, "Who the fuck even knew?"

Austin ignored him and continued, "And the other team won't do anything about it!"

Billy poked a finger at him, "But yours *will*."

Austin and I shared a glance. He had a point that I shouldn't have overlooked. I should have also kept my mouth shut and stayed away, but I didn't; instead, I voiced my excuse for my earlier behavior.

"I was just *so* close to making a touchdown, Billy. I wanted us to score against them."

Billy shook his head from side to side rapidly, staring at me in disbelief. "How long have you been playing football, Weston?" he asked.

"Four years."

"Four years," he repeated, pressing down on his matted brown hair.

"Yeah," I said with a nod.

Billy leaned closer to me, arms folded. "And you still haven't learned that you aren't out there alone? That you aren't the only one who can score? That you'd have other opportunities later, because your teammates would work their asses off, play after play, to make sure you got them?" He pointed to the rest of our team as he asked that last question.

Billy certainly knew how to make me feel like an idiot, but I already had these morsels of wisdom he was handing out about team spirit drilled in my head from all the coaches from previous years.

"No, I know all that!" I said, looking him in the eyes now.

"You sure fooled me!" Billy snapped back, folding his arms again.

I pointed to myself, saying, "I do the same for them when I'm on defense! You've seen it!"

Billy scratched his chin and made a sharp observation, "So... then you just let Casten get the best of you."

I snarled, wanting to call him an asshole for showing me out in front of the other guys.

Billy narrowed his eyes, inching even closer to me. "You have something you want to say to me, Weston?" This guy was good at reading people – annoyingly so.

"Better take a deep breath and think it over before you do, though," he suggested.

Jack looked over at me and rubbed the back of my neck gently, a sure way to make me relax instantly. He knew it, too.

"Ah... Jack..." I whispered, letting out a sigh and closing my eyes for a moment.

"Just relax and take a breath, okay?" Jack suggested.

I closed my eyes again and took a deep breath. As I exhaled, the tension left my body, along with most of my anger. It only left me with the realization as to why I had reacted to Jimmy the way I did. I wanted to be a hero for the team – show off in front of the guys – and when Jimmy took that away from me, especially by how hard he hit me, I'd lost my chance to shine. It was as though he wasn't just tackling me, but shoving my defeat right in my face.

I didn't know if I'd be able to lose face and admit all that to Billy and my teammates. Although, when I looked back at Billy and saw that his expression had softened, I felt I could trust him.

"Yeah, I did let him get the best of me," I admitted, leaving it at that; however, I did add a sincere, "I'm sorry."

I felt the energy levels lift in the team, and Billy cracked a smile, "Good. Now you don't have to run laps to realize it." This

made many of the guys, including Jack, laugh. Ryder came and rubbed my hair, making me smile.

"Miller, you following this?" Billy asked Austin.

Austin threw his palms up, "I got it, boss."

"You seventh graders will get to know what real football is all about in middle school," our captain went on to say, "if you want to take your game further, that is." Ryder and the other senior players nodded in agreement.

"But the further you take it, the better you get, and the more fun it becomes... not to mention all the glory and respect that you get. Even as seventh graders, you'll see. It's awesome."

We walked over to the benches, where Jack sat with me. When Billy left to talk to Calvin, Jack leaned over, placed his hand on the side of his mouth, and whispered, "You know, between you and me, I would have probably tackled Jimmy to the ground as well."

"Yeah?"

He nodded, then smiled and said, "Yeah. That asshole did deserve it. Glad you learned that lesson on behalf of the rest of us, though... thanks." I gave him the finger, which made him cackle.

"Billy's a pretty good team captain, isn't he?" I asked, thinking about how he handled the situation.

"He's awesome," came Jack's reply. I began to understand why Jack admired him.

We watched the game, and the desire to just go out on the field and score some touchdowns made me battle a sharp pang of envy toward my teammates. I wondered if Jack was here with me just to make sure I didn't try to sneak in for a play. We scored, but we could never catch up. Although, we Warriors came in second amongst our four sub-teams, and that made us proud enough.

chapter four

Practice was now over for the day, so we headed back to our lockers to grab our stuff and get cleaned up. Ty's locker stood next to mine, and he was already getting changed when I came in.

"Wow, he got you good!" said Ty, cupping his palm under my chin and moving my head to scan my swelling.

"Don't touch... Ow, *Ty!*" He had pressed his fingers against my bandages.

"Still sore?" he asked.

"What the fuck do you think?" I snarled back.

"Gotcha!" he cackled.

I growled and pushed him against his locker. In retaliation, he grabbed and held me in a headlock, his odor way worse than Jaden's.

"You stink, man," I said through a cough, punching him in the ribs and kicking him in his shins enough times for him to loosen his grip. I pulled myself away from him as he yelped.

"Fucker, that hurt!" he said. I gave him a sly grin, and he put me in a headlock again. This time, the stench of his body made me cough.

"Smell my victory!" he yelled.

Boys were filing in and out of the locker rooms, laughing as they watched Ty and me rough-housing around. I could hear some of them muttering among themselves, wondering what had happened between me and Jimmy.

"I heard Calvin made Jimmy do laps until he actually threw up," I heard one of the kids say. That made me feel even better.

When Ty and I were done horsing around, we finished changing, swung our backpacks over our shoulders, and made our way out to meet Jack and Jaden by the bicycle racks.

"Hey thanks for letting me stay with you, Scott," said Ty.

He was staying at my place for the weekend while the rest of his family went on a visit to his grandparents. He had said that all he'd be doing there is tossing the football with the neighborhood kids or playing on his tablet; so, his time was much better spent at camp. At least, that's how he had spun it to his parents.

"Dude, it's gonna be fun!" I replied, giving him a fist bump, "You wouldn't want to stay at home for five days by yourself, anyway."

"My parents made it clear that there was no way there were gonna let that happen, even though I'm already twelve years old. I would've had to miss most of the first week of camp."

"Yeah, that would've sucked."

I heard my name being called, and Ty and I turned to spot Jimmy and Ryder walking out of the eighth-grade locker room together, Calvin a few steps behind them. Jimmy looked beaten to hell; his face showed all visible signs of exhaustion. Ryder had his hand on the kid's shoulder, as if to guide him. The mere act of walking appeared to be difficult for him. It certainly seemed like the rumors were true about how hard Calvin had made him run.

I stared at them for a few seconds before Jimmy said, "You gonna make me walk over to you?"

Ryder motioned to me with his other hand, and I strode over to them, my fists clenched. If Jimmy wanted to start something, I was ready. Ty followed, and Calvin leaned against the outside wall, watching us.

"Hey, man," Jimmy started, "You okay?" His calm, friendly voice surprised me. This made me relax my fists and drop my arms to my sides. I nodded.

"I got you pretty good, huh?"

I sighed in annoyance. "I wish everyone would stop saying that."

Jimmy showed me the left side of his head. A deep scratch had made its way from his ear right down the side of his neck. I winced when I saw what I had done.

"You got me pretty good as well," he said, "You're strong for a seventh grader."

"Yeah, sorry for that," I said, "You did get the best of me there though."

Jimmy held out his arm for a shake, and I took it.

"I got a bit over zealous there myself," Jimmy admitted, "But you do realize that when we're in pads, that's gonna happen... but even worse, from guys bigger than me. Can you handle that?"

"Of course, I can," I responded confidently.

He rubbed his chin. "We'll see. It's different facing your teammates in a scrimmage than it is facing giants from another team."

I let out a sigh at being lectured at again.

"I experienced that last year," I said, "I'm not a rookie."

Jimmy grinned. "Yeah, that's *exactly* what *I* said last year as well. But, I can tell you this much from my experience, the differences in middle school can be huge. I'm a lot stronger now, though – we eighth graders got your back."

Calvin looked over at me with his bright, green eyes and began, "By the way, Scott?"

"Yeah?"

I was drawn to his birthmark. It stood out; but the way it blended it with his lighter skin, it actually looked pretty cool.

"I'm having you transferred over to my team, starting tomorrow – both you and Ty."

My eyes widened. Ty and I shared an exasperated look.

"*What?*" we exclaimed in unison.

"You guys were told this on the first day – trades could happen," Calvin declared.

"Cool!" Ty responded. He was obviously having a different reaction to this news than I was. "We get to be on the same team now, Scott!"

That was true, but it'd have been better if I had just stayed with Billy, and Ty was transferred to us instead.

"Yeah," I said, looking down at the ground, "But I want to stay on Billy's team... with Jack and Jaden and Ryder."

Calvin didn't react, but Ty's face fell. "Seriously?" my friend exclaimed.

Ryder grinned. "Well, thanks, but I'm being transferred to Calvin's team too, and I love it."

Jimmy flashed a smile at that as well.

"And what about Jack and Jaden?" I asked.

Calvin shook his head. "No. Jack's one of Billy's squad leaders, and I don't know who Jaden is."

"But why am I being transferred?" I whined.

As if on cue, Billy suddenly appeared from the eighth-grade locker room and answered, "Because the coaches wanted to even out the teams and fill some gaps. I already have a few guys who can

play offense and defense the way you can, but Calvin doesn't. And those other guys are eighth graders, and they get seniority – none of them wanted to move." Sensing my disappointment, he continued, "It's actually a compliment to you and your abilities. And you know, all of us are really one team. We're all Putnam Panthers. It's not like you're being shipped off to another school or something."

My frown didn't let up, which seemed to irritate Billy. He let out a sigh. "Look, Weston," he said, "we'll all still be here. Come regular season, we'll all be playing together, and that includes your boyfriends, Jack and Jaden." Ryder burst out laughing; even Calvin cracked a small grin.

"That's really funny, Billy," I said, my flat tone betraying my words, "I'll probably have to make the A-Team for that to happen."

"Then *make* that happen," replied Calvin.

"And speaking of your boyfriends, Weston," Billy continued, looking between me at Ty, "Aren't you two supposed to meet them at the bicycle racks?"

Why was he busting my balls all of a sudden? Was he trying to show off in front of the other eighth graders?

"They're not my boyfriends."

"Tough breakup, huh?"

I decided to throw Jack under the bus. "No, Jack already has *you*, Billy. I wouldn't take that away from him."

If Jack found out what I had said, I'd just have to apologize to him, and probably even endure a noogie or two. The other eighth grade players joined our little group, encouraging Billy to continue with the teasing.

"You *couldn't* even if you tried," he corrected me, flexing his muscles and then, pointing to his dick, "No kid – boy or girl – can resist this meat. Wanna see why?" That stirred up a round of

34

laughter from most of the older players, except for Calvin, who was shaking his head. He did let out a smile, though.

"Jesus, Billy," exclaimed another kid.

Billy sure acted differently outside of football – like a regular kid. Okay, fine, if he wanted it that way, I was going to play along.

I stared at him for a second. The eighth graders, including him, with grins on their faces, waited for my response. The perfect response came to me – a quote from an R-rated teen flick that I had seen on TV a while back.

"Sure, Billy," I said, "Whip it out. Let's see that small sausage you call a dick." A roar of laughter followed from the rest of the group, especially Jimmy and Ryder, who nearly fell backward. Ty joined in, giving me a high-five. Calvin laughed this time, shaking his head again. "Home run, Scott," he praised.

Billy chuckled, but I couldn't tell if it was out of anger or if he was glad I stood up to him. "If you only knew," he said. "You've got some balls there, Weston. Unfortunately, I'm gonna have to crush them at our next scrimmage to teach you a lesson in respect."

That made me flinch. My new team captain walked over to me and patted me on the head. Then, he pointed at himself, Jimmy, and Ryder. "You gotta get past us first," he challenged Billy.

Calvin then pointed his thumb over to Ty, as my fellow seventh grader was about to open his mouth and include himself. "And Ty, too," said Calvin. I grinned.

"Piece of cake," was Billy's response.

Then, he walked over to us, his eyes locked on mine. His looming body instinctively made me edge back. Billy glanced at me for a second before ruffling my hair and asking, "You like picking fights with bigger guys, doncha?"

"You guys kinda started it," I replied, looking at Jimmy and then, back at Billy.

35

The team captain thought for a moment. "You're right. I guess I did. I'll have to end it, too," he said.

He winked at me, gripped my shoulder hard enough for me to wince, and then walked away.

Calvin now turned to Ty and me, "Welcome to middle school football, boys."

chapter five

Jack and Jaden had already taken out their bikes. Jack, the oldest of us, sat stationary on his, moving the pedals backward while Jaden sat on the ground next to his.

"What the fuck took you guys so long?" complained Jack as we went over to them.

While Ty and I were unlocking our bikes, we narrated our encounter with the eighth graders and then told them that we had been transferred to Calvin's team.

"Yeah, Billy told me after the game," nodded Jack, "He was supposed to announce that tomorrow... Jaden knows, though – slipped it to him while we were waiting for you."

"I wonder who Billy ended up with?" I asked.

"Some other seventh graders." When Ty told him about Billy's change in attitude and the insults I hurled at him, Jack began to laugh. "Wow, Scott," he exclaimed, "That was pretty ballsy."

"You think he got mad?" I asked, mounting my bike.

"Would *you* get mad if someone made fun of *your* dick?" A fleeting flash of anger flowed through me when I imagined some kid doing that. "Yeah, I guess I would," I admitted.

"But good for you," Jack said, "He deserved it... calling me your boyfriend."

"You're not my type anyway, Scott," Jaden stood up and chimed in, "Too flat-chested. And you smell like B.O."

"Keep talking, stink-boy," Jack snapped back.

The four of us headed back to my place. We were going to hang out for a few hours before Jack and Jaden went home. We rode up to the front driveway of my two-storied red brick house, standing among dozens of other similar two-storied houses. Ty lived three doors down, and Jack and Jaden lived in the same neighborhood as well, about four blocks over.

When Jaden dismounted, he let his bike fall into the flowerbeds near the porch, where my mom's precious azaleas had fully bloomed. "Don't let my mom see that," I said, pointing to the bunch of shrubs and flowers that she had planted, "All those flowers are like her children. They get more attention than I do."

Jaden moved his bike away. Then, in a poorly dubbed English accent, he delivered a quote from a British comedy that we had seen on television last year. "Even the shrubs?"

"Of course, the shrubs," I played along in an equally bad accent, "You can't forget the shrubs."

Jack cried out, "No one is to forget the shrubs!"

Finally, all four of us shouted in unison, "ALL HAIL THE SHRUBBERY!" as we headed inside.

We cackled as we kept our backpacks down near the stairs. I called out to my mom to let her know that we were home. Only silence in response, I began to move around the house, calling out to her. I spotted a note from her on the kitchen counter, twenty-five dollars and a pizza coupon lying next to it.

"Oh, sweet!" I exclaimed, reading out the note.

"What is it?" Jack shouted from the other room.

"Mom's gone for the evening. She left us money for pizza!"

All three of them shouted in glee. "I'm *starving*," I heard Ty say. Jack and Jaden concurred, and my stomach rumbled in agreement as well. I walked over to the den, where my friends were sitting idle on the carpet, leaning against the couch. We knew better than to sit on my mom's furniture after football practice.

"Get one with lots of meat," Jack suggested, leaning his head back so he could see me.

"Get them *all* with meat," Jaden corrected him, "Football players need meat."

"And breadsticks," added Ty.

"Mom says we have to have veggies on it too," I said, searching for my phone in my backpack.

My friends shrugged. "Just no mushrooms, olives, or fruit, and I'm good," came Ty's request.

"Yeah, we like the same toppings," I agreed.

"I don't care – just have meat," repeated Jaden.

After placing the order for pizza, we went upstairs to my room and played video games against each other until the doorbell rang.

"Food!" we all exclaimed in joy.

I ran downstairs, grabbed the money, and opened the door. Instead of the pizza guy, the nine-year-old kid from next door stood smiling up at me. He was dressed in his red football jersey, minus the shoulder pads, along with his white padded football pants and black cleats.

"Hey, Scott!" he called out, a gleam of joy in his bright, blue eyes. He looked clean, and his short blond hair wasn't matted down with sweat. I figured that he hadn't been to practice yet. His expression turned to worry when he noticed my injury. He pointed to the bandage on my face and asked what happened.

"Football injury," I responded. It was only half true; I did not want to admit being knocked out cold.

"Cool!" he said with a smile, pointing to a scab on his arm, "I got one, too!"

"Here's to football injuries, Max," I smiled, holding up a hand. He gave me a high-five, and I tousled his hair.

"So, Max," I asked, "Whatcha need?"

"Did you just get back from football camp?"

I nodded. "Sure did."

He leaned into the doorway, searching intently for something. "Yeah. I noticed the bikes. Jack and Ty are here too, aren't they?" His eyes widened in excitement as he asked.

"Yep."

"Can I see them? I haven't seen Jack in forever!"

"Sure," I shrugged, "You want to come in?" That was all he needed. He darted into my house, shouting out for Jack.

"Up here, Max!" Jack shouted back.

The boy raced up the stairs, skipping a few on his way. I followed him up and saw him jumping on Jack and hugging him, making Jack lose the game he was playing against Ty.

"Hey, kiddo!" said Jack, ruffling his hair, "Who's the Shield, huh?" Then, he pinned Max to the ground, tickling him and repeating the question as the boy kept giggling in glee. Max answered every time through fits of laughter, "You are! You are!" Once Jack paused, Max tried to tackle him down; Jack obliged and let the kid win.

"I sacked our quarterback twice at last week's practice!" said Max, sitting on top of Jack, his chest swelling with pride.

"That's awesome, kiddo!" came the reply, with Ty and I echoing the same ovation.

"I'm gonna be the next Shield!"

Jaden looked confused. "Who's the kid?" he asked.

"This is Max," I said, introducing him to Jaden, "He lives next door to me, and two houses down from Ty's." Max smiled at him.

"We've been his hero," Ty added, "well, more so Jack... ever since he saw our game against the Mustangs last year."

"Oh, that kid," said Jaden, picking up a controller and handing the other to Ty, "Yeah, I've heard you guys talking about him."

"Really?" Max asked, overjoyed at hearing this.

"Jaden played in that game too, Max," I informed him.

Max looked over at Jaden, but he didn't look back. Our friend seemed to be more interested in the video game than Max.

"What position do you play?" Max asked him.

"Safety, mostly," replied Jaden, not taking his eyes off the screen.

"Just like you, Ty," said Max.

"Yup," responded Ty, grinning as he knocked out Jaden's character. "Haha!" he gloated.

"Dammit!" Jaden exclaimed, throwing up his arms in disappointment.

There was another knock on the door. "Hopefully, it's the pizza this time," said Jaden, "I think I'm about to pass out from hunger."

I walked downstairs and opened the door. Again, it wasn't the pizza man but Leo Walker, Max's father, a thin, black-haired guy with a young face that made him look like he was still in his teens.

"I suppose my son wouldn't be here, would he, Scott?" he asked through a sigh. The grin on his face didn't show any worry; it was as if he knew.

"Yep," I smiled back, "He saw our bikes and ran upstairs to say hi to us."

41

Mr. Walker rolled his eyes. "He was supposed to just get the mail. He's got football practice in like fifteen minutes. We need to get going."

"Sure," I replied, motioning for him to come in.

"Thanks," he said, shaking my hand. Exactly like his son, he pointed to my bandaged bruise. "Got yourself in a fight today or something?" Unlike his son, however, he could tell a fight when he saw a bruise.

"Yeah," I admitted.

"Hope the other guy looks worse," grinned Mr. Walker.

"I got him pretty good, yeah." I left it at that.

He shouted out for his son, and within a few seconds, Max bounded down the stairs, high-fiving me before heading for the doorway.

"Can I come back after practice, Dad?" he asked, "I want to hang out with Scott and his friends and play video games!"

I chuckled.

"Son, don't you have Zach coming over to spend the night?"

"Oh, yeah! We can both come! He can meet them!"

Mr. Walker and I laughed.

"Son..."

Max interrupted him and turned to me. "Zach's a safety like Ty and your other friend," he said.

"Is he on your team?" I asked.

Max nodded. "Yep. And he'd love to meet you guys!"

"He might, but that probably won't work, pal," Mr. Walker cut in, placing his hand on Max's shoulder, "These guys don't need two younger kids hanging around them tonight."

Max looked dejected; joy went out of him like a deflated balloon.

"You can see Scott and Ty another time," Mr. Walker reassured him, and I agreed.

"But, what about Jack?"

Max's dad raised an eyebrow. "Who?"

When I explained, Mr. Walker slapped a palm to his face. *"That's* the Jack you're always on about, Max?" he exclaimed, "The Shield? The greatest kid linebacker in football?"

"Who's the greatest kid linebacker in football?" Jack interrupted, appearing from the top of the stairs.

"You are!" said Max, pointing at him.

Jack puffed out his chest and thumbed himself, saying with a grin, "Damn right, I am!"

"Bullcrap!" disputed Jaden and Ty. I thought about mentioning Billy, but decided not to steal this moment from Jack.

Mr. Walker asked, still confused, "You only saw him play that one time when Scott's mom was babysitting you, right, and took you to their game? The night your mom and I had to leave town?"

"Yup!" nodded Max. His dad sighed and rolled his eyes again.

"Kids," he sighed, looking at me.

I grinned and reassured Max again, "I'm sure you'll see Jack again." The kid smiled up at Jack, and he winked back.

"Go get your helmet and shoulder pads, and get in the car," Max's dad directed, guiding his son down the front path, "Your Aunt Veronica is going to be there tonight to watch you."

Veronica? I wondered if I had heard it right. My face froze in shock.

"Yay!" Max exulted. Then, turning to me, he waved, "Later, Scott! Bye, Jack! Bye, Ty! Bye, other kid!" Max sped away, running as fast as his little legs could carry him. What had happened a few

hours back suddenly returned to the forefront of my mind. I started to scratch my head.

"He has an aunt named Veronica?" I asked Mr. Walker.

"She's my sister-in-law," replied Mr. Walker, looking back at me.

"What does she do?" I asked, praying for it not to be nursing.

"She's a nurse." My mouth dropped open. "Works with kids. Loves it."

Then, winking, he added in a hushed voice, "She's *really* hot."

"Have I met her?" I asked, my voice began to squeak.

Mr. Walker shrugged. "Possibly," he said, "She's been to our house a few times, so you've probably seen her come and go. Catch you later!"

I didn't wave back. Instead, I stood still in the doorway, trying to rationalize all this. My brain froze for a second. I thought of what could be the only rational explanation. I *had* seen her before - even though I don't remember where or when - and dreamed her up when I was unconscious. That's what it had to be. Nothing more.

A small, yellow car pulling up in front of my house shook me out of my daze. A glowing sign with the words "Pizza Place" was tied on top. I walked back inside to get the money, hardly even noticing Jack coming down the stairs and following me.

"Hey, you okay?" he asked me, his arms folded, "You just went quiet."

I passed the money to the driver as he came walking up to the front door. "Do you have the coupon?" the man asked. Jack handed it out to him. I didn't even notice that my friend had taken it. Then, Jack took hold of the food for me and said to the driver, "Sorry, my friend seems to have gone into a trance." The man shrugged and walked back to his car, and I locked the door behind me and followed Jack upstairs into my room.

chapter six

We gorged on the food, devouring it like hungry wolves. It probably took us only about ten minutes to finish just about everything off. Jaden and Ty had paused their next bout to eat. I needed something more than a video game to distract my mind, so I suggested we watch a movie.

"No," said Jack, placing his hand on my shoulder, "I want you to tell me what's going on with you."

"Nothing's going on," I responded, wriggling away from him.

Jack picked his teeth and sucked in whatever was stuck in between. Then, he started, "You wake up after Jimmy hit you asking about some nurse named Veronica who was never there, and then you go completely stiff when Max's dad mentions his sister-in-law, who also happens to be a nurse named Veronica."

"What?" asked Ty and Jaden, looking at each other puzzled. I sighed.

"It was just a dream, Jack," I said, "You said so yourself."

Jack folded his arms, his muscles bulging again. He looked at me in the eyes and said, "You never did tell Billy or me what that dream was all about."

"Does it matter?" I asked, looking away from him.

Ty pushed me with a friendly shove. "I bet you had hot sex with some chick!" he teased.

Jaden chugged down his second bottle of water, let out a loud burp, and pointed the bottle at my face. "You just looked away when Ty guessed that," he suggested, "He's right, yeah?" When I didn't respond, Jaden became even more convinced. "Come on, man," he insisted, "You can open up to us. We're your friends."

"But it was just a dream," I said.

"Tell us!" demanded Ty.

"If I do," I said, "it doesn't leave this room. *Ever.*" All three nodded in earnest promise. "I mean it!" I said, peering at them.

Jack held out his arms, his palms facing up. "We got it, buddy," he affirmed.

"Fine," I surrendered. My fellow seventh grade boys immediately huddled next to me. After drawing in a long breath, I leaned back against my bed and explained everything, starting with waking up half-naked and finding the hot nurse. I made sure to present her as closely as I could recall.

"Like those Miranda Dallas pinups," said Ty, referring to the girly mags we looked at.

"Exactly," I agreed.

"Oh, Wow."

Then, I mentioned the way she spoke to me, how she had said she loved young, strong boys our age, especially football players, and the smell of our sweat and body odor. Their mouths began to fall open; I knew their jaws would hit the floor when I got to the good part. Jack and Ty sniffed their armpits. "Well, we have that covered," said Ty. Jaden didn't budge, but he was leaning as forward as he could toward me. "Go on," he urged, nudging me.

I told them that she had kissed me on the lips, put my hand on her breast, and then confessed that she had peeked at my dick while I was still knocked out.

Jack's eyes were as wide as saucers. "Why did she do that?" he asked, surprised.

"Because she wanted to see what it looked like," I replied, "Then she told me she wanted me to fuck her." Exactly then, all three of them exploded in shock.

"Holy fucking mother of God," Jaden exclaimed, exasperated.

"What a fucking awesome dream, Scott," Jack insisted.

"So... did you really do it?" asked Ty.

I nodded. "She put my dick inside her, and we... we started to do it." Just how I'd predicted, the guys had their jaws on the ground.

"How'd it feel?" Ty asked again.

"Wonderful, man," I confessed and continued to explain it without boasting. I simply narrated it as I had experienced it.

"I felt so alive... so much a boy, connected to my manhood – my masculinity. She kept calling me her dirty boy, how much she needed me. Then, I came inside her... and she screamed." Both Ty and Jaden wiped the drool away from their mouths.

"Woah," Jack blinked, "And then you woke up?"

I shook my head. "No," I continued, "She lied down on my chest, and I held her for a while, and then, I kissed her." Jaden began to stare at me in awe.

Ty crawled closer. "And then what?" he persisted.

"She told me that I'd make a girl very happy one day... and not to worry about smelling bad as a young boy and that some women like her really like it. That part confused me, really."

"Considering what the volleyball girls said earlier, yeah, I can see that," Ty agreed.

"Then, she said she'd call Jack and Billy and took out some type of gas canister and sprayed me in the face with it. I immediately passed out."

Ty gulped and said, "Awesome."

Jack had a different opinion. "That's weird."

"Yeah," I said, "and then suddenly, I woke up to you yelling my name and pushing my shoulder, Jack."

"I wish I had dreams like yours."

"No shit," said Jaden and Ty in unison, exchanging another glance.

"That's the thing, though," I said, "It felt *so* real. You sure the real nurse was some old lady?"

"For sure, man," Jack nodded, "No hot woman in sight."

"Dude, did you smell your dick afterward to make sure?" suggested Ty.

Jack deduced, snapping his fingers, "That's why you went into the restroom on our way out."

"Yeah," I confessed.

"And?" Ty asked.

"It just smelled like me. No other scents, really."

"No wonder you freaked out," said Jack, rubbing his chin, "when Mr. Walker mentioned Max's aunt and how she looked."

"Maybe she washed you or something," Ty suggested.

"Ty, there was no hot chick there," Jack chided, frowning at him, "Stop encouraging him to think it was real."

About then, a text alert went off on my phone. Thinking it had to be my mom checking up on me, I looked at it. Surprisingly, it was from some unknown four-digit number with a hyperlink that

had the title 'veron_scott'. Without hesitation, I tapped the link, and a video popped open. It showed me waking up in the nurse's office, with Veronica sitting at the desk next to me.

"Holy shit!" I cried out at the top of my lungs, "Guys, look at this!" In an instant, all four of us had gathered around my phone, and what we saw there happened just as I remembered and described – audio included.

"She does look like Miranda Dallas!" exclaimed Ty, and then, we all went silent, our eyes glued to the screen. When it got to the part where she gassed me, I saw myself letting out a sigh and my eyes fluttering; they rolled up and shut as my body came crashing down on the pillow, my mouth slightly open and one arm extended out of the bed.

Ty gasped, and without looking away, said, "Woah. She really did gas you!"

"Yeah," I replied.

Veronica leaned over and raised my right eyelid. She looked at the pupil that had rolled back to my skull. Then, moaning and touching herself, she leaned toward my face and kissed me on the lips.

"Oh my God!" shouted out Jaden.

Jack gave me a quick glance. "Dude..." he started. I didn't know what to say.

Then, she walked over to the sink, moistened a paper towel, and slowly washed my crotch – she even used a dry one to take sweat from different parts of my body and dab over it, masking her own scent.

"See, I knew it!" exclaimed Ty.

At the end, Veronica dressed me up, sniffing my right armpit as she did and moving that arm to my side. Looking at the camera, she smiled and declared, "The best is yet to come, Scott. For you

and your fellow football players." Then, she exited the frame, leaving the camera pointed at my unconscious body for a few seconds before switching off. A message then popped up on my phone, lingering only long enough for us to read: "The footage has been deleted." This left us staring at a blank screen, mum for almost a minute.

Suddenly, Ty grabbed my phone and tried to reload the link, but the video didn't start playing again. "No, no, no!" he cried, "I need a copy of this!"

"Dude, you got fucked by a hot chick!" said Jaden to me.

Jack stared out into space, saying, "That was all *real*? But that doesn't make any sense. The nurse was an old lady. She even sounded like an old lady."

"Ooo!" Ty exclaimed, snapping his fingers in rapid succession and addressing Jack. He said, "Unless she wore a disguise... concealed her voice too – just for you and Billy – and took it off after you dropped him off."

"And no one except Scott was there when you went to pick him up, though, right?" asked Jaden.

Jack's face froze. "Woah... you're right. She wasn't there."

Jaden grabbed the last breadstick that had almost made it through the night untouched. "This is like Twilight Zone or some shit," he said, shoving the breadstick into his mouth. He didn't bother to swallow before saying, "Either way, you're one lucky son-of-a-bitch, Scott."

"Did you guys miss the part where she included the rest of our team as well?" I asked.

"Oh man, I gotta get injured," said Ty.

"So," I said, folding my arms, "Just to be clear, this isn't a dream." My friends shook their heads.

"Nope, Scott," Jaden assured me, "This is all real – fucked up, but real."

"You gonna tell your mom?" asked Ty, as he got up to use the bathroom next to my room. He kept the door open so he could hear us.

"He fucking better not," declared Jaden, picking up a controller and tossing the other one to me, "I don't want him ruining this opportunity for the rest of us."

"Yeah, me either," Ty yelled over the sound of him peeing.

I looked down at the controller, not really in the mood to play. Jack took it from me, and then, pulling down one of his sleeves, began scratching his bare armpit. I was immediately drawn to it, taking in the strong odor that it emitted.

"Well?" he asked with a grin, glancing into my eyes; his bright, blue ones showed no hint of persuasion. "Are you?"

I shook my head, "I don't think she'd ever let me go back to that school, but don't you guys say anything to anyone, either. Not even the rest of our team." I took a count on my fingers and looked between Jack and Jaden as I said, "Billy, Calvin, Austin, Ryder, or anyone. This stays between us."

Jack nodded, and Jaden grinned.

"Sure thing!" assured Jaden.

"Got it!" Ty affirmed over the sound of the flushing toilet.

We played some more till about nine o'clock, the time my mother had written that Jack and Jaden needed to go home. I felt my eyelids begin to droop; exhaustion from the day's hard workout began to affect me. Jack and Jaden both started to yawn, and Ty and I bid goodbye to them as we walked them out to the door.

My two friends mounted their bikes, and Jack said, "We're starting in full pads tomorrow, so you and Ty better be prepared for us!"

"Don't worry, " I responded through a yawn, "Us Colts will kick your Warrior asses." Ty pointed to them and nodded in agreement.

"As long it gets me a visit to the nurse's office," Jaden said before he rode off.

chapter seven

Ty and I headed back upstairs and got ready for bed. After brushing my teeth, I stripped down to my cupped underwear and hopped on the bed, folding my arms behind my head and closing my eyes.

I heard Ty take a sniff at me and say, "Man, your armpits still smell terrible." I didn't respond, and suddenly, Ty's strong odor hit me. I opened my eyes and saw him dressed down to his cupped underwear as well, smiling and lowering his armpit on my face. He had curled up his hand into a fist and bent his elbow so that his biceps bulged and exposed most of his underarm.

I began to get lost in it, thinking how awesome it looked and how strong an odor came from it – just like Jack's. My penis began to swell, but the odor was just too much. If he got it any closer, I thought, I'd pass out. He laughed as I swatted his arm away. My exhaustion dissipated as I caught my second wind. I jumped out of bed and threw the other boy to the ground, making a loud thud.

"Ow!" he exclaimed, laughing.

I raised my armpit and lowered it close to his face. He began coughing.

"Ugh!" he exclaimed, punching me in the ribs. We traded blows, trying to pin down and stick our armpits in each other's faces. I nearly passed out when Ty thrust his pit into my face; I fell to the ground, disoriented.

"Dude, stop faking!" he shouted.

"I'm not! You just stink!" I replied as I recovered, springing up, ready for round two. We went at it for a bit, before he pushed me back down and pecked me on the cheek.

"Hah!" he said, his chest moving up and down rapidly as he breathed. I stared at him in shock, my own breaths heavy as my heart was racing from the wrestling. He had never kissed me before.

I wiped off my cheek and grumbled, "Ew, why did you do that?"

Ty shrugged, sweat dripping down his face, "I dunno. I like you."

"Yeah, I like you too, Ty," I said, feeling sweaty myself, "but boys don't kiss each other."

"It ain't like I kissed you on the lips like a girl," he said, wiping his face with his arm. Then, he put his head on my chest and started tracing it like Veronica had done. It felt really good, but the energy was different with Ty, him being a boy. It was almost as if he were trying to connect with some part of me. Either way, my penis began to harden again.

"You're really strong, Scott," he said, his voice soft as he felt my muscles, "and an awesome player... and I love how you gave it to Billy today. That was some hilarious shit."

I placed my hand on Ty's brown hair, stroking it gently. "Thanks," I responded, "You're a pretty damn good player yourself."

He looked up at me with his green eyes. "I love being a football player," he said.

"Me, too."

He pointed to his biceps and then his crotch. "This is what it's all about."

I didn't get that. "What do you mean?" I asked. His breathing became stronger, and he started to trace the curves and bumps of my body all the way down to my underwear.

"I've been wanting to do this for a while," was all he uttered as I watched him, wide-eyed, pulling my underwear down, exposing my rock-hard boner. My mouth dropped open. "Ty... what... what are you..." I hesitated.

"Wow!" Ty exclaimed, raising his eyebrows, "You've got a big dick there, Scott! The cock of a real boy." He slid himself down by my legs, stationing his head at eye level with my cock. The feeling of his warm breath on it made it pulse. Then, he gently flicked it a few times, watching it bounce back like a rubber band as he made 'pew pew' noises. I lifted my head and watched in confusion. He had a dick of his own; why did he need to play with mine? For some reason, I wasn't uncomfortable, even though we had never done anything like this before. We certainly didn't have romantic feelings for each other. Although I did feel some kind of deep bond with him – I always had – but what he was doing then was bringing that bond to the forefront. If Ty wanted to play with my dick, I'd let him. It didn't seem to care, either, as it reacted to his touch, giving me a wonderful feeling.

"You really do stink, though," he declared, "Even your cock."

"Looks who's talking, Ty-yyy!" I groaned as he grabbed my dick firmly and began to stroke up and down. I closed my eyes and threw my head back on the floor. My heart started racing; an intense, incredible feeling hit me.

"Yeah, that's right," he teased, "You just shut up and lie there, B.O. Boy. I'm in control here." He massaged my nuts and moved them around. When he stopped, I opened my eyes and saw him staring at my nearly hairless crotch.

"Yeah, I want your energy too," he said, caressing my penis gently with the back of his hand. My heart started pounding again, this time in anticipation of what he might do next.

"Ty, what do you mean by my ener-" Suddenly, he put his mouth around my dick and began to suck on it.

"Aa!" I squealed, grabbing his sweaty, short, brown hair as the intense feeling returned. With the smell of our sweat combined, I felt my energy, as a boy, as a football player, being siphoned into Ty, enhancing his own. I couldn't understand why, but it felt so good... so right... that I couldn't hold out. I reached out a hand, and he grabbed it. I closed my eyes as the sucking of my dick, combined with the incredible massage his tongue was giving it, made me lose it.

"Ty-yyy..." I moaned in ecstasy as I orgasmed, shooting my load into his mouth while he swallowed it. I focused on our smell and the feeling of his body as I squeezed his scalp and tightened the grip on his hand. He squeezed back, and for a brief instant, I felt myself become one with him, combining our strength and our being. I let out moans of pure bliss, and when it finally faded, I found myself back in my own body, my heart pounding.

I hardly had any energy left to open my eyes. My arms dropped to my side, and the exhaustion now started to overwhelm me. I slurped the sweat from my lips. If I didn't make any effort to stay awake, I would've fallen asleep immediately, and it wasn't time yet. I finally summoned enough energy to open my eyes. Ty was sitting next to me, looking at me with a smile.

"Felt good, huh?" he asked.

"Fuck yeah," I replied, "I've never experienced anything like that before." That made him grin even harder.

"Even with Veronica?" he said, helping me sit up.

"No, it was different with her," I replied, "Felt great, but different. Not sure how I can explain it." Ty looked confused, maybe even disappointed that his wasn't better.

"Because she's a girl?" he asked.

"I think so."

"Well, then I gotta try that."

"What?" he asked when I stared at him with a mock glare. It was time to get *his* energy. I growled and leapt on top him, pinning him to the floor. He didn't resist.

"It's *my* turn," I declared. His face turned serious, and his breathing began to speed up. I scanned his body and moved his left arm behind his head to expose his bare armpit; the strong odor made my nose crinkle.

"Talk about B.O. Boy," I grinned, tracing his biceps down to his pit. He smirked but didn't say anything. His muscles looked as big as mine. I leaned my head down on his chest and licked his left nipple, looking at his armpit and welcoming the strong odor. That made him start moaning. I placed my ear over his heart and listened to it pound. Then, I copied what he had done – traced his body down to his underwear. I pulled it down slowly, taking my time to get a good glimpse of his hard penis; it sprang up when it was finally freed. It looked a bit smaller than mine, but I noticed a big vein running up from the base of his balls to the tip of dick. I decided to lick it, enjoying the musky scent of his cock as I did.

"Uuuuhhh... Scott..." he gurgled, extending his hand, "Not... gonna... .last..." I took the hint and grabbing his hand, put his dick in my mouth. As soon as I began sucking and licking it, Ty started moaning loud, "Ohhh... my... Goddddd." This time, I felt his energy

flow from his body into me, making me feel at one with him again. He felt my biceps and screamed, "Oh, Scott... SHIT!" as his sperm spurted out and into my mouth, almost making me gag. When he'd stopped ejaculating, he lay quiet for a moment before saying, with his eyes closed, "Scott. That... you... oh that felt so... goo..." Ty couldn't finish his sentence before passing out. I pulled up his underwear and crawled next to him on the floor. I wrapped my arm around him, gave him a hug, and fell asleep next to him.

chapter eight

My alarm went off at six-thirty with a rising loud buzzer. I opened my eyes and saw Ty sprawled out on top of me. I reached over and pushed him off.

"Get offa me!" I said. He groaned and pushed me back with his eyes still closed. "Go turn that damn thing off," he ordered. I stood up, made my way groggily over to the alarm, and smashed the off button. I stretched and yawned and rubbed my eyes.

"Scott?" I heard my mom's voice from downstairs.

"Mom?" I shouted back.

"Good, you're awake. How's Ty?" I looked down at my friend; his inert body showed no intention of moving.

"I'm about to kick him awake," I informed her. Ty opened one eye, stared at me, and snarled. "You do that, and I'll shove your face in my pit this afternoon," he threatened, "Seven hours of practice in the heat with full pads, buddy."

"Yeah, yeah, whatever," I dismissed him, reaching down to help him up. He grabbed my hand; and when I pulled him up, he nudged me hard on my shoulder. Then, headed into the bathroom and closed the door.

I put on my practice clothes from yesterday and checked my phone. No new messages. I tried the link from yesterday as well, but the video still wouldn't play again.

I needed to hit the restroom, so I used the one downstairs since Ty occupied mine. Looking in the mirror, I saw the bandage from yesterday still staring at me from my face. I ripped it off and assessed the damage – my cheek was still sore and swollen, but it didn't throb like it did yesterday.

The smell of eggs and bacon lured me into the kitchen; my mom, a tall, lean woman in her mid-thirties, was standing by the stove, making our breakfast.

She had long brown hair and had on blue jeans and a light blue checkered shirt with a collar. I walked over to her, scratching the back of my neck. She leaned down to kiss me on the cheek. That's when she saw my face.

"What happened to you?" she asked, her expression showing worry. I told her that I got into a fight at camp, but that everything was cool now.

"'Cool', huh?" she grunted, mocking my choice of words. She cupped her hand under my chin to examine it further. "I thought football was all about sportsmanship."

"Well, it is," I said, jerking my head away, "The other kid and I reached an understanding."

"Thanks to Billy Thompson," came Ty's voice as he entered the kitchen and sat down at the table.

"Who?"

"The eggs are going to burn, Mom," I said, pointing to the pan.

"Ah, shit," she exclaimed, turning to the food and scrambling the eggs around in the pan, "But don't change the subject."

I explained everything in more detail, omitting getting knocked out and the affair in the nurse's office.

"Boys," she complained, "What would your father say?"

"That I learned my lesson," I replied, "And that boys have to sometimes learn things on their own, through experience."

"We do," Ty nodded.

"Oh, good Lord," she wailed, her tone indicating annoyance, "Okay, first off, not *just* boys, Scott. Second-" She sniffed the air, smelled my neck, and crinkled her nose. Looking at my body, she rebuked, "You still have dried mud on your arms and legs, Scott. Didn't you two shower last night like I asked you to in the note?"

Oops.

"Uh, no... I sorta forgot about that," I said while Ty shrugged; he didn't know he was supposed to.

"And you're wearing the same smelly clothes as yesterday?" she groaned.

"Well, yeah, I'm just going to sweat in them again today, Mom... except I won't be wearing my shorts under my football pants." Ty nodded in agreement; the same applied to him.

She doled out a heap of eggs and bacon on three plates with a few slices of toast.

"Thank God you two aren't going to be out in general public," she said, motioning for Ty to come get his food.

"Just around other stinky boys," Ty responded with a grin as he grabbed his plate.

"I wish I had a daughter," she complained, handing me mine.

"Hey!" I said, curling my lips and furrowing my brows in a frown.

She smiled and planted a kiss on my forehead, saying, "I meant in *addition* to my wonderful, stinky son."

Ty chuckled, and I grunted an "Uh-huh."

She watched us sit down before filling a few glasses with orange juice. "I found you two sleeping on top of one another on the floor again," she let us know. Ty and I glanced at each other and then shoveled a heap of eggs in our mouths.

"We never made it to the bed," I admitted through chews.

"Fell asleep playing video games again?" she inquired.

Ty and I shared another quick glance. "Yeah," I nodded.

"Some things never change," she declared, handing us our juice, "I keep telling you that you're going to get a sore neck or a sore back sleeping on the floor like that." She took her plate and a cup of coffee and began to walk out of the kitchen. "Enjoy," she said before leaving.

"Aren't you gonna eat with us?" I asked.

"I'm not sitting close to two stinking twelve-year-old boys," she announced, not mincing her words at all.

"Yeah, yeah, I get it, Mom," I heaved a sigh. I couldn't really blame her for not wanting to be near us, but she could have at least stopped harping on me.

"She sounds like *my* mom," said Ty, shoveling more food in his mouth and drinking his juice.

"Oh, did you boys enjoy the pizza?" she asked, before disappearing into the den.

"Yes!" we shouted back; I added what I figured she wanted to hear – "Thank you, Mom!"

"Yes, thank you, Mrs. Weston!" Ty echoed.

"You're welcome. Jack and Jaden stayed back to eat and hang out, too?"

"Yup!" I said.

"Good," she replied and turned on the TV.

We gobbled down the rest of our breakfast, finishing up just as Jack and Jaden showed on their bikes to ride with us to school. We grabbed our backpacks, and I opened the door. Jack and Jaden said hello; they had on the same clothes they were wearing yesterday too.

"Later, Mom!" I shouted out, and Ty added, "Later, Mrs. Weston!"

"Aren't you forgetting something?" my mom asked, staring at me from her seat on the couch. I thought for a moment and opened my pack. "No," I replied, rummaging through it. "I have my phone, protein bars, drink bottle, mouth guard, towels, the lucky football that Dad gave me-"

"Scott..." my mom said, interrupting my inventory check-list. I looked over at her. She was tapping her cheek with a finger and making a pout. Ty sneered, and I felt a twinge of embarrassment at having to kiss my mom in front of my friends. I folded my arms and argued, "I thought you didn't want to be near a stinky boy like me?"

"Mister, quit your backtalk and give your mom a goodbye kiss," she insisted.

"Yeah, Scott, go kiss your mommy goodbye!" Ty teased, shoving me toward my mom. He looked over at my two other friends with a grin, encouraging them to pester me as well. Jack and Jaden chuckled back.

I shot Ty a glare and then walked over to my mom. I bent down, and we kissed each other on the cheek. "Have fun, be careful, and don't get into any more fights," she said.

"Don't worry, Mrs. Weston," said Ty, strapping on his backpack, "Billy or Jack, or actually Calvin, will make him run laps if he causes any more trouble."

"Calvin?" she asked.

"He's Scott's and my new team captain."

"What about the coaches? Don't they do anything?"

I rolled my eyes. "Of course, Mom. We gotta jet."

"Okay, whatever," she said, peering back at the television, "See you later tonight. You and Ty be sure to shower when you get home, especially if you want to go out to see that movie." The four of us looked at each other with excitement. Jack's dad said he'd pick us all up and take us to the mall so we could grab dinner and watch a flick.

"Sure, Mom," I replied.

"I'll leave money on the table again for you and Ty."

Ty and I said thanks, and then, the four of us hopped on our bikes and sped toward the school, Jack leading the way.

"I can't wait to put on our pads!" said Ty, riding in weaves between us.

Jaden slowed down to get beside me. "Any more messages from you-know-who?" he asked. Jack peered back.

I shook my head. "No. Nothing," I replied.

"I still might fake an injury," said Jaden.

I thought Jack might rebuke Jaden, but instead, he said, "Man, I'm tempted, too."

We made it to the school about twenty minutes early, waving to the other kids who were arriving then. We stowed away our stuff in our locker room before heading to the adjacent seventh grade boys' war room, where we junior kids met every morning with a coach before practice began. The room reminded me of those small college lecture halls I'd seen in movies. Several rows of tables spanned the back of the room, with each row split down the middle to form a walkway to the elevated coach's platform in the front. It also had a door on the side that exited into the hall.

Many other boys were already there when the four of us arrived, and more began to show up as the clock got closer to eight

o'clock. We sat near the middle, but Jack and Jaden didn't stay seated long; they huddled in a corner with some of their squad members. Ty had his head down on the desk, his eyes closed. I shook his shoulder, but he didn't react; I decided just to leave him alone and look around.

Dozens of closed cardboard boxes lined the walls at the back and front of the room, each one with a kid's name and his jersey number. A wave of anticipation washed over me, as I figured they must have contained our football equipment.

I stood up to stretch, and that's when everything went black.

chapter nine

I felt dizzy for a moment after regaining consciousness. I noticed that I was sitting in a chair, my arms around my head, and my head resting on a desk. I could hear my teammates talking. I opened my eyes and lifted my head, and I saw that I was still in the war room in the very same chair I was sitting in before I had stood up to stretch.

How had I gone from standing up and stretching to sitting down with my head on the table? Did I pass out? I must have, but as I looked around, none of my teammates even seemed to take notice. They were all talking to each other or sitting quietly; some were even reading a book. We weren't allowed to use our phones or other electronics for entertainment in here, but only for note taking. So, if I *had* passed out, *someone* would have noticed; unless, of course, if I had landed really neatly in my chair.

That's when I thought about Ty and glanced next to me. I saw that he still had his head down between his arms, and his eyes shut. Had the same thing happened to him? I shook him harder this time, calling out his name and not relenting, until he finally opened his eyes, groaning.

"What happened?" he groaned, lifting his head slowly and looking around.

"Did you pass out, too?" I asked, placing my hand on his shoulder.

Ty thought for a moment, scratching his head. "Yeah, I think so!" he said, "I was just sitting there, and then, all of a sudden, you were shaking me."

"Do you feel dizzy?"

He shook his head. "Not anymore. I did at first, though." "Wait," he continued, looking at me, "Did you fall asleep as well?"

I nodded and explained what I experienced.

"That's fucked up!" he exclaimed, which made some of the other boys glance at us, "No one noticed?"

"Nope."

"How long were we out?" he asked, rubbing his nose.

"Well, I think you passed out just moments before I did. We weren't obviously out that long, because the meeting hasn't started." I pointed to the digital clock on the wall; it read seven fifty-five.

He looked around the room and asked, "No one else passed out?"

"Doesn't look like it."

He lowered his voice and asked, "You think it has to do with what we did last night?"

"You mean between us?" I replied, matching his volume.

He nodded.

"I don't know why it would. Maybe? I feel fine now, though. You?"

"Yeah."

"Well, if it happens while we're on the field, Ty, someone will help us."

Then, I tried to lighten the mood by saying, a wise grin on my face, "Maybe we'll wake up in the nurse's office." That didn't seem to help, so I said, "Hey, don't worry too much about it, Ty. You feel fine, and so do I."

The side door squeaked opened, and I expected Coach Thimbleton to enter. Instead, Coach Sim King, Thimbleton's assistant, entered the room. His baby face and medium build made him look twenty-five or so. He had bright green eyes and brown hair cut to a buzz, almost like an army man. I had yet to talk to him, but every time I saw him, I felt instantly at ease, like I knew him well.

The other kids took their seats, with Jack mussing my and Ty's hair together as he passed us. Ty smacked Jack's arm, and I blurted out, "Hey!"

"It's on, buds," said Jack, the defensive linesman, winking at us before sitting down next to me.

"Gonna kick yer butts," echoed Jaden, dropping himself down next to Jack.

"Bring it on, ladies," I hissed back. Jack nudged me in the shoulder. I winced and shoved him back harder, making him yelp. Then, he grabbed my shirt by my neck and pulled me next to him.

"You really wanna mess with me?" he jeered, giving me his best war face. The strong smell of dirt evidently meant that he hadn't showered yesterday either.

"Fuck yeah," I said, glaring back and flexing an arm to bulge a bicep.

Jack and I had squared off at pee-wee and youth football scrimmages for years, with him nearly always winning. Even though he had somehow managed to develop even stronger muscles than mine, I wasn't going to be a pushover. Jack looked at my biceps, smirked, and flexed his own; they out-bulged mine.

"You know I can knock you into next week, especially with these bad boys."

"Save it for practice, guys," came the coach's voice.

"We know, Coach," Jack said, releasing me and mussing my hair again, "I just gotta warn him of his ass-kicking beforehand. Being a friend and all that." That last jeer made Coach, and most of the other boys, laugh. "Murphy, right?" he asked, flipping through the roster.

Jack nodded, the smile still plastered on his face, saying, "Yes, Coach."

"MLB and squad leader for Billy Thompson's Warriors?"

Jack nodded again and repeated, "Yes, Coach." Then, Coach turned to me.

"I don't need to look up your name, Weston." Some of the other kids chuckled. I figured why. I looked down at the table, frowning. "Yes, Coach," I responded.

"Your face looks swollen."

"It's fine, Coach," I said, wanting to end the subject as quickly as possible. Plus, I wanted to look tough.

"Look at me, Weston," he barked. I obeyed him, looking into his green eyes. They twinkled, and again there was something about him that made me feel good.

"Remind me what position you play."

"Halfback on offense and DT on defense, Coach."

He looked down at his papers. "It says here that you got traded from the Warriors to Holden's Jets? That can't be right."

"No, Coach. Calvin..."

King interrupted me, holding the paper closer to his face. "Oh, read the wrong line. You're on Calvin Williams' Colts."

I stretched my back, pulling each arm towards my chest. "Yes, Coach."

He shuffled his papers. "That's what I had thought. Williams and Thompson told me you like to pick fights with bigger kids. Wasn't sure I believed it, until I just witnessed you challenging Murphy here." Jack nodded in rapid succession. He clasped a hand on my shoulder.

"They start it, Coach," I defended myself, looking over at Jack and pulling his hand off me. Jack stuck out his tongue. "Each time," I said, my eyes narrowed.

"Then you need to learn how to end it," he replied, his face stern, "Properly, as Thompson told you yesterday."

I forced myself to squeak a "Yes, Coach."

"The team captains are proving to be outstanding leaders. You should listen to them."

I agreed, repeating "Yes, Coach."

"That statement goes for the rest of you guys, too. Got it?"

"Yes Coach!" everyone else shouted in unison.

King pointed to the dozens of boxes and said, "We're starting in full pads today." Loud cheers arose from all of us, making the coach smile at our enthusiasm. "Each box contains a full uniform, including pads, jersey, and helmet. Your name and jersey number are printed on the box, and they should be in numerical order, starting from the back of the room." He continued, "We'll get to them soon, but there are a few things we need to take care of. However..." Coach looked over at my direction again.

"Weston, Williams requested that I let you suit up as soon as possible. He wants you to meet him out in the field."

Some of the guys let out "oooh" noises. One of them, sitting a few rows in front of me, said, "He's gonna work you hard, Scott. I'm

on his team too, and I've seen one-on-ones with Calvin already. He usually means business."

I actually didn't mind that. Having some individual time for him to get to know my skills, and me his leadership style, would be good. At least, that's why I assumed he wanted to see me alone.

Coach then looked at Jack and said, "Murphy, since you're a squad leader, you need to suit up as well and get out to your field to assist Thompson."

Jack grinned and shouted with enthusiasm, "Yes, Coach!"

"Sweet!" he said to himself, pumping a fist.

"Lucky bastards," Jaden whispered with a frown.

Ty gave me a high-five as Jack and I stood up. "See ya out there, Scott!"

"One quick announcement, though," added King, freezing Jack and me in our tracks, "Today is Coach Thimbleton's last day. He's moving on to grander things. I know you seventh graders don't know him very well, but he is an amazing coach, not to mention a wonderful person. Wish him luck when you see him today, okay boys?"

"Yes Coach!" we all shouted back, again in unison.

A kid raised his hand, and when Coach called on him, he asked, "Does that mean you'll be the only coach?"

"Starting Monday, yes. At least for the duration of the camp," he replied.

Jack and I found our boxes quickly and took them to the locker room, our arms trembling with excitement. The boxes were folded in a way that they closed without needing tape; all it took was a pull in the middle to open them up.

I smiled at seeing my equipment waiting for me. I lowered my nose in the box and sniffed, relishing the smell of clean plastic, mesh, and padding. Of course, it wouldn't be long before they

reeked of my sweat, but I looked forward to that too. Jack, whose assigned locker stood on the other side of the room, did the same thing, putting his face into his box.

"Nothing like new equipment, huh, Scott?" he shouted over to me with a smile, his voice echoing in the empty room.

I took off my cleats, shorts, and practice shirt, storing the last two in my locker. I removed the helmet from the box and looked through the facemask to the padding at the back. I sniffed it as well, and then I placed it neatly on the bench next to me. I noticed that the helmet had my number, fifty-five, in small black letters on its rear, near the bottom. After that, I took out my jersey, white with red sleeves and also with the number fifty-five, printed in large red letters on the front and back. I hugged the jersey close to my chest, feeling a strong connection to it, to that number. This was *me*; *my* number, one I'd had for years. I folded the jersey back and placed it next to the white helmet. The shoulder pads came out next, then my white football pants with belt, and then, finally, the knee, thigh, hip, and tailbone pads.

My hands trembled in excitement as I put on the knee and thigh pads in the pants packets and attached the slotted pads with the belt. Once that was done, I put on the pants and laced up the crotch. Afterward, I tied the belt; the cleats came on next.

By this time, Jack had almost completed suiting up. His jersey, colored like mine, had the number sixty-four on it. He looked like a warrior. My friend smiled at me; after putting on his helmet and strapping on his chinstrap, he said, "See you on the battlefield, Scott."

I nodded, and he turned away, showing sixty-four printed on the back of his helmet. As he jogged out the exit that led to the fields, I wondered if he had felt the same way about the equipment as I did.

Alone now, I took a slow, deep breath, allowing this moment to sink in; I had the urge to look at myself in the mirror before putting on the rest of my uniform.

I walked to the end of our row of lockers, carrying the rest of my equipment, where a full-sized mirror stood attached to the wall. A handsome, well-built twelve-year-old boy with green eyes, a swollen cheek, and semi-curly black hair stood staring back, his bangs almost covering his thin eyebrows. I curled my upper lip into a snarl and narrowed my eyes. I then rolled my hands into fists and flexed my muscles, admiring the amazing physique I had.

The muscles on my chest moved up and down as I breathed, and my abs formed a six-pack. I stared at my bare underarm and the large muscles surrounding it, then bent my head down to the side and sniffed it, relishing in the strong odor. My body was still a little stinky and dirty from yesterday. I liked it that way. Which other boy here wouldn't be this way? We were all football players.

My mind flashed back to yesterday with Veronica, and I thought about what she said about me being a boy, and what that meant; more so, how she made me *feel* like a boy, more masculine than I had ever felt. And now, in this uniform, I began to feel it with almost as much power. I gazed at myself in the mirror as I put on my shoulder pads over my bare chest, snapped them in place, and stretched the jersey over them. I then put on the helmet, snapping the chin strap in place, attaching the mouthguard to it, and putting it in my mouth. The coaches always compared a football uniform with that of an armored knight, a warrior, or an ancient Roman soldier, ready for battle, ready for glory. I posed in the mirror again, growling and flashing my best war face. This was fucking awesome.

I started to rub my crotch then, feeling the cup against my hardened dick and balls. I couldn't take it anymore. I ran into the bathroom, the noise of my cleats against the hard floor echoing

throughout the quiet locker room. I went inside a stall, untied my football pants, moved my cupped underwear down, and took out my boner. I concentrated on being in my football uniform as I began stroking my dick; of what Veronica had said yesterday; of being a boy.

I groaned in bliss as I orgasmed swiftly, my sperm shooting into the toilet and my body trembling. Afterwards, I made myself presentable again and on the way out, grabbed my face towel and an empty Gatorade squeeze bottle. I broke into a full sprint towards the Colt's field, where a suited-up boy, with the number twelve on his white jersey, waited for me. That had to be Calvin.

chapter ten

Calvin didn't say anything when I approached his position. Instead, he motioned at me to follow him. Upon reaching the edge of the field, he had me do stretches and some warm-up routines with him for about ten minutes. Other kids, all suited up and ready to dive in, started to make their way to their teams' side of the home field, while I was still running a few short sprints with Calvin.

The heat of the morning summer sun, combined with our pads, had started to make us sweat like pigs in saunas; I could already feel it dripping down my face as Calvin led me to 'the pit', a circular area, outlined with chalk, on the field. My team captain walked up to the circle and threw his Gatorade bottle to the side. I followed his move, facing him.

"We're gonna face off," he declared.

I could feel my heart rate pacing up, a knot was forming in my stomach. This kid was big, bigger than Jack. Sure, I had faced stronger kids before, but the opponent facing me now had at least twice the muscle power as I did.

I nodded, my facial muscles straining to hide my fear.

"Put in your mouthguard and get in position," he ordered, biting down on his own. I bent down, assuming a three-point

stance, with one hand touching the ground and the other back by my thigh.

Calvin bent his knees and lowered his shoulder pads, holding out his hands. It could be mere co-incidence, but it looked as if he were out to get me.

"On three..." he barked.

I drew in a breath and psyched myself up, geared to knock him out of the circle.

"Two!"

I narrowed my eyes. *I can beat this kid!*

"One!" he shouted.

We lunged at each other, loud grunts filling the circle. I knew I had to try and hit him under the chin to gain advantage. But Calvin was faster. *Much* faster. He dropped his head and hit me under the chin instead, knocking me back harder than Jack ever had. I felt dizzy momentarily. He had bought himself enough time to push his palms into my chest and thrust me right outside the circle, throwing me to the ground. The pads cushioned the blow, but it still hurt, making me wince and knocking the very wind out of me.

"Not good enough!" he yelled as I stood up, "Is this what will happen between you and someone like Jimmy in a real scrimmage?"

I knew the answer was yes, but I needed to save face; and since Jimmy wasn't there to argue back, I shouted between catching my breath, "No!"

"Bullshit!" he snarled.

Calvin pointed to the ground. "Give me twenty, Scott! Now!"

Exasperation was all over me, but I wasn't going to be *THAT* kid who whines or argues. I got down on all fours and did the twenty pushups, grunting as I breathed out for each one and

watched my sweat drip down and into the dirt. When I was done, I stood up to find a few other players looking at us while walking by.

"We're going again, Scott," Calvin snapped.

I followed him back into the circle and got back to the three-point stance. He counted down again, and when he shouted "one", I wasted no moment to launch at him. But he got the better of me. Again. This time actually lifting me off the ground and tossing me down, as if I were a useless mannequin.

"NOT GOOD ENOUGH!" he exploded. I was moaning in pain. He didn't even wait for me to recover before ordering twenty pushups again. This was starting to suck.

The third time, I decided to pay attention to his movements, well aware that concentrating on this instead of my strength would make me lose again, but I needed to first study him to attack better. I did lose, allowing myself to trip to lessen the impact, hoping Calvin wouldn't sense that.

"What in the *fuck* was *that*?" Calvin yelled, taking out his mouthguard and letting it dangle from his facemask.

When I stood up, he marched over to me, grasped my jersey, and brought his facemask up against mine. His odor made me edge back.

"Are you giving up on me?" he yelled, his face seething in anger, and his eyes narrowed into slits.

I didn't take my mouthguard out as I held his gaze and yelled back, "No way, Calvin!"

"Are you a fucking baby seventh grader who can't take it? Because I've NO need for pussies like you on my team!" In youth football, coaches would say things like that, too, although in a more kid-appropriate manner, when they thought kids were giving up. If a kid really was throwing in the towel, the boy would give some

excuse, and the coach would bench him. But, I wasn't planning on being that kid either. I just needed to figure out how to beat Calvin.

"I'm not a pussy!" I yelled out, pushing him back, "I *can* beat you!" The boy cocked his head, stared at me for a few seconds, then pointed to the ground.

"Twenty."

"FUCK!" I was sick of that. I complied, nonetheless, spending that time go over his movements in my mind, trying hard to find a weakness. When I hit the penultimate pushup, an idea struck me. However, when I stood back up, Calvin didn't move. He even had his mouthguard out. I ignored that, but just as I was about to get in position, Calvin stopped me, a hand on my bicep.

"Go back to our team for warmups, and tell Ty Green to get here." My eyes narrowed. Was he kidding me? His command had no emotion, so I couldn't tell if he was testing me, or just what was going on in that head of his.

"What? Why?"

"We're done here for now," he said, matter-of-factly.

I took out my mouthguard and spat, "The fuck we are!"

He gave me a hard stare. More than surprised, he looked pissed. "Excuse me?" he hissed.

"Let's go again!" I demanded.

My team captain shook his head and folded his arms. "Go. Get. Ty," he commanded, his voice lowered.

A part of me was pushing me to obey him, but the stronger part wasn't going to let me leave without that last go-around.

"No!" I said firmly.

Calvin gritted his teeth. "*What?*"

He came right up to my face again, but I was still not ready to back down.

"I said no! I'm not leaving until I try again!" I demanded. Calvin banked his head again and looked at me. This time his face only showed disbelief.

"One more time!" I begged, "Just *one* more!"

He looked me over for a few seconds, our heavy breathing echoing in the surrounding silence; the only other sound was that of our teammates warming up on the other side of the field.

"Last one," he relented with a sigh, "After this, *you do* as I tell you."

I nodded. We put in our mouthguards, walked into the circle, and got into our positions. When our eyes locked, I suddenly felt this connection with him. Something that hit my masculinity. Boy against boy. Warrior against warrior.

When he started counting down, I channeled all my energy into my legs; and when he finished, I made a quick, short sprint at him, lowering my head and thrusting my arms toward the sides of his chest, close to his armpits. This time, the sound of our helmets crashing boomed through the circle and both our arms grabbed the other's jersey. My cleats dug into the dirt, I grunted as loud as I could, trying with all my might to push Calvin off balance. I managed to budge him, just an inch, before my legs gave out, his brute strength overwhelming mine. He fell flat on top of me, his face landing on my chest, while my helmet hit the ground hard.

I saw stars. Calvin stood up and waited for me recover. When I did, he reached down and helped me up.

The order for pushups that I was expecting never came. Instead, in a calm voice, he said with a nod, "Go get Ty. And tell him to fill up my Gatorade."

I wasn't going to push it. "Okay," I replied, dejected. He tossed his squeeze bottle at me, which had his name and jersey number

neatly Sharpie'd across. "And make sure you hydrate as well," he added.

I looked away from him and grabbed my bottle.

"I will," I assured him.

"By the way, Bryce Winters is your squad leader. Number Sixty-Two. Join him after you send Ty my way."

"Okay," I affirmed. I wanted to add something like, *"I'll beat you next time, Calvin,"* but I felt that wasn't necessary. It seemed like something a coward would say at this point. I'd just had to show him by *beating* him. Period. Just like a warrior would.

For the first time, the feeling of the sweat streaming down my face irked me. I wiped myself off with my towel, holding it against my face as I walked to my fellow Colts, who were still doing their warmups.

I spotted Ty in his number forty-two jersey, doing agility drills in a line with other players. When he saw me, he motioned for me to join him.

"Man, you look like Calvin just kicked your ass," he said as I approached.

"Thanks a lot, Ty," I replied.

He switched to a back-pedal drill with the rest of the group. "You okay? What happened out there?" he asked.

"Yeah, I'm fine," I replied, "but I couldn't beat Calvin in the pit."

"Oh. That's too bad."

"He says it's your turn," I continued, handing him Calvin's bottle, "He wants you to meet him at the pit, and fill up his bottle. Yours, too."

"Sweet!" Ty replied, putting a hand on my shoulder pads, "Don't worry, buddy. I'll get even for ya."

"Good luck with that," said a sweaty, brown-eyed kid approaching us; his jersey had number sixty-two on it. That must have been Bryce Winters, my new squad leader. He stood a little taller than I did, and had bigger muscles; but he didn't look any older. I wondered if he was a seventh grader.

"Are you Bryce?" I asked.

"Yup," he acknowledged, extending his hand. We shook hands, and Bryce asked Ty to get going.

"Are you Ty's squad leader as well?" I asked as Ty ran off towards the watering stations to fill up his and Calvin's bottles.

He shook his head. "That would be Derek Edwards," He clarified. Bryce led me off the field, following Ty.

"Calvin told me that he was going to feel you and Ty out separately, with you first on defense and then on offense."

I looked to the ground and grumbled, "Offense? He never ran any patterns with me. We only did some warmups and then the pit."

"He probably figured you needed a break," he continued, before adding, "and by the look of you, you need it." When I didn't respond, Bryce asked, "What's wrong?" We reached the watering stations, and I filled my squeeze bottle with cold Gatorade.

"I couldn't beat him," I said, "He was just too strong."

"Who? Calvin?" he asked, filling his own bottle.

I nodded, unstrapping my helmet and lifting it enough to pour the entire content down my throat, finishing it in only a few gulps.

He laughed for a good five seconds, which made me grunt in annoyance. Then, he said, "Dude, did you seriously think you could beat him in the pit?"

I glared at him. "Yes! Why not?"

He started laughing again. "Scott, hardly anybody can beat Calvin in the pit. Even our own starting offensive line has problems

when he plays defense." Bryce squeezed his bottle so that the liquid went through the bars of his facemask and into his mouth, negating the need to lift up his helmet. A look of confusion came over me, and I wondered what it was that Calvin had expected out of me.

"So, tell me what happened out there," my squad leader asked. I explained my trials in the pit. He looked impressed when I told him about the last play.

"You actually held your own against him for a few seconds?" he asked in disbelief.

"During that last round, yeah," I confirmed.

He patted my back and said in an upbeat tone, "Good for you, man! I bet that impressed him."

My eyes lit up, and I felt a wave of relief wash over me, even though I wasn't sure I believed him. "Really? Even though I didn't beat him?"

Bryce downed more Gatorade. "Hell yeah," he said, wiping his mouth, "Dude, I promise you, there's no way he was expecting you to beat him. Just to improve after each try. Sounds like you did at the end there. Good for you!"

I smiled, "Thanks, Bryce." The familiarity with which he talked about Calvin, I figured that they actually were in the same grade.

"You in eighth grade?" I asked to confirm.

"Yeah," he said, "You're in seventh, right?"

I nodded. "How long have you played with Calvin, then?"

"Three years. That kid's a monster."

"So is Jack Murphy."

"That's what I hear. Anyway, middle school football is a lot of hard work, but it's also fun – much more intense than youth football, but the payoff is worth it. You'll see." Then, he motioned

for me to follow him. "Let's get you back into conditioning. We're about to do our sprints. You up for that?"

I pulled down my helmet and strapped it back on. "Fuck yes," I grinned. I was thankful for the way Bryce treated me and the thought that, perhaps, I had impressed Calvin.

"Good," he said, leading the way again, "We've got a lot of work to do."

chapter eleven

Ryder, Jimmy, and some other kids welcomed me as I joined our team on the field. "How'd it go?" Jimmy asked, his sweat now beginning to cover the eighty-five printed on his jersey.

"It was rough," I replied.

The boy who had warned me about Calvin this morning, now suited up in jersey number eighteen, said, "Told ya."

"He held his own in the pit against our team captain at the end," Bryce added, patting my back again, "so he deserves some credit."

"No way he did that!" Jimmy gasped, looking me over, "Even *I* can't beat Calvin."

"I can't either," Ryder said, number thirty printed on his jersey. He then asked me, "Did you really beat him?"

"Well, no," I said, "but I held him back for a few seconds."

"That's awesome, man!" Ryder said, shaking my facemask from side to side.

Jimmy sighed in relief, "Don't scare me like that, Bryce. No offense, Scott, and it's great that you were able to hold him off. But there's no way you'd be able to beat him."

"*Someone's* ego gets hurt easily," Ryder sneered, coughing with one hand and pretending to secretly point Jimmy with the other. Jimmy, in retaliation, gave him the finger. Bryce let out a chuckle and adjusted his shoulder pads. "Time for sprints," he announced to our squad, "Everyone, line up with Derek's squad."

"What number is Derek?" I asked as I followed my squad over to our starting line. Bryce pointed to a boy with the number twenty-seven on his jersey.

"Oh. What position does he play?" I asked.

"Linebacker. Outside," came the answer.

"And you?"

"Running back," he said, holding out his fist for me to bump, "Good to have a skilled halfback like you on my squad."

I smiled as I bumped his fist. "Thanks."

"With Nicholas as our tight end and Calvin as our quarterback, we have a great offense going," Bryce said, before trotting off to meet Derek. I knew that Calvin played quarterback on offense, but I had no idea who Nicholas was.

"Nicholas?" I asked.

"Yo," responded the kid with the number eighteen jersey, walking behind us.

"Nicholas Schmidt," said Number Eighteen, "Tight End." We shook hands.

Bryce and Derek led us in sprints down the field, then started the conditioning work. That meant the usual classic agility ladder drills, crawls, and other exercises to get us into optimum shape. This was the least favorite part of practice for just about all of us, as it was the most demanding, but it certainly developed our strength, speed, agility, and endurance.

When that ended, we broke up into offensive and defensive groups. I normally only played defense as a backup, so Bryce put

me with him for offense practice. As we were about to start, Calvin and Ty joined us, the seventh grader looking as beat up as I had been after my stint with our team captain. Calvin sat down on a nearby bench and had a talk with our two squad leaders, while Ty walked over to me.

"Good God, that kid is fucking strong," Ty complained to me with a scowl on his face, "I don't know how the fuck you managed to push him back at all, Scott." Apparently, his mood had soured just like mine had, but I had to ask him how he knew what I did.

"Calvin told me, of course," Ty replied and spat on the ground, "He ordered me to quit after only four tries, but I refused. I wasn't going to give up that easily. He said you did the same thing."

"He wanted me to quit after three," I said, doing some leg stretches, "but, yeah, I sort of threw a fit."

"Well, so did I. But he didn't give me another chance. He said that the time was up, and that if I didn't stop whining, he'd make me run laps." Ty's voice carried over to our team leaders, who looked over at us.

"Calvin looks tired, Ty," I said, looking back and noticing Calvin bent over, face down, with his elbows on his knees, "Maybe he just needs a break too."

Then, I relayed to him what Bryce and the others had told me about how hardly anyone could beat Calvin in the pit.

"Well, you actually held your own against him, though," he said, "And I'm stronger than you!"

"The fuck you are, man!" I dismissed him, laughing and nudging him on the shoulder.

Ty growled, raising his upper lip and clenching his fists. He put his facemask against mine, and I got a close-up view of the sweat streaming down the kid's face and a smell of the odor reeking from

his body. He took a deep breath and said, "I think you and I need to spar in the pit, Scott. After I beat Calvin, that is."

"Keep dreaming, Ty," I replied, snarling myself, "But I'll humor you."

Ty pretended to be chewing on some tobacco. "Noon," he said, mimicking a very bad Southern accent, then spat on the ground beside me. "Tomorra," he stated. He was re-enacting a famous scene from an R-rated, blood-soaked comedy Western that both our parents had specifically forbidden us from watching. But, Ty had cable in his room, so it was fair game to us.

"How about right na," I retorted, "You got yer pistol?"

Ty pointed to his crotch. "Right here, mother fucker."

A loud burst of laughter near us caught our attention. It came from Derek Edwards, Ty's squad leader. He must have walked over to us during our re-enactment. Derek was a tower of muscle with hazel eyes, and I could see some of his light brown hair, which was not covered by his helmet, matted down by sweat. As big as he was, though, he still had a prepubescent voice. "You guys seen that movie, too?" he asked.

We both nodded, even though we hadn't made it through the whole flick.

"My dad took me to see it," Derek said, "but made us leave after the pig scene."

"Yeah, that was really disgusting," I said, then admitting, "Ty and I turned it off in the middle of that."

"He also made me swear never to tell my mom," Derek continued, "She'd kill him."

Ty and I chortled.

Derek then turned to my friend. "You're with me on the defensive team, Ty. You and I will do some drills together." My friend pulled each arm to stretch his back, the way I had done

earlier this morning. "Okay. But really, all I can think about right now is having another shot at Calvin."

I thought Derek would get upset at Ty for not being able to focus. Instead, the bigger boy chuckled. "Take a number, man. There's not one kid on this entire team who's gone up against Calvin that doesn't want to beat him."

"Hasn't anyone beaten him?" I asked.

"Well, of course. Calvin isn't invincible. But losing to him only makes you want to beat him that much more, doesn't it?"

chapter twelve

Ty and Derek left for the defense side of the field, while Bryce walked over to me.

"Calvin said he will run you through some one-on-one offensive drills after lunch," Bryce said, "So that should make you happy, huh?"

"Sweet," I grinned.

We were about fifteen minutes into our offensive line drills when I heard my name being repeatedly called out from a kid far away.

It sounded like Max, my next-door neighbor's kid. I turned to look across the field, and sure enough, it was him, dressed in shorts and a shirt with some cartoon characters on it. Another young boy, with short, brown hair, was walking with him, and both the kids were being escorted by a football player with number eight on his jersey. That had to be Mason Holden, the Jets' team captain. Some of my fellow teammates looked over there as well, including Calvin and his squad leaders. I had no idea what those two kids were doing here, but I figured it was best to go and find out.

"I'll be right back, Calvin, Bryce," I said.

"Hurry," reminded Calvin.

I jogged over to Mason, and when I was a few yards from him, Max ran over and hugged me.

"Scott!" Max exclaimed, looking up at me with his big, blue eyes. "This is Zach," he continued, pointing to his friend, whose hair had been styled so that the front was spiked up. He had on a red football jersey with the number forty-eight on it over his blue shorts. He appeared bigger than Max and taller by about a few inches, but he only came up to my nose. His green eyes looked into mine.

"Hi," he greeted in a southern drawl, holding out his hand. I shook it, feeling a hard grip.

"These kids wanted to see you and Jack Murphy," Mason informed me, folding his arms. The Jets' team captain had a round face and looked about as tall and strong as Billy. His eyes were the same shade of green as Zach's. I felt a twinge of embarrassment and anger at Max having bothered us at practice.

Mason continued, "Coach Thimbleton said that as long as they didn't get in our way, they could watch. But only today." That quelled my anger.

"Where's Jack?" Max asked, looking around. I held up a finger for him to be quiet.

"I'm surprised Coach made *you* bring them here," I said, "considering you're a team captain, Mason."

Mason shrugged. "I need to talk to Calvin anyway, but he's not answering his team phone. I think his battery died or something, so I'm bringing him a new one. Kills two birds with one stone."

"Three, actually," Zach pitched in, holding up three fingers, which made Mason chuckle.

"Yeah, I guess you're right, kiddo," he said, mussing the kid's hair.

"I want Zach to meet Ty," Max began.

"You're in luck, then," I replied as we walked back towards the Colts' section of the field, "He's on my camp team."

"Sweet!" he exclaimed, grabbing my hand, "And Jack?"

I pointed to the other end of the field, where the Warriors were practicing. "Over there."

Max looked up at me again. "Will you take me to him?"

"If my team captain lets me."

The Rams, led by Number Ten, Damian Jackson, and the Jets had been assigned the high school field for practice, which was further from mine and Max's house than the junior high.

"Why did you go to the high school field?" I asked Max.

"Because Zach and I first rode our bikes to the store, and we took the route back here that passes by the high school. We saw football players there, so we thought maybe you were among them."

When we reached our area of the field, Calvin met Mason at the benches, and Ty, standing among the defending team, said, "Max?"

"Hey, Ty!" the kid replied, running over to him and giving him a hug. Many of my teammates watched with smiles on their faces, probably thinking that Max was Ty's little brother.

Ty gave him a high-five and asked what he was doing there. Max introduced him to Zach and said, "This is my friend Zach. He's a safety as well on our football team."

Ty shook Zach's hand. "Nice to meet ya, kiddo. Man, you have a strong grip for a little kid."

"Thanks. Do you care if I watch you play?"

I told Ty that the coaches had allowed them to be here, but only for today.

"Sure," Ty shrugged.

"I wanna see the other guys on defense too."

Jimmy walked over to us and towered over Zach, making the kid's eyes widen and his jaw drop. "Woah! What position do *you* play?"

Jimmy grinned and flexed his arms. "I'm a cornerback."

"Woah!" Zach repeated, "You're big!"

That made our cornerback grin even wider.

"Our cornerback is strong too," continue Zach, "but not nearly as strong as you. In fact, I think even *I'm* stronger than he is."

"Yeah," Max seconded, patting Zach on the shoulder, "Zach is probably one of the strongest kids on our team."

"Good for him!" said Jimmy, patting the kid's head.

"Go sit on the bench watch us from there," Derek, Ty's squad leader, told Zach, "I don't need you getting hurt."

"Okay!" said Zach and ran over to the bench, sitting next to where Calvin was standing and talking to Mason.

My team captain looked over at him, upon which Zach held out his hand and introduced himself. Calvin shook it and shot me a quizzical look before turning his attention back to Mason.

Max tugged at my jersey. "Will you take me over to Jack now?"

I didn't want to interrupt Calvin, so I shouted over to Bryce and asked if I could escort Max to the Warriors.

"Sure," he replied, "Just hurry back."

Max let out an "Awesome!" and we made our way to where the Warriors were playing.

I took to the sidelines to avoid Max getting hit accidentally, but we didn't have to get very close before I saw Jack stare at us in surprise. He held out his hand to stop whatever he and his group were doing and trotted over to us. Billy, wearing number four, followed.

As soon as Max saw Jack, he darted off and gave him a hug and a high-five and fist bump.

"Hey, little man," said Jack, "What are you doing here?"

"You're number sixty-four, too?" Max asked, looking at Jack's sweaty jersey in awe.

"Yup! You?"

"Yes!" Max exclaimed, jumping up and down and giving Jack another high-five.

"Family reunion?" asked Billy.

"He's Scott's neighbor," replied Jack, squatting down to get eye level with Max, who hugged Jack around his shoulder pads.

"Did you seriously bring your neighbor's kid to our practice, Weston?" questioned Billy, shooting me an irritated look.

"Do you seriously think I would?" I snapped back.

"Well, he's here, so don't cop an attitude with me," he warned, "or I'll shove a sweaty pit in your face."

Max laughed. "Ew!!"

"Yeah, no kidding," I said.

"What's the deal with the kid, Weston?" Billy smirked.

"He and his friend just showed up wanting to watch us, and Coach Thimbleton agreed to let them for today."

The team captain cocked his head. "And you brought him to my Warriors' field because...?"

"Because he wants to watch Jack play."

"Yeah!" said Max, "I *really* want to watch him!"

Billy shrugged. "Fine, whatever. Just don't get in our way, okay, kid? I don't need you getting hurt."

"He won't," assured Jack, ruffling Max's hair.

"I won't!" Max reassured Billy as Jack stood up, "Besides, if I do get hurt, my aunt will take care of me!" My face froze; so did Jack's.

"Your aunt?" asked Jack.

"Yeah. She's a nurse."

"Is she here?" I had to ask.

"I dunno." Max shrugged, "She left early this morning, though. She's the one who encouraged Zach and me to come see you guys." Jack and I exchanged an exasperated look.

"Really?" asked Jack, "This wasn't *your* idea?"

"Well, I thought we'd get in trouble, but Aunt Veronica said we should try."

Billy looked at us in confusion. "What's the problem?" he asked.

Jack shook his head. "Nothing, Billy. Let's just get back to practice."

"Good enough for me," Billy said before walking back.

Jack gave me a perplexing look, and I raised my shoulders as a mutual feeling of bafflement. Billy only took a few steps before he turned around and addressed me. "How did your one-on-one with Calvin go this morning, Weston?"

"I didn't beat him in the pit," I answered, "but I pushed him back a few inches."

Jack slapped me on the back and expressed, "Nice!"

"No shit?" Billy exclaimed, his eyes widened.

"No shit."

"Damn, Weston," he whistled, "I should have kept you and traded Adams." Jack rolled his eyes but couldn't hold back a laugh.

"Thanks a lot," I said, giving Billy the finger. Max laughed. Oops, I forgot the kid was there. "Forget I did that, Max," I told him.

"We flick each other off all the time," Max admitted.

Billy stared at me for a few seconds before pointing at his sweat-stained armpit. "Just wait for it, Weston. This will be the last thing you smell for a while."

"Ew!" Max cringed, "Do you guys really make each other smell your armpits?"

"Sometimes," Jack laughed.

The thought of Billy's odor making its way to my nose made me gag. He was probably just being Billy – the one I had confronted the other day. Either way, my own stench wasn't something to dismiss.

"Yeah, I guess we'll have to see about that, Billy," I replied, thumbing my own armpits.

Billy smirked. "Yeah, I guess we will, Weston."

chapter thirteen

After morning practice, we all filed into the cafeteria, ready to gorge down lunch. The school had ordered pegboards with hooks on to be placed on the walls for us players to hang our helmets while we ate. Each hook had a number, in sequential order, that corresponded to our jersey. So, we all knew from what peg we could place our helmets. Since our helmets also had our numbers on the back, we could spot them easily after lunch.

The cool air inside was a blessing against the sweat of our bodies, and the delicious smell of hot food made our mouths water. Our coaches asked us to wash our hands thoroughly, which meant a mad rush to the bathrooms to clean up as fast as possible to allow ourselves more time to eat. Fortunately, the catering people that the athletic department hired knew how to handle hungry kids; so, they made sure to have four queues.

They brought food specifically suited to athletes – an equal balance of meat, veggies, and starches, usually a baked potato, but sometimes rice or pasta. The coaches never allowed us to have any fried or sugary foods during camp, which meant no desserts or sodas. Even our protein bars for afternoon snack had to be approved. We were drilled for an hour on the first day of camp about the importance of good nutrition, and how our performance

would greatly suffer if we didn't properly feed ourselves. That included breakfast and dinner, and it wasn't just regulated to when football was in season.

Coach Thimbleton let Max and Zach eat with us. Zach wanted to sit between Ty and Jimmy at my table, and Max, of course, insisted on sitting next to Jack at his. Soon, the cafeteria was filled with the sounds of eating, chatter, and laughter, not to mention the smell of the combined stench from around a hundred of us sweaty, twelve and thirteen-year-old boys in equally sweaty football pads.

"This is great, isn't it?" I asked Ty, who was seated opposite me.

"What? The food?" Ty asked in return, before scarfing down baked potato.

I pointed to my chicken wing with my fork and said, "Well, the food is good, but I meant the football camp. I love being in pads."

"Oh, yeah," said Ty, "This is great. Kinda wish we could have camp every day and skip school."

Bryce, seated next to me, grinned, "Yeah, that would be awesome."

"Yeah, me too!" said Zach, scooping up some potato as well.

Jimmy pointed to Zach's tray, which was still full of food. The portions had been set up for middle school boy football players, not elementary ones. "Can you finish all that, lil' man?" Jimmy asked, his own tray nearly empty already.

"No way," Zach responded, shaking his head, "This is way too much for me."

Jimmy patted him on the head. "No worries. I'll finish what you don't."

Ryder, sitting on the other side of Jimmy, protested, "He's gonna share that with the rest of us, Jimmy."

"Don't overeat," came an emotionless directive from Calvin, sitting between Bryce and Derek, "Unless you want to throw up like you did on Tuesday, Jimmy."

"I tried to make up for skipping breakfast that day," was Jimmy's excuse. Then, he bent down toward Zach, who looked up at him with chicken hanging from his mouth.

"It didn't work, kiddo. Don't skip breakfast and definitely don't overeat to make up for it. Got it?"

Zach nodded, soaking in every word that the older kid said. "I can't believe that the coaches here let your team captains do most of the coaching," he replied, "Our two team captains don't really do anything."

"But your coach relies on them a lot, though, right?" asked Jimmy, "To make sure the other players know what's going on? And they spend lot of one-on-one time with the coaches too, don't they?"

Zach thought about that for a moment. "Yeah, I guess so," he answered after drinking some water.

"It's not *too* different with us," Calvin said, "I'm a player, but we team captains are given a lot of responsibility in middle school. Right now, I handle a lot of the little things so that our coaches can handle the bigger things, like coming up with offensive and defensive strategies."

"Yeah but you also boss everyone around," replied Zach; the matter-of-fact manner of the reply made our entire table laugh.

"And you have two sub-captains that work under you too," he continued, looking at Bryce and Derek.

"Middle school football is serious around here," explained Calvin, "There are almost a hundred of us at this camp, and each one of us is passionate about the sport."

"Are the other middle schools around here the same way?"

"Yup." Jimmy was the one to respond.

"Cool," the kid said, "Max and I will be in seventh grade in a few years ourselves. Can't wait!"

Then, he turned to Ty. "Are you finished eating, Ty?"

My friend looked down at his empty plate. "I guess I am."

Looking at Zach's half-eaten tray of food, he said, "But you don't look like you are."

Zach wiped his mouth with his napkin. "I can't eat another bite."

That's all Jimmy needed to hear.

"Mine!" he jumped in. His hand struck out like a cobra and grabbed the remaining half of the boy's chicken.

"Hey!" whined Ryder, elbowing him in the gut, "Share that with me!"

"Fine!" grunted Jimmy and handed him half of it.

"You said that, after lunch, you'd go over some techniques you learned about being a safety," Zach reminded Ty.

"Yup," said Ty, "Let's go in our war room." He stood up and grabbed their trays.

"Don't be late on the field," warned Derek.

"Yeah, you won't like what Derek will make you do," said Jimmy.

"No problem," shrugged Ty, "I'll be out of here once the speaker bell goes off."

"Don't forget your helmet," reminded Ryder.

"Oh, yeah. Thanks!" replied Ty, and after putting the trays away and grabbing his helmet from the pegboard, he led Zach toward our war room.

Calvin called out my name, and when I looked over to him, he told me, "I'm going to call some patterns for you to run once we're outside. I want to see how well we mesh."

Some one-on-one offense time with him – finally! "Awesome," I let him know.

Calvin actually smiled. "Also, good work out there this morning.".

My chest swelled with pride.

"You and Ty don't know when to give up, but I like that. Usually."

Another kid on Bryce's squad asked if I had really held my own against our team captain.

"He did," confirmed Calvin, then turning to me again, his expression turning serious, "But let's see if he can actually beat me next time."

Jimmy laughed, nearly spitting out his food, "That'll never happen." Then, looking at me, he said, "No offense."

I frowned. We'd see about that.

chapter fourteen

My one-on-one offensive practice with Calvin had been smoother than our pit practice in the morning. We had all learned a bunch of routes on Tuesday and committed them to memory; so, I was able to run every one that Calvin had called. His tosses were nearly perfect, spiraling in the air and landing in my hands almost every time. The ball slipped in a few instances, but I was able to recover. When that happened, Calvin didn't fail to remind me that I'd normally have at least one defensive player on my ass, so I wouldn't always have the luxury of second chances.

That gave him an idea. He had Ty cover me, and we re-ran the routes, while Zach kept watching from the sidelines. Calvin was dead on about not getting second chances. I had already known there'd be a wide difference in pressure when someone is trying to tackle me to the ground. Ty and I ended up with about even scores. I had outrun, out-maneuvered, or overpowered him about the same number of times as he was able to tackle me. Zach celebrated each time I got tackled.

"Hey, where's my support?" I whined at him, half-jokingly, when he and Ty high-fived each other after one of Ty's successful tackles. Zach giggled.

"I really hope you're not that sensitive, Scott," said Calvin, visibly annoyed, "because even middle school fans can get... opinionated." He was evidently talking from his experience.

"Nah," I dismissed his concern, waving my hand, "Not really. Our previous coaches taught us how to shrug it off and just focus on the game."

"Good."

"Max would cheer you on if he was here, you know," Ty said to me.

I wiped some sweat off my arms with a towel. "Unless I was up against Jack."

"Yeah, that's true. You need a kid halfback rooting for you, like in the movies."

Ty looked over at Zach. "You got one on your team?" he asked the kid.

"Two, actually," replied Zach, rubbing his chin, "I think one of them, Shane, would really like to watch Scott."

I shook my head. "Ty was kidding, Zach. I'm fine."

"Oh."

"But you guys are welcome to come and cheer for us on our games."

We finished our practice with Calvin, and afterwards, he gave both Ty and me a thumbs up, making us both grin at each other.

"This *is* going to be fun," Ty whispered as we sat on a bench for our water break.

We spent the next few hours practicing team defense and offense in our individual camp teams. Calvin had me playing defense and offense in turns, which meant I got to play a lot more. It also began to wear me out; I had gone a few months without this much activity.

When I made one too many mistakes and eventually allowed Calvin to get sacked, he yelled at me, asking where my head was at. I didn't want to admit that I felt exhausted; otherwise, he'd have bench me.

"Williams!" shouted Coach Thimbleton, a thin, older man whose mirrored sunglasses hid his eyes. The gray that peppered his black hair showed his age. Calvin looked over at him. "Assess your player's condition before you yell at him!"

My team captain looked me over, my heaving breaths becoming labored. He softened his expression and said, "You need to sit out for a bit. I've played you too hard."

I frowned.

Calvin then motioned for Bryce Winters, our running back and my squad leader, over to us. "I'm benching Scott right now," he told Bryce, "I'll call up Billy and borrow a halfback from him."

My squad leader took this opportunity to wipe his face with his towel. "Sounds good," he said.

I knew I needed a break, but I didn't like leaving on that screw-up. I also hated being benched, especially now that there wasn't anyone else sitting out. Calvin noticed that I had looked at the benches and then, back at him. When I began to open my mouth, he must have figured I that was going to protest, because he said, "I'm not going to have a player pass out on me, and I'm not going to argue. Go take a break, have some Gatorade, and get over yourself."

Ouch.

"You sound like Billy," I told him.

"Good," Calvin replied, "Then we're both doing our jobs as team captains."

Calvin gave Bryce a quick nod, before turning his attention toward the other players.

"He's right," Bryce said, his face turning serious, "You look really worn out."

Bryce put his hands on my shoulder pads, spun me toward the sidelines, and gave me a light shove toward the benches. "Go sit down. I'll check up on you in a bit." I took off my helmet, sat on the bench, and sipped Gatorade as I watched the other guys play. Ty, Ryder, and Jimmy waved to me at various times. I smiled back, but really, it just made me want to play even more, despite my body telling me otherwise.

Coach Thimbleton came over to me. "You feeling okay, son?"

I looked at myself in his sunglasses, noticing almost my entire uniform, arms, and head covered in dirt. My hair was completely matted with sweat, which was still dripping down my face. Bryce was right; I did look completely worn out.

"Yeah, I'm fine," I replied.

"Calvin didn't overwork you?"

"I can handle it, Coach," I shrugged, "I want to play."

He smiled. "I know you want to, but Calvin made the right decision. Mind if I sit down?" I blinked. I wondered why he thought I'd mind and shook my head to let him know that I didn't.

"Thanks," he said, sitting next to me.

I remembered what Coach King had said and wished him well.

"Thanks, kid," he said, "You know, here at Putnam Middle School, I have never seen young boys like yourselves have so much passion for the game. Way before this, I was at a prep school up north, and while kids there liked to play football, it was more of a hobby or fun sport than anything halfway serious. If things got too hard, they wanted to get benched – to take it easy."

"It's different here, Coach," I said, putting my elbows on my kneepads and going back to watching my teammates.

104

"No kidding," he replied, mimicking my posture, "When I was told this school always had the team captains handling their teams and players like coaches, I thought they were crazy. No way thirteen-year-old boys had enough experience to be an authority figure in football or anything, really. But these captains, including young Calvin Williams over there, can put many *high school* coaches I know to shame."

Eighth grader Lucas Colby, one of Billy's halfbacks, made his way onto the field as my replacement and gave me a high-five as he passed. He had twenty-one printed on his jersey.

"Football's in our blood, Coach," I answered back, watching Lucas jump into the fray, "We're all here because we love the game, and we want to be with other kids who feel the same. We take it very seriously."

"That's exactly what I was told," he said, smiling at me, "I joked every year at the captains – don't take my job away. Billy Thompson teased back that he wouldn't get paid enough anyway." We both laughed. "There is some irony in that," he said.

I didn't understand what he meant and asked, "What do you mean?"

"Nothing," he said with a shake of his head and a smile, "Just an inside joke." He adjusted his sunglasses on the bridge of his nose. "Last year, Billy and Calvin were two of the best players we had," he continued, "and they were seventh graders. Hell, Calvin was a squad leader last year at camp and an all-star quarterback the year before." Just like Billy had said the previous day. The bit about Calvin being a squad leader reminded me of my Warriors friend. "Like Jack," I said, "Well, the part about being a squad leader." I watched as Calvin threw a touchdown pass to Lucas, which made Derek yell at his defensive line.

"Oh yeah," Thimbleton said, "Like young Jack Murphy. He seems to have taken a liking to Billy."

"Billy's his hero."

Coach nodded. "I can see why. That kid is an amazing player. Never, *ever* misses practice, either."

"He's a bit of a smart-ass, though," I said through a grin.

"*A bit?*" Coach replied with a laugh, "Well, as captains go, both of them are still learning how to assess the needs of their players." He pointed to my Gatorade as an indication to hydrate more.

"And that just takes experience. But, you need to listen to your body as well. I could tell yours needed a break."

I drank some more and then said, "Calvin noticed it too, Coach. After you said something."

"Good, then maybe I can rest easy leaving this team in their, and Coach King's, hands." Bryce Winters got his attention from the field and pointed to his wrist.

"Must be time for us to go in for our afternoon break," said Coach, checking his watch. Then, he gave a thumbs up to Bryce as an acknowledgement.

He looked back at me and said, "As a coach, it was a dream being able to focus on strategies and administrative duties and let the team captains and their squad leaders handle just about everything else."

"Yeah, I bet."

I could see Coach Thimbleton stare longingly at the field.

"I'll miss this. It's definitely been the highlight of my coaching career," he said. My teammates began jogging toward the benches. Coach stood up and stretched, placed a hand on my shoulder pads, and winked at me.

"Take care, son," he said.

"Thanks," I replied, "You, too."

With that, he joined the Colts' leaders in a circle. They removed their helmets, revealing Bryce's short, brown hair and Derek's messy brown mop.

"Time to head in, Colts," said Calvin, motioning with his thumb toward the school.

Ty came over to me, and we walked side by side, following everyone else. The kids on the other sub-teams were heading inside as well, reminding me of an army of ants heading to their mound. I felt a hand on my shoulder, and turned to see my squad leader looking me over.

"You look better now," Bryce concluded.

"Yeah, I'm feeling better," I replied.

"Good. Just checking on ya."

"Thanks."

He nodded, then flared his nostrils. "You two are certainly beginning to smell like middle school boy football players," he grinned, pointing to our stained armpits.

I could certainly smell my own odor, not to mention Ty's and Bryce's.

"You have us beat," I snapped back at Bryce.

"By a mile," added Ty.

"Yup!" he agreed with pride. Then, rubbing his hands together, he said, "I can't wait until next week."

Ty and I blinked.

"Why?" I asked.

"It's gonna be hella fun," he said with a wink before trotting off to catch up with Derek and Calvin.

When he got far enough, Ty asked me, "What'd he mean?"

I shrugged. "I guess we'll find out on Monday."

chapter fifteen

We were mingling around in the locker rooms, eating our protein bars, and enjoying the cool air hitting our hot and tired bodies. Max and Zach became minor celebrities, hanging out with us seventh graders before being invited by Jimmy to the 'big boys' locker room', as he preferred to call it. We talked non-stop with the two fourth graders about football, their own experiences, and how much more fun and intense the game would get as they get older.

After break time, Max got a call from his mom, asking him and Zach to go back. Zach and Max hugged Ty and me; Zach even gave one to Jimmy, followed by high-fives and fist bumps to just about everyone before they left.

In the war room, our entire team split into offense and defense, regardless of camp team or grade. Along with us offensive players, Coach King took Calvin and Damian Jackson, the Rams' team captain, and went over previous routes as well as some new strategies they had come up with. Then, we hit the gridiron again, doing some quick warmups before practicing the new routes. The Warriors and Colts teamed up, placing our offensive and defensive guys together, while the Jets and Rams did the same on the other field. Calvin only threw the ball to me once, but I caught it just as Jimmy and Ty sandwiched me. The rest of the time, I concentrated

on helping protect Calvin from the defensive line, which meant I had to go up against Jack sometimes.

Whenever Jack and I squared off, we always grunted as loud as we could when he faced off, like warriors clashing in battle. We lived for these moments, and even though he mostly got past me, I hardly ever failed to slow him down, at least.

A few plays later, before the snap, I noticed Jack's eyes, normally fixed on the quarterback, looking from side to side. My instinct told me that they were going to try a blitz. As soon as Number Thirty-Four, center Austin Miller, snapped the ball back to Calvin, the defense did blitz, with Jack rushing straight up the middle.

I sprinted toward him, but he noticed me and prepared for the tackle. I snarled, biting down on my mouth guard and hit him dead on, letting out a loud howl. The collision thrust Jack off his feet, but couldn't knock him down. He growled at me, twisting his body and lunging back. His odor hit me, and conversations about armpits, body odor, and Billy's threat went through my mind. An instinct came over me – maybe I could stun him with my odor. At the very least, it'd throw him off guard. So, before he could grab my jersey, I raised my arm up to his facemask. My entire day's sweat and odor slammed into his nose.

"Ugh!" groaned Jack as his head snapped backward. He sank to the ground; his upper body fell first, with both of his arms out to the side. His head turned right as far as it could go, before his helmet's facemask bumped up against his shoulder pads. After that, his legs fell to the ground, and his feet rotated sideways. I looked down at his dirt-smeared face, dripping with sweat; his eyes were shut and his lips pursed together against his mouthguard. He wasn't moving.

I wondered if he was faking it. No, he wouldn't do that during real practice. I bent down and shook his shoulder, but he didn't

react. Then, I raised one of his arms, only to see it flop back to the ground when I let go. I squeezed in my fingers through his facemask and lifted one of his closed eyelids. Jack's eye had rolled all the way up to the back of his skull. The realization hit me – I really had knocked out a kid with one whiff of my armpits.

I looked up and noticed that my teammates were flocked around me. The eighth graders who saw what happened started cheering and slapping me on the back, moving my head around by my facemask and congratulating me on the first armpitting of the year. The seventh graders stood still in shock, asking each other what everyone else was talking about.

"Woah, Scott," said Ty, "What did you just do?"

"Yeah," Jaden, wearing number seventy-six, replied, "Why'd you knock him out?"

All I could do was look at my unconscious friend, wondering when he'd wake up. Calvin asked me to stand up and everyone else to give Jack some air. Billy grasped my shoulder pads with one hand, his patent smirk plastered on his sweaty face.

"Nice move, Weston," he said, "But you're only allowed to pit a kid at a scrimmage or a real game. Not anytime else. Got it?" He motioned for a few eighth graders to move Jack to the benches.

"Pit?" I asked, watching Jack get carried away and set down against the benches.

"Yeah," nodded Calvin Williams, "That's what shoving your armpit into another boy's face is called."

"I didn't think it'd actually knock him out," I replied, looking at Jack, slumping and unconscious, "Is he going to be okay?" That question made Billy and Calvin laugh.

"Oh, for sure!" grinned Bryce Winters, "He'll probably wake up in half an hour or so."

"That's what being a football player our age is all about," added Billy.

"But I've never even heard of that happening," pitched in Austin Miller.

"Like Billy said," replied Bryce, "it's a middle-school boy football thing."

"Don't worry, Miller," said Billy, putting an arm around Austin's shoulder pads, "Just wait until next week."

chapter sixteen

We practiced for another thirty minutes before Jack woke up, disorientated. Billy had Travis Bower, the other Warriors squad leader, run over to check up on him. Jack looked over at me and yelled out my name; his eyes were narrowed, his teeth mashed together, and his upper lip twisted in a snarl. He marched over to me, quivering his fists by his side, as the other kids made a path for him. Travis was following him closely.

Fuck. Jack was in a fury.

"What did you do *that* for?" he yelled, fixing his facemask against mine.

"Sorry, Jack," I said, rubbing the back of my neck, "I didn't think you'd actually pass out."

"Yeah, well, you better believe your ass is mine!" he threatened, bashing his helmet against mine.

"Ow!" I cringed.

"He did stop your blitz," Ryder prodded him with a laugh.

"Well, you're next, pal," Jack seethed back at Ryder.

Ryder cracked his knuckles and pointed to the sparring pit. "How about now?" he challenged, "I have some anger to work out against you." He and Jack looked over to our team leaders, who

nodded in agreement. Our entire two teams surrounded the pit, murmuring with excitement as the two contenders entered it.

"Best two out of three," declared Billy.

"How about whoever loses gets to run laps until practice is over," Ryder suggested, a smirk on his face.

Jack's eyes lit up, and when I was about to open my mouth and tell Ryder how bad an idea that was, Jack interrupted me. "You're on!" he declared.

Ty, Jaden, and I looked at each other and shook our heads. Poor Ryder. We knew this eighth grader didn't stand a chance. When Jack got mad, he was basically a monster on the field, and a bully off it.

Calvin counted down, and then, Jack and Ryder slammed into each other, their pads ramming in a stunning loud crash. As I figured, it wasn't much of a contest. Jack hurled Ryder out of the circle both times with a loud cry, and both times, it prompted cheers from the crowd, including me.

Ryder bawled out a loud curse word as Billy pointed to the field. "They don't call him The Shield for nothing, Banks," he asserted, "Get moving."

The tight end glanced at Calvin, his team captain, but Bryce, his squad leader, stood between them and yelled out, "You lost, Ryder! Now move your ass!" Ryder cursed again and began jogging around the field, evoking laughter from a lot of the guys.

"That guy has a big mouth," a kid remarked. Another said, "I can't believe he got beaten by that seventh grader."

"Wasn't a surprise to those who know Jack," said Jaden, "It was inevitable."

Then, Jack looked into my eyes, his face in a scowl and his chest moving up and down as he took deep breaths. He didn't

budge from the circle. Instead, he pointed a finger at me and then, used it to beckon me into the pit.

I sighed. "Is he serious?" I wondered aloud.

My teammates 'ooh'ed and clapped, shouting "Yeah!" and slapping me on the back. Jack marched around inside the pit, punching a fist into his other hand, letting out a growl each time.

"It's on!" shouted a few more kids. Billy and Calvin looked over at me expectantly as well.

"Jack-" I began, but he spun around, took out his mouth guard, and yelled, "No! You get your ass in the pit, *right now!*"

There wasn't any use arguing with him. He was super pissed. I felt a wave of fear flow through me, something that I had only experienced a few times when we went up against each other. Each time, something had been bothering him, and he kept it bottled up, ready to explode as soon as he was given permission to proceed. This was the first time, however, that the rage was directed toward *me*. I could feel the tension – the fury – in his body, in need of release.

"Scott..." urged Calvin. I looked over at him. "Yes or no?" Billy waited for my answer as well.

I wasn't going to back down, even though I didn't stand much of a chance. Jack wouldn't have let it go until I faced him. If I could just hold him off for a few seconds, like I did Calvin, I'd be happy.

The field was filled with loud cheers as I stepped into the circle. Calvin gave me an approving nod, while Billy shot me a look as if I was crazy.

"It's your funeral," said Billy, "but I admire your balls."

"I'm not running laps if I lose," I declared. Calvin frowned for some reason. I shrugged back.

"No one's asking you to," replied Billy.

"Let's get this over with," growled Jack, getting into his position and biting down on his mouthguard.

I did the same and peered at Jack. His eyes were narrowed and focused on me, his breathing, deliberate and even. I readied myself for our clash, directing nearly all my strength on my legs, and when Billy finished counting down, Jack let out a howl, and we leapt at each other. He struck me with enough force to stun me, grabbed my jersey under my arms and kept pushing me backward, grunting out a primal scream of rage all along. I tripped over another kid's cleats and fell backward, Jack crashing on top of me. His sweat-soaked armpit landed over my facemask. I only got a short whiff of his strong body odor before I felt my body go limp; my arms out by my sides. I blacked out.

chapter seventeen

Jack's horrid stench stayed in my brain as I awoke; it took quite a few seconds before it went away, allowing me to open my eyes. Like Jack, I found myself against the bleachers, looking at my lower body, my arms by my legs, my palms facing up. I felt the sweat running down my face. As I lifted my head, I heard Billy shout from the field, "Hey, Weston's awake!" Most of the boys clapped, especially my friends – even Jack. Bryce ran over to me, made sure I was okay, and helped me up to my feet.

"How long was I out?" I asked.

"Almost thirty minutes," he said, "Same as Jack. You still have some time to practice if you want."

"Yeah."

"I bet Jack's armpit smelled terrible," Bryce chuckled.

"It sure did."

Calvin motioned for me to join them on the field, and Jack met me halfway there, giving me a smile when he reached me. I could feel that the anger he had toward me had dissipated. He was now back to his usual self, and that was a relief.

"So, now we know what each other's sweaty pits smell like," he said, pulling my facemask around, "Although, Billy told me we can only do that at scrimmages or at games."

"Same here," I said.

"We cool?" Jack asked, holding out his fist for me to bump.

I smiled back and bumped his fist. "Sure are."

"Thanks for not backing down," he said, "Hope you aren't hurt."

"No," I replied, "Just my pride."

Calvin wasn't smiling, however. Neither was Billy, standing next to him. "Scott, I didn't like your attitude back there in the pit," my team captain said, "You basically gave up even before you tried." I felt my excitement draining away and replaced with dread at having to explain myself.

"I just *knew* what I was getting into," I said, looking at Jack, "When he gets mad, all hell breaks loose."

"Oh, really?" Calvin scowled, folding his arms, "What the fuck happened to that never-give-up attitude you had when going up against me, huh?" I couldn't believe this conversation was happening. Why couldn't he just let this go? Calvin squinted his eyes at me. I took it as a warning that if he didn't like my answer, or if I didn't answer, he'd make me do pushups; or run laps; or do both.

"Because I know him," I replied, "He needed to vent out his rage with me. Besides, I felt guilty for knocking him out like that. I guess a part of me *wanted* him to win." I gave Jack a sidelong glare. "I didn't think he'd pit me back, though." Jack laughed, and Calvin and Billy exchanged a glance.

"Just be aware of your attitude, Weston," replied Billy, "You don't lose until you've actually lost... or you think you have – whichever comes first."

"That's right," Calvin added. Even Jack added his two cents by nodding to that.

"Okay," I said, hoping that would end this conversation. With that, Calvin motioned for me to rejoin practice, and I was relieved that I wasn't going to be punished. We practiced for the next twenty minutes, and then, we ran our finishing sprints. Calvin made Ryder participate in those as well.

"We're a team," Calvin reminded him, "Don't forget that."

After that, both Coach King and Coach Thimbleton stood in the middle of our school's field and had all one hundred or so of us form a circle around them, sitting with our legs crossed, and facing the center. Jack was seated on Billy's right side, and I sat next to him, with Ty beside me, and Jaden seated next to him in the circle.

We were told to put the back of our left hand on the right knee of the boy next to us and hold the hand of the boy to our right. I put my left hand on Jack's knee, which he clasped. When I felt Ty put the back of his left hand on my right knee, I took hold of it.

When we all held hands, Coach King shouted instructions into a megaphone, "Close your eyes. Take slow, deep breaths. Focus on the energy coming from the teammate on your left. Hold your breath. One. Two. Sense his energy coming through, mixing with your own. Exhale. Slowly. Move the energy along to the boy on your right."

I did as I was told. As I breathed in, I focused on Jack's grip, feeling the warmth from his hand and the intimate connection from my own hand resting on his knee. I held my breath, sensing his warmth mixing with mine, spreading throughout my body. Exhaling, I passed on this energy to Ty, who responded with an

immediate squeeze. At that very moment, I felt a powerful, concentrated flow of energy coming from Jack, like it contained not just his energy, but Billy's, and Travis Bower's, sitting next to Billy, and so on down the line. I found my own hand, almost instinctively, squeezing Jack's.

As we kept repeating this, our breathing became synchronized, and the air filled up with the harmony of one-hundred warrior boys breathing rhythmically. I felt our collective energy grow, cumulate into an incredible warm, loving feeling in my heart. After a few minutes, Coach King shouted, "Let go and open your eyes."

When I did so, I immediately planted both hands over my crotch, feeling Jack's, Ty's, and everyone else's energies mixing with my own, triggering an amazing mini-orgasm that made me moan and shut my eyes for a few seconds. When I opened them again, I noticed that almost every other boy had done the same thing, including Jack, Ty, Jaden, and even Billy.

"Stand up," yelled Coach King through the megaphone. As we all stood, Damian Jackson, the Rams' team captain, walked to the center of the field to Coach King, who handed him the megaphone with a wink.

Damian removed his helmet and held it up high. The rest of us followed suit.

"On three, boys, we will shout 'Panthers! Panthers! All as one!'" he announced. "One! Two! Three!"

We filled the sky with one hundred shouts in unison. *"Panthers! Panthers! All as one!"* When the echo finally died down, Damian prompted, "One more time! One! Two! Three!"

This time even the coaches joined in.

"Panthers! Panthers! All as one!"

"Excellent!" shouted Damian while we cheered, whooped, and hollered.

Both King and Thimbleton had wide smiles across their faces, and when Damian attempted to hand the megaphone back to King, Coach refused and ushered Damian to continue.

"Great work this week, kiddies!" the Rams' captain concluded. "Have a good weekend and see you on Monday, which starts the first five-day overnight camp!"

More cheers erupted, and we patted each other on the back and shoulder pads – or even rubbed each other's hair before heading to the locker rooms. I only made it a few steps when Ty put me in a headlock and gave me a noogie, making Jack laugh. "Yeah, get him good, Ty!" he prodded him on.

Once Ty let me go, instead of going after *him*, I decided to tackle Jack for his betrayal, catching him completely off guard and knocking him to the ground.

"Ack!" he gasped, dazed for a moment. I took that opportunity to squat on top of Jack's chest, giving him a noogie and rubbing his scalp hard.

"Traitor!" I said to him, a smirk on my face.

"Ow!" he yelped, "Get offa me!"

I suddenly found another kid reaching under my armpits and holding me against my chest. Whoever it was, he lifted me onto my feet. I turned my head to see Billy's grinning face.

"Hey!" I shouted, struggling to be let loose, but for the life of me, I couldn't break free. The kid had an iron grip.

"Let me go, Billy!" I demanded. Jaden laughed and gave me a noogie.

"Jaden, you asshole!" I cursed, but that only made Jaden laugh some more. Jack stood up and wiped himself off.

"You wanna get him back, Murphy?" asked Billy, looking at Jack. The other boy nodded in rapid succession.

"Well, you better hurry. I don't know how much longer I can stand Weston's stench." Jack growled, bent his body to lower his shoulder pads, and bolted for me, digging his pads into my gut. Billy held his ground.

"Oomph!" I gasped as Jack knocked the wind out of me. My head dropped forward, and my eyes nearly popped out of their sockets. As if on cue, Billy let me go, and I fell to the ground on my hands and knees, gasping for breath.

"You assholes!" I said, wheezing, "That hurt!"

Billy stood over me, arms folded, and said, "You smack one of my guys like that, Weston, you pay the price." I gave him the finger in response. Then, Jack put me in a headlock and returned the noogie, the pain making me whimper.

As Calvin walked past me, we locked eyes; my expression gave him the hint that I wanted his help.

"I saw what you did there, Scott," Calvin said with a shake of his head, "Pick fights with the big boys, and you're gonna get hurt."

Jack put me in a choke hold, and I begged, "Stop lecturing me, Calvin, and help me for fuck's sake! He smells terrible!" Everyone burst out laughing.

"You would know!" said Billy, high-fiving Travis Bower.

"Say you'll let me come over and be the first one who gets to play Asher's Legend, Scott," demanded Jack, referring to the new video game coming out next month that I had been saving to buy.

"Ooo! I want to play that game too!" exclaimed Billy.

"No way!" I whined to Jack.

"Have it your way, then," he said, increasing the pressure on my neck, making it harder for me to breathe.

"Urk!" I gurgled, "Okay, okay! Fine! But only for ten minutes."

Jack squeezed even harder. "Two hours, fuckface."

If this continued, he'd choke me out. I had no desire to be knocked out twice in one day – and both times by Jack, no less.

"Fine!" I relented and Jack released me with a chuckle.

Even my team captain had a big grin on his face by then, which irritated the hell out of me. I knew what I was about to do was stupid, but I couldn't help but allow my emotions to take over.

"This is for not helping me, Calvin!" I exclaimed, putting him in a headlock and giving him the patent noogie burn.

"Ow!" he yelped, "Fuck!"

I had enough sense not only to stop before he escaped and retaliated, but also to jog a few feet away to be clear of any knee-jerk reaction from him. As I did, I nearly tripped over my helmet. I picked it up and grinned at him as I tossed it in the air to myself.

"Holy fucking shit!" Billy exclaimed, his eyes as wide as saucers, and his mouth agape. "You did *not* just do that!"

Calvin brushed his hair to side, then steadily looked over at me, slit-eyed.

I strapped on my helmet and bit down on my mouthguard, in case he came after me. Calvin strapped his helmet on as well and then dashed after me like a bullet.

"Oh fuck!" I exclaimed, running off in the other direction.

"Get 'em, Williams!" shouted Billy, behind me.

I looked behind and saw Calvin gaining on me quickly. I wasn't watching my course and slammed into Bryce Winters, which knocked both of us off balance and slowed me down. Then, the hit from Calvin struck. I don't remember exactly what had happened, except that I found my body tumbling over on the ground, like a car that had just been T-boned.

The pain, with all its groans and gasps, escaped my lips each time I hit the dirt, and when my body had finally come to a halt, I found myself lying motionless, twisted like a pretzel, looking

sideways at the grass. Calvin's cleats and dirty socks came into view as he stood over me. I heard shouts, gasps, and laughter roaring from my teammates.

"Holy shit!" Jack, Ty, and Jaden exclaimed in unison. I heard their footsteps rushing toward me.

"Now *that* is how you tackle someone," said Billy, walking slowly toward me.

"I think you broke my everything," I wheezed to Calvin through the pain, spitting out my mouthguard. My attacker had used his cleats to turn me over on my back.

"Pain," I moaned.

Then, Calvin bent down and placed his facemask inches from mine, his mouthguard dangling free. With a stony, cold face, Calvin looked into my eyes and asked, "Was it worth it?" I stared back, silent for a few seconds.

"Oh, fuck yes," I finally said, laughing and groaning with pain. Calvin burst into a laugh as well, unable to hold his seriousness any longer.

"You're crazy, Scott," he grinned, helping me back up, holding on to my body to stabilize me. Everyone around us clapped.

Billy cocked his head. "Do you have a death wish, Weston," he asked, "or are you just stupid?"

"I dunno. Both?" I quipped, making my three seventh grade friends laugh.

Billy placed his hands on his hips and said, "Yeah, I can believe that, since stupid is doing what you just did to a kid twice your size."

"It's not like I picked a fight with him, Billy," I explained, "I was just messing around."

That did make him chuckle, though. "You are something else," he said.

Calvin removed his helmet, his pooled sweat spattering everywhere. He shook my facemask around and removed my helmet for me.

"Can you walk?" asked Calvin.

"I think so," I said, but when he let go of me, I started to wobble and wince in pain, and all Billy could do was chortle.

Jack put a hand on Calvin's shoulder pads and said, "Ty and I can help him get back, Calvin."

Calvin shook his head. "Nah. I got him," he said, "Have to admit I'm impressed. Very few guys have ever had the balls to do that to me before."

"And lived to tell about it," added Bryce.

"Yeah, no kidding," said Derek Edwards, joining us.

By the time we got to the entrance of the locker rooms, I was walking on my own. Before we seventh and eighth graders went into our separate locker rooms, Calvin said, "You're an interesting kid, Scott."

"Thanks," I smiled.

"You got balls," he continued, "even if they end up getting your ass kicked."

"I think Weston here just likes pain," Billy interjected before shaking Jack's hand and leading the other eighth grade Warriors inside their locker room. Calvin smacked my hand, gripping it in a handshake.

"See you guys Monday," he said to us Colts seventh graders before turning to the eighth graders and saying, "Let's go."

chapter eighteen

Inside our own locker room, most of the fifty or so seventh graders were already changing out of their uniforms, the loud clangs of the lockers and excited chatter filled the air, along with the strong smell of mud and sweat.

A few unconscious boys lined the walls, some with their pads on, some only in their cupped underwear. Apparently, they wanted to see if they could take another player's body odor and found the answer quickly enough. Jack and I were bombarded with questions from the other boys about being armpitted; we said it wasn't fun being the victim of, but a joy to dish out.

"According to the team captains, we're only allowed to do that at certain scrimmages or on rival teams in the game," Jack warned, "Otherwise, we'll be running laps. We need to be conscious to practice."

Some of the guys, mostly members of the Colts, passed comments to me about me noogie-ing Calvin and the incredible retaliation tackle he struck me with.

"I wish I had my phone to video that," said Nicholas Schmidt, our tight end, "That would have become a meme in no time."

"Yeah," added another boy, "and the title could be, 'Kid takes acrobatic tumble after dead on collision with fast moving defensive tackle'."

"Waddya think, Scott?" a third kid asked, a smirk on his face.

"Well, there are worse ways of becoming famous," I replied.

"Hah!" Nicholas chuckled, "That's true."

When I got to my locker, Ty was already undressing.

"We're supposed to leave our pads here," Ty said to me, removing his shoulder pads. Ty left the jersey attached as he placed it in his locker.

I followed suit, placing my jersey-covered shoulder pads and padded pants neatly in my locker, my helmet on the top shelf. I took a whiff of the strong odor coming from my sweat-soaked uniform and grinned. That was *my* locker and *my* equipment. Ty stepped up right next to me.

"I can't tell who's stronger," he started, comparing our bodies, now that we were both stripped down to only our cupped underwear and socks. I flexed my muscles and looked between the two of us. We seemed to be about even. Then, I flapped a hand over my nose. "You are, obviously," I said, grinning a wide one.

"Oh, ha ha," he said, pointing to my armpit, "Jack passed out from your stench, you know."

"I know," I replied, "It was kind of awesome. I didn't know I could do that."

Ty smelled his own armpit and grimaced. "Ugh. That's pretty bad," he admitted, "I bet you'd pass out from mine too."

Billy Thompson stuck his head in to our locker room. "Murphy!" he called out. We all turned to a now bare-chested Jack, who had only managed to change out of his shoulder pads. He looked over at his team captain.

Billy tilted his head, gesturing him to meet in the eighth graders' locker room.

"Catch you at the bike racks, guys," he said to Ty, Jaden, and me, and then followed Billy out.

I wiped the sweat off my torso before putting on my shorts and gray practice shirt. My body was still so hot from practice that I continued to perspire. It didn't matter, though; my mom would be washing my clothes this weekend anyway.

Jaden, now changed into his shorts and practice shirt, came over to our locker, his backpack slung over his shoulder.

"You guys aren't done changing yet?" asked Jaden.

"Working on it," replied Ty, throwing on his own clothes while I laced up my cleats. Jack came back into the locker room as Ty finished up.

"Yo, Scott!" called Jack, "Calvin wants to talk to you in the eighth grade locker room."

I raised an eyebrow, wondering what he wanted. "He does?" I asked.

"Yup."

"About *what*?"

He smiled. "Just go see him, Scott."

Then, he told Jaden he needed to talk to him in private and asked Ty to wait by the bike racks.

"What the hell's going on?" Ty whispered to me, as Jaden met Jack by the linebacker's locker.

I shrugged, watching Jack change as he and Jaden started talking. "Hell if I know, Ty," I said.

"What-the-fuck-ever," Number Forty-Two said, grabbing his backpack.

"Mind taking mine as well?" I asked, handing mine out to him.

"Yeah, sure," Ty said, taking it before walking away.

I made my way to the eighth grade boys' locker room, which smelled just as bad as ours. Calvin was standing bare-chested in his shorts by his locker, a few feet from the entrance to the hallway. I didn't think I'd ever seen a kid his age as muscular as he looked. No wonder he hit so hard. Billy stood next to him; he was bare-chested as well. While not *as* muscular, he would certainly give another kid a run for his money.

Billy pointed me out to Calvin when he noticed me.

"Come here, Scott," Calvin asked.

On the way to his locker, I passed the other two team captains, Mason Holden and Damian Jackson, who had already changed and were heading outside together. Mason was a little taller than Damian, and both had short hair; although, Mason's was brown and Damian's was black. Freckles dotted Damian's face.

"You're one crazy son-of-a-bitch, Weston," said Damian, raising his hand for a high-five. I followed though, and he winked at me with one of his hazel eyes.

"Your neighbor's kids go home?" asked Mason.

"Yeah," I replied, "Sorry if they bothered you, Mason."

"Nah," the Jets' team captain grinned, "Like I said, it's all good. I got a little brother too, around their age."

"Does he play football?"

"No. Just basketball and baseball. He's too scared of getting hit by bigger kids." Mason laughed at that last remark and said, "He said he'll leave that to me." I laughed as well, and the two team captains waved goodbye.

When I joined Calvin at his locker, he simply acknowledged me with a simple, "Hey."

"Hey," I replied back, removing my shirt.

"What are you doing, Weston?" Billy asked, looking quizzically at my body.

"I don't want to be the only one of us with a shirt on," I teased, making Calvin chuckle. I looked between the three of us, comparing our muscles. Billy gave my body another glance and moved my torso from side-to-side.

"Yeah," he said, "that's about how muscular I was last year too."

"Woah, really?" I asked, hopeful that the next year, I'd be as strong as he was.

"Yup," nodded Billy.

"How about you, Calvin?" I inquired, reaching for the stars on that question. Billy simply laughed.

"I looked like you did about two years ago," he replied nonchalantly as he finished changing.

"Oh bullshit!" I exclaimed. Calvin gave me a sidelong glance.

I flexed my arm, looking proudly at my bulging muscles. "No eleven-year old has guns like this!" I declared.

He pointed to a younger picture of himself taped on the inside of his locker. The kid in the picture, covered in dirt and sweat from his head down to his football pants, stood in a locker room, shirtless and looking as strong as I was now. A muddy, sweat-stained red and blue number twelve jersey, still covering the shoulder pads, sat on the bench next to him. A scratched helmet was next to that. He was holding a large trophy in his hands, wearing a smug grin on his face.

"That's you two years ago?" I gasped, taking a closer look.

"Sure was," he said.

His fingers were covering the year, but I could read the rest of what was written on the trophy – Southwest Youth Division One Football Tournament: Regional Champions.

I snapped my fingers. "I remember my dad showing me the article in the paper about that game!" I said, "About you, Calvin!"

A smile formed on Calvin lips. "I still have a copy of that paper," He said fondly.

"You were the quarterback," I rambled on, "and made, like, six touchdown passes *and* managed to hold off two blitzing defenders!"

"Five touchdowns, actually," said Calvin.

"But who's counting, right?" quipped Billy, now entirely dressed.

"Man, am I happy to be playing with you," I said, star-struck.

"Thanks."

"Looks like you got yourself another rabid fan, Williams," said Billy.

"So that's what you and Coach Thimbleton meant," I turned to Billy, "when you guys referred to Calvin as an all-star quarterback."

Billy nodded, strapping on his backpack and asked, "So I guess you aren't upset anymore that you got traded, huh?"

"Nope," was my sharp reply, shaking my head.

"Good to know." Then, he smacked Calvin on the shoulder, "See you tonight, Williams." Calvin waved goodbye, and Billy gave me a light noogie as he left.

Calvin watched him leave, and then, he leaned against his locker and asked, "You know how we eighth grade players are getting together this Saturday night at The Edge of the World club?"

"Yeah. Jack mentioned it on Monday," I replied, "He's a squad leader, so he gets to go, even though he's just twelve."

He lowered his voice. "Would *you* like to go? As my guest?"

My mouth dropped open. "Seriously?" I cried out. Calvin gestured for me to keep my voice down, but he nodded.

The Edge of the World was a popular teen hangout, which served all types of interesting food and drinks, played the latest hit music, and had tons of video game consoles to play on. Plus, it had a large dance floor and a stage for live bands. You had to be at least thirteen to get in by yourself or twelve if one of them brought you in as a guest, and each summer, they hosted a Saturday night party only for eighth grade middle school football players. Of course, they also had one for the high schools the week after, which I heard always ended up as *the* place to be for teens if they were lucky enough to get in.

"You'd really take me as a guest?" I asked, my excited voice now hushed.

"Sure. Why not? Like I said before, you're an interesting dude. I kinda want to see what you're like outside of football – Billy does too."

I couldn't believe it. The two coolest eighth graders wanted me to join them at the (second) most happening event of the summer.

"I know I probably shouldn't ask this," I said, which made Calvin look at me quizzically, "but would you mind inviting Ty Green too? He's a good friend of mine."

"Yes, I know," said Calvin, a small smile curling at the corner of his lips, "I figured you'd ask. He's a cool kid too. Go ahead."

"Thank you!" I shouted back. My excited shout made some of the other kids look over at us. I covered my mouth. "Sorry," I whispered. Calvin just shook his head, but the smile didn't leave his face. I thought about Jaden and hoped that Jack thought of him first, and that's why Jack wanted to talk to him. If he didn't, Jaden wouldn't have gone, and he'd feel left out.

"You look worried," remarked Calvin, noticing the downturn in my mood. "What's wrong?" he asked.

I didn't want to come right out and ask if Jaden had been invited; Calvin might not even know.

"I was just thinking about my other friend, Jaden Ludge. See, he-"

"Billy's already told Jack that he could invite him," he cut me short, "So, don't worry." So that *is* what Jack wanted to talk to Jaden about. Oh, thank God!

"Awesome!" I said, all concerns leaving my mind, "Thank you, Calvin!"

Calvin smiled again. "You're welcome," he said, "See you there at seven?"

I nodded.

"Just be sure to wear a clean, sleeved Putnam Panthers football practice T-shirt, okay?"

"Okay."

He looked at the football practice T-shirt I had on, which had begun to soak in fresh sweat.

"Emphasis on clean, Scott. And make sure you are too – so you don't smell like a dead animal like you do now." What kind of kid did he think I was? Besides, he probably smelled worse than I did at that moment. I decided to play it off.

"You think I'm an animal? Huh?" I responded, imitating a popular TV gangster, "I'll show you what an animal can do!"

A bunch of laughs came from some of the other eighth graders, who had obviously seen the show, but Calvin just stared at me, his eyebrows furrowed.

"Never mind," I said, "I'll be sure not to stink on Saturday night."

"Good," he said, grabbing his backpack and slung it around his shoulders, "That's all I wanted to hear. Also make sure you guys

bring your student IDs and ten dollars each for the cover charge. I'll be sure to put you on the guest list."

A sense of self-importance surged through me. "You bet!"

"See ya then."

We slapped palms as a goodbye, and I trotted out toward the bike racks, head held high. Jaden and Jack were riding their bikes around in circles, and Ty was standing next to his, guarding my backpack lying at his feet.

"Jeez, what took you so long?" Ty complained, "What did Calvin want?" As there were several other kids hanging around, I told Ty that I'd tell the three of them when we got back to my place. On our way home, Jack and I let Ty and Jaden lead the way; the two of us hung back so we could exchange a few words without them hearing us.

"Did you invite Ty?" Jack whispered over the noise of the pedals. So, he obviously knew.

I nodded. "Jaden?" I asked to confirm. Jack nodded back. We shared a grin and fist bumped each other. We rode the rest of the way back in silence, waving to a few teammates who passed us by in their parents' cars. When we reached my house, Ty and I parked our bikes near the driveway, but Jack and Jaden stood still on theirs.

Jack looked at his phone. "My dad just texted me," he started, "and said we only have about half an hour to get ready, so we gotta hurry back."

"Yeah, hold up," said Ty, "What was all that about back at the locker rooms?" Jack and I explained everything to him. Jaden knew already, except for my inviting Ty.

Ty's mood skyrocketed, and, with a big grin, he made a fist and yanked his arm down, exclaiming, "Yes! That's awesome! That's

like the coolest party *ever* for middle schoolers!" He gave me a one-arm hug and a light noogie. "Thanks for thinking of me!" he said.

"Well, yeah," I replied, smiling, "I didn't want to go without you and Jaden either."

Jaden smiled at Jack, who waggled his eyebrows back at him and motioned for them to get going. As Jaden and Jack began to pedal away, Jack shouted to Ty and me, "Get cleaned up, guys. My dad will be at your house in about forty minutes, Scott."

Ty and I waved back and headed inside; we were getting ready for the amazing weekend that was just getting started.

chapter nineteen

When Ty and I were getting dressed, after we had cleaned up, I told him about Calvin's all-star status.

"Oh, yeah, I remember that now!" said Ty. He put on a T-shirt with a silhouetted young football player running with the ball; the tagline beside him read "Play Football". I decided to match him. So, I put on a red tee with a silhouetted football player boy reaching out to catch a football. The words, "Gotta Catch 'Em All" were printed below it.

"You think people will figure out we play football together?" asked Ty with a laugh.

"I hope so," I replied.

True to her word, my mom left money for us, along a note that told us to have fun, that she loved us, and that we were to be home by ten.

We played some video games until I got a text from Jack, which said their car was waiting outside my house. Ty and I hopped into the backseat of Jack's dad's silver SUV, Ty sitting in the middle between Jaden and me. Jack sat in the passenger seat and high-fived the two of us as we got in.

"You boys certainly love football," Mr. Murphy remarked as we drove off.

His slightly wrinkled face made him look older than my mom and dad and definitely older than Ty's parents. He had a graying mustache that covered his entire upper lip and a head full of black hair, which had, like Coach Thimbleton, hints of gray.

"Of course we do, Mr. Murphy," Jaden said. "What brought that up?"

"All four of you are wearing football-related shirts."

Jack pulled the vanity mirror down in front of him, and we saw that he was wearing his favorite shirt – a blue one with the football catchphrase "This Is My Number" and his jersey number, Sixty-Four, below it. Jaden wore a gray one with a football in the middle of the phrase "Give an Inch, I'll Take a Yard". The talk about shirts reminded me of what I was told in the locker room.

"Calvin said we have to wear a clean Putnam Middle School Panthers practice shirt tomorrow night," I said.

"Good to know," replied Ty.

"Yeah, I told Jaden already," said Jack.

Jaden nodded. "I gotta surprise for you two," he told me and Ty. Jack turned to face us, a huge smile forming on his face. He already knew apparently.

"I've got four tickets to White Water tomorrow," Jaden continued, "and I want you two to come with me and Jack!" My eyes instantly widened. I had been to that giant water park a few times over the years, but hadn't been able to go this summer. It had over a dozen huge slides and a mile-long lazy river, along with a wave pool and plenty of over-priced food and drinks – A kid's summer haven.

"Awesome!" Ty and I shouted together.

Jaden explained that his family had won them in some raffle, and originally, it was going to be Jaden, his parents, and Jack, but then his parents decided to allow Jaden to invite Ty and me instead.

"You guys just need money for food," said Jaden.

"No problem!" I said, "I'm sure Mom will give it to us."

"Thanks, Jaden!" said Ty, giving him a high-five. I added a thank you and reached out to give him a fist bump.

Jaden winked at us. "Just be at my house around nine tomorrow," he continued, "we'll be back around five, so we have plenty of time to shower, change, and eat dinner before the party." Excitement was simmering inside us, and I could feel the bond between us grow even stronger. Jack's dad dropped us off at the mall, and we made our way to the food court. We walked around with our chests puffed out, smiling smugly at the smaller boys and sizing up those who looked like football players our age, especially if they were wearing football related shirts. We could tell that they were sizing us up as well, and, like us, I bet they had hoped we'd run into each other on the field. We checked out the pretty girls we passed, giving them grins. Some of them giggled and flashed us smiles; the others just rolled their eyes. We didn't care either way.

We each ended up getting a large burger and fries, scarfing them down in no time. The coaches had said that we could cheat a little on the weekends, limiting most of the sweets to just Saturday. So, even though we wanted milkshakes, we decided to pass and get water instead.

In the middle of our meal, a hulking older kid wearing a Gunner High School Cougars football tee came over to us with his food, bringing another boy with him wearing the same shirt and two girls around their age.

This giant of a boy had a voice as deep as a man's. "You guys must be middle school football players going to camp," He said. He had short, blond hair, lighter than Jack's, and the bulge of his muscles reminded me of an NFL player. Not even Calvin came close to this guy's strength.

"Yeah," Jack replied, smiling as he looked the kid over, "Putnam Panthers. I'm a squad leader."

The high school player reached out his bear-sized hand and shook each of ours, saying, "Hey, that's where Grossfield and I went!" He pointed to the boy beside him, and we shook hands with him as well. They introduced themselves as Denton Cryer and Elliott Grossfield.

"And we both were squad leaders too!" Denton exclaimed.

"Our T-shirts gave our status away, huh?" I asked.

"Not at first," said Denton, sitting down at the table next to us with his friends, "You were all drinking water with your burgers. No kid does that unless his parents make him or he's a football player, and it's football season."

"But yeah, we looked at your shirts, and they gave it away," Elliott added with a grin.

"You four boys are cute," remarked one of the girls, with short, blond hair.

"So are you two," I blurted out, making the two older boys laugh.

Then, the girl pointed to Jack and said, "This one reminds me of you four or five years ago, Denton."

"Yeah," Denton nodded, "Looks as strong as I was too." That made Jack smile.

"How is high school football camp?" Ty blurted out before he put a handful of fries in his mouth, an obvious attempt to divert the attention away form Jack.

The two older football players looked at each other with a smirk, and Elliott said, "Let's just say it's different than middle school."

"More intense?" I asked, biting into my burger.

"You'll see," said Denton, "Middle school is all about discovering who you are."

Jaden looked confused. After gulping some water, he asked, "It is? I was always told that was what college was all about."

"Not for football players," he replied, "Just trust me."

We talked about football for a bit longer, which bored the girls, who I assumed were their girlfriends, and they ended up just talking to each other. Denton played middle linebacker, just like Jack, and Elliott played wide receiver, so he and I talked about playing offense.

I lost track of how much time had passed, but eventually, Jaden looked at his phone and said, "Guys, we gotta jet *now* or we're gonna be late for the movie!" We shook hands with the high school players again, wished each other luck, and said goodbye to their girlfriends before running off to the theater. Luckily, we made it in time and got decent seats, just before the theater quickly filled up.

After the flick, we ran into Stephanie Williams, Calvin's sister, and her volleyball teammate, Jean, while exiting the theater. It turned out they had only been a few rows in front of us while Calvin and Billy, who were now using the restrooms, sat near the back. The crowd inside the theater and the low lighting must have made us miss each other.

The lighting outside and around the parking lot pierced the darkness. It had been sunny on our way to the mall, and the sudden lack of light startled me at first. The time on my phone read exactly

nine-thirty; as long as Jaden's dad picked us up in the next ten minutes, Ty and I would be home in time for our curfew.

As we all waited for our rides, Jean remarked, "You boys clean up nicely."

"Yeah, you actually don't smell like B.O.," added Stephanie, leaning against a column from the overhang of the theater.

"Like I care," replied Jaden with a shrug. Ty and Jack just rolled their eyes at each other.

I laughed, though. "Well, thanks, Stephanie, I think," I said.

"You're welcome, Scott."

She and I exchanged a long gaze. I stepped a bit closer to her and rested my hand on the column, placing it by her head, so that she could smell my body. It turns out that I could smell her too, the sweet aroma of apples and spice coming from her neck.

"You smell good yourself," I said, "Like apples."

"It's my body wash," she replied, looking at my muscles.

"Yo, Scott," said Jaden.

"Hey, Scott!" shouted Jack.

"Pssst!" hissed Ty.

All three of my friends were looking past me, and even Jean's face was turning red. I felt a finger tap me on the shoulder, and I turned around to see Calvin inches from my face, his arms folded. Billy, wearing a T-shirt with an 8-bit image of a football, stood by him, shaking his head.

"A *little* too close to my sister there, don't you think, Scott?" asked Calvin, sporting an NFL T-shirt.

He wasn't visibly upset, so I replied a little cheekily, "Not like I'm on top of her, Calvin."

"Could have fooled me." Calvin clasped a hand on my shoulder and walked me a few feet away from his sister and closer to Billy. "There," said the Colts leader, "Much better."

"He's very protective of his sister," Billy whispered to me, although Calvin could easily hear him.

Stephanie rolled her eyes. "Don't listen to Calvin, Scott," she said.

"I kinda need to," I said with a shrug, "He's my team captain."

She rolled her eyes in exasperation, placed her hands on her hips, and shouted, *"Seriously?* You're *not* playing football right now!" A few other kids around us turned toward us. I didn't understand why she'd gotten upset over what I said.

"What does that have to do with anything?" I asked, "He's still my team captain – on or off the field. Besides, you *are* his little sister." Stephanie just let out a groan.

"Why does everything revolve around football for boys around here?" Jean asked, "I mean, I lost count of the number of them wearing football related shirts in this mall." She pointed between all six of us guys. "And all of you prove my point," She finished. We all looked at our shirts.

"It's the best sport in the world, that's why," replied Ty.

"You girls just wouldn't get it," added Jaden.

"Don't bother, Jean," said Stephanie as Jean gave Jaden the stink eye, "It's in the stupid part of their DNA."

"Hey!" said Calvin, crossing his arms.

Stephanie smiled at him, teasing, "Hah hah!"

"My mom said the same thing to my aunt, actually... about my dad and me not too long ago," confessed Ty.

Jack switched the subject by telling Calvin and Billy about the conversation we had with the high schoolers and their football experiences.

"I guess we'll find out for sure next year," said Billy, "Huh, Calvin?"

"I guess so," he replied.

We chatted a bit more about the movie before Calvin's mom arrived to pick him and Stephanie up, along with Billy and Jean, who were sleeping over. Billy let the girls climb in the backseat first before getting in himself.

"See you all tomorrow," said Calvin to us, before he gave me a nod and got into the passenger's seat. The back window rolled down, and Billy gestured a fist, sticking out his pinky and thumb.

"Yeah, see ya tomorrow, dudes!" said Billy, waving his wrist from side to side. "Wooo!!! Surf's up!" he shouted, as the car rolled away. Some of the kids around us laughed.

"You can take the kid out of the beach," Jack chuckled, "but you can't take the beach out of the kid." His dad arrived soon after and dropped Ty and me home. Exhaustion suddenly took hold of me when we walked in through my front door, and I let out a big yawn.

"I'm beat, too," said Ty, yawing as well.

We said hello to my mom, who was in the kitchen making brownies. I told her about White Water and our invite to The Edge of the World while she licked the spatula.

"I was hoping to spend some time with you boys," she said, giving me a light pat on the shoulder, "You've been busy all week."

"That's the life of a football player," I quipped, sticking my finger in the bowl and wiping the chocolate off the edges, "Besides, there's always Sunday." As soon as I did that, she smacked the back of my hand with the spatula, making Ty snicker.

"Hey!" I exclaimed.

"When was the last time you washed your hands, Mister?" she asked. I thought about that as I licked my fingers.

"Um..." I said, "In the shower before we left for the movie?"

"And did you use the restroom between that time and now?"

I raised an eyebrow at her. "Really? I'm not a little kid, Mom."

She folded her arms, hiding the spatula behind her back. "Yes, really," she said, "Until you get a wife or a girlfriend who nags you about all that, it's gonna be me."

I rolled my eyes. That didn't make me look forward to having a girlfriend. "No, I didn't use the restroom, Mom," I declared.

"Thank God for that," she said, making Ty laugh again. Although Mom called him out. "Yeah, you laugh, Ty," she said, "but I bet you're in the same boat."

"Yeah, pretty much," he admitted, leaning against the counter.

She took a spoon, put a glob of batter on it, and handed it to Ty. He nearly put the entire thing in his mouth. When he took it out, it was practically clean.

"Mmmmm!" he moaned in delight, "You make the best brownies, Mrs. Weston."

"Thank you, Ty," she said, handing me a spoonful as well. I hadn't had her brownies in a few months. The sweet taste of the chocolate put me in heaven, and I closed my eyes to savor it.

"Why are you making these?" I asked, handing the spoon back.

"Well, they were for tomorrow, but we can wait till Sunday."

I had a better idea. "How about a snack for in-between White Water and the party?"

"We'll see," she laughed, "Get to bed. I'll leave money out for lunch at White Water."

"Will you take us to the party?" I asked.

"Well, can I go too?" she asked without any hint of joking around, "I think it'd be fun to see you with all your football buddies."

My jaw dropped. "You can't be serious."

"It's just for teenagers, Mrs. Weston," Ty explained.

"Which neither of you are yet," she pointed out, emptying the batter in a deep baking pan.

"I told you we could go because we were invited by the eighth graders!" I clarified, throwing up my hands. I couldn't believe this. There was no way I was going to allow her to be at a club with God knows how many seventh and eighth grade football players. I'd be a complete laughing stock.

She sighed, put her hands on the counter, and turned her head toward me.

"I won't embarrass you, Scott," she said, "I promise. I'll just sit at the bar and drink my blues away. Maybe I'll even strike up a conversation with one of your friends." I gave her a very confused look, as that didn't make any sense, but then it struck me – she was quoting, with small changes, from an R-rated comedy that we had watched on TV together last month. I wondered if Ty knew the reference. I looked over at him, and his troubled expression told me he had no idea. That meant Mom and I could have some fun at his expense.

"Oh yeah, Mom?" I said, going along the script, "And end up in bed with one like last time?"

Now, it was Ty's jaw that dropped. He couldn't say a word, though.

"He was bit young for me, I admit," she said.

I didn't miss a beat. "Mom, he was *thirteen*."

"What the hell?" Ty whispered to me, but I ignored him.

"He looked eighteen to me," came the reply, right on cue.

"Your mom had sex with a thirteen-year-old boy?" Ty gasped, his eyes as wide as saucers and his jaw practically on the ground.

Then, it was our turn to burst out laughing. We high-fived each other and grinned at Ty, who still didn't have a clue what was going on.

"I had you going there for a minute, Scott," she said.

"Until that drinking line, yeah," I admitted.

"Wait," said Ty, folding his arms, "Were you guys quoting a movie or something?" I waggled my eyebrows as an answer. He laughed out of relief. "I swear you're the masters at that."

"You weren't so bad yourself out on the field today, Ty," I said.

"Yeah, that's true."

Then, I told Ty and Mom my gangster show reference, and how Calvin didn't get it while a bunch of other eighth graders did. That got both of them laughing again. After that, Ty and I headed up to bed, brushing our teeth before falling asleep almost immediately afterward.

chapter twenty

Although it seemed like the entire city had showed up at White Water, the four of us had a blast, the least of which amounted to running around bare-chested and showing off how muscular we were for our age. We got grins from more than one of the young female lifeguards. On the lazy river, Jaden would flex his muscles every time our inner tubes passed this one chick with long, brown hair and a small, dainty nose. She would normally just shake her head at our antics, but once, I caught her gazing at Jack.

"Dude," I said, paddling my way over to him, "That lifeguard chick totally checked you out!"

That made Jack grin. "I don't blame her," he said.

"Uh-huh."

"Well, that other one, with dark hair, the one that sat by the Totally Tubular slide?"

"What about her?" I asked, spinning around in circles.

"She was totally checking *you* out."

"No way!" I exclaimed, stopping my tube. I sat on the edge to see if I could spot her.

"Yup! Ty noticed it first," said Jack. I glanced back behind us. Ty had gotten pushed out of his tube by Jaden, and he was now trying to pull Jaden off of his.

I frowned at him. "That idiot. Why didn't he tell *me*?"

"Because you were too busy fighting for King of the Mountain with Jaden." Oh, that's right. Ty and Jack had gotten knocked off their tubes in that round, leaving Jaden and me to battle it out, with him winning. It looked like they had already started round two, even though Ty wasn't supposed to fight back after he had lost.

"You lose!" Jack suddenly shouted, and I turned to see his foot slam into my chest, knocking me into the water with a large splash. When I came up for air, Jack was howling with laughter. I wiped my face, grabbed my inner tube, and snarled at him.

"You fucker!" I hissed, loud enough for only him to hear.

"Bwahahaha!" he snorted, "I got you!"

"Looks like Scott just lost to Jack!" Jaden shouted as he and Ty looked over at us. I swam over to Jack and grabbed his leg.

"Nah-uh!" he said, kicking my head with his other foot, "You know you just have to take the loss like a man!"

"The hell I do!" I growled, lifting his tube up. A whistle from a male lifeguard caught my attention, and when I looked over, he shook his head at me.

"Haha! You got in trouble!" Jack sneered as I dropped his tube.

Then, I spun his tube around, jumped on the side and put my arm around his neck. I started giving him a hard noogie.

"Ow ow ow! Stop!" he yelped, "You lost fair and square!"

"Fair, my ass!" I retorted. A few people chuckled at us as they passed us by. When I finally let go, he leapt off his tube and lunged at me, growling and baring his teeth.

"Oh, shit," I exclaimed.

"Oh! Jack got out of his tube!" shouted Jaden, "That means I win round two too!"

"I don't care!" said Jack, grabbing me and holding me in a headlock.

He then proceeded to alternate between noogieing and punching me on the shoulder, gnashing his teeth all the while and saying, "Gonna cheat on me, huh? Gonna twink out on me *again*, huh?"

I cried in pain and shouted, "Stop it!"

"Yeah, get him!" shouted a younger boy who caught up with us, "I saw what he did to you!"

"Thanks, kiddo!" said Jack, pausing the torture long enough to give the kid a high-five. I took that opportunity to twist the skin of his shoulder, making him shriek as well. He started to tighten his grip around my neck. Then, I heard a whistle and saw him look up at someone, probably a lifeguard.

Jack grunted, saying, "Fine, fine." He let me go, and then he poked a finger on my chest with one hand and pointed over to a cute female lifeguard with another. She had a scowl on her face and was shaking her head at Jack.

"You're lucky that lovely lady there requested that I take it easy on you, Scott." said Jack.

In an instant, her scowl changed to a smile. I looked up at her again as we passed by. With my masculinity challenged, I had to respond. "I could have taken him, you know!" I lied.

"I don't think so," she replied, giving Jack a wink and making him blush. I grunted and plopped down in my tube, my arms folded across my chest and a frown on my face. I wondered why Jack always got away with getting physical with me, while I almost always ended up in trouble, and why he had to be so much stronger than me. *If he hadn't lied to me about that other lifeguard...*

Jack interrupted my thoughts. "Hey, man," he said, holding out his fist for me to bump, "No hard feelings. I won't allow it." I shook my head, glaring at him. Jack frowned and said, "Stop being such a sore loser!"

Ty and Jaden had caught up to us by then, both sitting in their respective inner tubes.

"Was that Totally Tubular lifeguard really staring at me, Ty?" I asked him, while making a side-long glare at Jack.

Ty nodded. "Oh, for sure. She seemed to like you."

Jack raised his eyebrows at me. "You owe me a fist bump, Numbnuts, and a smile."

"Fine," I said, fist bumping him and managing to form a small grin.

"Good. Now... you cheat on me like that again, Scott," he warned, wagging his finger, "and I'll wait until we're alone before I give it to you."

"Sounds pretty fucking gay to me," joked Jaden, spinning in his tube.

"You only *wish* I would give it to you like that, Jaden," Jack quipped back.

"Hah!" exclaimed Ty.

We continued our King of the Mountain game in the lazy river for a bit longer, with Jack being the ultimate winner and Jaden coming in second. Afterward, we ate lunch, hit the main attractions again, and then, went into the wave pool to play King of the Mountain there. We got into pairs, with one guy on top of the other's shoulders trying to knock each other off, a point each going to the pair who won. The waves were an added obstacle, and it actually knocked Jack off twice. His lack of agility made me laugh. We switched positions and partners so that each of us fought the other at least once. Before the last round, Jaden and I were tied for

first place. I was on Ty's shoulders; Jack was on Jaden's. If I knocked Jack off, I'd win, making Ty and him tie for third place. If Jack knocked me off, Jaden would win and Jack and I would share second place.

"This will go just like it did at the pit yesterday, Scott!" Jack declared, cracking his knuckles.

The four of us let out war cries as Jack and I clashed, locking hands and trying to push the other off. Jack had as much strength as Billy, which meant I didn't stand much of a chance. I could only hope that the next wave would push him off Jaden's shoulder. But, he had learned from his previous experiences, directing Jaden to turn his back toward the wave. When it hit, it merely pushed Jack against the back of Jaden's head, and he used our clasped hands to stabilize himself.

"Yeah!" he shouted, "I ain't going down that easily anymore!"

He gritted his teeth, snarled at me, and began to push me with all his might. I felt myself beginning to fall backward. Ty grunted as he tightened his grip on my legs and turned his body; the next wave hit us from the back, giving me a little support. I noticed that every time a big wave hit them, Jaden would immediately wipe his face, regardless if he was on top or not. It meant that in this round, with him holding Jack, he'd momentarily let go of one of Jack's legs, which would give me a small, but convenient, opening.

"Get closer to Jaden, Ty!" I shouted over the squeals of the other kids playing in the water, "and let go of my legs as soon as the next wave hits!"

Ty looked up at me, squinting. "You sure?"

"Yes!" I confirmed.

"Sure thing, boss!" Ty shouted back and got as close as he could. That meant Jack was able to increase the force in his arms against me, and I began to lose balance again.

Jack laughed and taunted, "Glug glug!" as an indication that I was about to swallow a lot of water.

Miraculously, the next wave hit immediately after, and when it did, Ty let go of my legs just as Jaden started wiping his face. I swept a leg under Jack's free knee and flipped his leg over Jaden's head. Jack fell unceremoniously into the water. He tried to pull me in with him, but by then, I had crossed my legs around Ty's neck for balance, and Ty immediately grabbed them to further stabilize me.

Jack was forced to let go of my hands to come up for air. Ty and I whooped and hollered and exchanged high-fives. Jack pushed me off of Ty out of spite, and I plunged into the water. It didn't matter to me, though, as I simply laughed after I surfaced.

"I win!" I said, shooting my arms up in victory, "I am King of the Wave Pool!"

"I got to admit, that was pretty damn clever of you, Scott," said Jack, "Seizing an opportunity like that and not giving up. I'm actually proud of you."

"Yeah, you would have lost otherwise," said Jaden, "I can't believe you caught me off guard like that."

"I just wanted to get back at Jack for kicking me off my inner tube."

Jack laughed, and as we exited the wave pool, he said, "It's just like what Billy said yesterday. 'You don't lose until you've actually lost... or you think you have – whichever comes first.'"

"Yeah, I thought you were a goner myself," admitted Ty, slapping me on the shoulder, "Too bad Billy and Calvin weren't here to see this."

"We'll all have plenty of opportunities to bring our A game to football," said Jack.

It was time to go home at that point, so we dried off and waited for Jaden's dad to pick us up in his Beamer. He appeared to be in his mid-thirties, with a head full of brown hair and a short beard.

"Did you guys have fun?" he asked.

"Absolutely, Mr. Ludge," said Jack, "Thanks for letting Jaden invite Ty and Scott, too."

"Yeah!" Ty and I added together.

"You bet. Diane and I got to spend the day alone, since Laura is at a friend's for the weekend." Diane was Mr. Ludge's wife and Laura was Jaden's older sister.

Once we arrived at their house, Ty and I waved goodbye to Jack and Jaden and told them we'd see them at the club. We quickly biked back to my house, where we took a shower and changed into clean shorts and Putnam Panthers football practice shirts, just as we were told.

We ate a quick dinner of macaroni and cheese with beef, downed a brownie, and then, Mom drove us to the first big party of our lives.

chapter twenty-one

My mom pulled up to a large, one-story structure covered in a colored mural that depicted a building on the very edge of a flat Earth. The words, "The Edge of the World" covered a part of the facade in large, white letters. A large sign on the door read, "Middle School Football Night. Pre-Authorized Guests Only!" That sense of self-importance came flooding back.

"Well, this looks cool," remarked my mom.

We saw kids being turned away at the door by the bouncer, a big dude who looked to be in his early twenties. Whenever he did open the door for someone, loud music blared out of the bright entrance.

"Double-check to make sure you have your IDs and the thirty dollars I gave you for the cover charge and snacks," she told us as she pulled into the drop-off zone.

"We got 'em," I assured her, holding them out. I looked back at Ty from the front seat, and we exchanged a grin. Excitement started to flow between us again.

"You ready?" I asked, raising my eyebrow.

"Born ready," he replied, winking back.

My mom smiled. "You two have fun," she said, "I'll be back to pick you up at eleven."

I had asked her to extend our time to midnight – when the club closed – but my mom would have none of that. She said she wasn't going to have two twelve-year-old boys out on the prowl at midnight. I could have told her how ridiculous that statement was, but that would have risked her not allowing us to go at all. My dad had taught me the importance of knowing when to leave well enough alone, especially when it came to my mom.

"Thanks, Mom!" I said.

"Yeah, thanks, Mrs. Weston!" echoed Ty.

We hopped out of the car and strode up to the bouncer, while a few rejected kids looked on.

"Football players, huh?" asked the bouncer, noticing our Putnam Panthers shirts.

Ty and I nodded. Up close, he looked more like a bear, with his large beard and paw-like hands. No kid was going to cause this club any trouble.

"IDs then, guys."

We pulled out our IDs and handed them over. As the bouncer matched them against the list on his tablet, Ty and I glanced at each other again, feeling like celebrities – or friends of celebrities, at least.

"Scott and Ty," the bouncer continued, handing back our IDs and holding the door open, "Welcome to the Edge of the World."

"There's no way *they're* thirteen!" I heard one boy shout, "They were in my grade last year!"

"*They* were invited," the bouncer replied, giving us a wink.

The two of us puffed out our chests and grinned. We walked inside, leaving the rabble behind. Some kind of techno music

blared from speakers all around us. The entrance turned left, where a thin man standing behind a counter greeted us.

"Ten dollars, please, boys," he requested over the music. As we handed him the money, he looked at our shirts. "More Putnam Panthers, huh?" he asked.

"Yup," said Ty, and we both beamed with pride.

"You boys know Calvin Williams, then?" he asked after he stamped our forearms.

"Of course," Ty replied, with me adding, "He's our team captain."

The man leaned closer to us, "Between you boys, me, and the fence post," he started, "I think he's the best goddamn middle school football player here. And that's saying a lot, considering how good everyone else is here, including Billy Thompson and Cameron Gunner."

That made us grin even more, and I couldn't help but feel elated at just how lucky I was – not only to be on the same school team as Calvin, but that he had wanted both Ty and me on his sub-team and that he invited us both to this party.

"Yeah, he's awesome," I replied.

Although, Ty gave a confused look. "Um", he asked, "what's a fence post have to do with anything?" Both the man and I laughed at Ty's ignorance. My dad had used that phrase quite a few times with me.

"It's just an expression," the man clarified, "It just means, please keep what I said between us."

"Oh."

I had never heard of Cameron Gunner, but I wondered if his family was related to the one that Gunner High School was named after. Suddenly, the man gave us a quick nod and turned his

attention away from us, just as I was in the middle of asking what school Cameron Gunner attended.

"Riverwood Junior High," came Calvin's reply. He was walking toward us with Bryce and Derek in tow, all of them sporting new, clean Putnam Panthers practice tees. We gave each other high-fives, handshakes, and fist bumps.

"Cam's a team captain too," said Derek, "And a damn good football player."

"Yep," affirmed Calvin, "This year's game against Riverwood is going to be a challenge, and hell of a lot of fun."

As the eighth graders led us to the area the Putnam Panthers had claimed, Ty and I soaked in the atmosphere. A few hundred boys, all wearing football practice tees of their respective middle schools, mingled about, mostly keeping to their own team, but sometimes I'd spot a group of guys from one school interacting with those from another.

All seven schools were represented: The Riverwood Wolves, the Eastland Razorbacks, the Pioneer Bobcats, the McClain Lions, the Waterland Cougars, the Pinedale Cobras, and, of course, the Putnam Panthers.

In our art class last year, we studied minimalism in the post-war era, and this place fit that definition to a T. No decorations adorned the walls; they had the same bright shade of white. The same applied to the tabletops and chairs. Hell, even the bar and the cushions on the barstools were white.

The only real break from the single color scheme came from the back of the club. There, a multitude of large, mounted high-def TVs screened video games being played by kids sitting in front of them on couches and giant, brown beanbag chairs. Several sets of steps led down to that area; a large sign near one of the TVs read,

"The Gaming Pit". A set of three televisions in a triangle hung down from the ceiling in the middle of the club. All were currently off.

On the other side of the room, a vast entryway led to an enormous dance floor with a stage at the back. Darkness engulfed the empty stage, and although music played in the dance floor, it stood devoid of people – not really a surprise considering there were only boys here tonight. I didn't think any of us were about to dance with each other, or worse, by ourselves.

"This place looks kinda futuristic and strange," Ty observed.

"Yeah," said Derek, "My dad came here once to pick up my older brother a few years ago. He said this place looked like the last scene of *2001: A Space Odyssey*."

"Never heard of it," Ty admitted.

"It's very white in here," I added.

"That's also what my dad said," Derek continued, "But he hinted he wasn't just talking about the decor." I hadn't really thought of that, but he was right, we were all Caucasian.

We passed a taller, muscular kid wearing a Riverwood Wolves shirt. He had short black hair, brown eyes, and a few freckles dotting his face. A large scar marked his left bicep.

"Cameron!" shouted Derek, giving the kid a high-five handshake combo.

"Derek!" the kid shouted back in an adolescent voice. Then, he shook Bryce's and Calvin's hands, saying, "Dude! Calvin! Bryce!"

"Heya!" Calvin shouted back.

"Isn't this, like, the fucking best?" asked Cameron, holding up both his hands in a thumbs up, "This year is going to be *so* much fun!"

"Oh, hell yeah!" exclaimed Calvin, pointing a finger at the other kid, "Our game against each other is going to be the most intense!"

"This is our time, man," Cameron grinned. Then, he turned toward Ty and me.

"Seventh graders?" he asked, his voice high-pitched, as if he was surprised to see us.

Calvin stood between Ty and me, placing his hands on each of our shoulders. Then, Bryce placed his hand on my other shoulder and Derek on Ty's.

"These two guys are the best seventh grade players on my Panthers' Colts," said Calvin. My chest swelled.

Cameron shook our hands and sized us up. "You guys look well toned. You've been training well," he observed. A smirk formed on his face. "But my Wolves' Gunners have some good seventh graders as well," he said, "so I think a few scrimmages are in order."

Bryce shook his head. "Did you really name your camp team after yourself, Cameron?" he asked.

"Nah, man," Cameron laughed, "After Gunner High School."

"Well, that school *was* named after your grandfather, Cameron. So, in a way, you did."

"Huh. Yeah, I guess you're right," said Cameron, winking at me. He turned to Calvin next. "So, what do you think about a scrimmage, Calvin?" he prompted. A large grin appeared on Calvin's face, and I could see the hunger in his eyes.

"You know," started Calvin, "I love that idea. Next Tuesday?" They shook on it.

"Fully off-rails, right?" asked Cameron.

"We wouldn't have it any other way," replied Calvin, looking at his two subordinates, both of whom grinned and nodded in agreement. Ty and I could just look at each other confused.

Cameron's smile grew wider as well. He pulled down on one of his sleeves to reveal his bare armpit, flaunting it at me and Ty. There was a subtle hint of body odor.

"Look closely, boys," he urged, "This is the only time you will get this close to my armpit without passing out." After that, he winked at us and walked away. Calvin watched Cameron leave, not appearing fazed at all.

Bryce snickered. "Looks like we get to show him what we're made of, huh, guys?"

"What's he talking about, Calvin?" asked Ty as we headed over to our teammates.

I scratched my head. "Yeah, what's off-rails?"

"You know how you and Jack Murphy pitted each other yesterday?" reminded Bryce.

"Yeah."

"That's what off-rails means. It's football where armpitting is allowed."

"Never heard of that rule," said Ty, "Or seen it."

"You will," said Calvin.

The other Panthers spotted us and waved us over to their tables. Jack, Jaden, Ty, and I exchanged fist bumps. Ty and I said our hellos to the rest of the Panthers, all eighth graders.

"Glad you made it, Weston," said Billy, nudging me on the shoulder.

Then, he began to shadow box me, punching me lightly in ribs. I punched back, but he blocked. I then went for his face. The Warriors captain grabbed my arm and twisted it behind my back, holding the other one by my bicep.

"Hey!" I protested.

He didn't put too much pressure on it, but it certainly wasn't comfortable.

"Why you always gotta try to one-up me, huh, Weston?" Billy asked, smiling at Jack and Travis Bower, his squad leaders.

Calvin put his hands on his hips. "Billy," is all he said.

Billy stared at his friend. "What?" he asked, "I can't play around with one of our star seventh graders?"

"I wouldn't underestimate him if I were you."

I seized the opportunity of Billy being distracted to prove Calvin correct. I flipped him over my shoulder, and he landed with a thud.

"Ack!" spat Billy.

The other Panthers burst out laughing. Even the kids from the other teams who had witnessed it started cackling. I grinned ear to ear.

"Nice one, Scott!" said Ryder Banks, giving me a high-five. Even Jimmy Casten gave me one.

Calvin slapped me on the back and said to Billy, "Told you so."

Billy snarled, jumped up, and got into my face, pursing his lip. His breath smelled like tacos.

"You..." he seethed, curling his fists and flexing his biceps.

My smile faded. I didn't think he'd make a scene here, but he seemed furious. I glanced over at Calvin, who folded his arms but otherwise, didn't intervene.

Suddenly, Billy turned his snarl into a grin, saying, "...you got me." The others started laughing, and I started smiling again.

"Yeah, I did, didn't I?" I sighed in relief.

Billy glanced over at Calvin; his expression turned to worry. "Uh oh, Scott," he said. "I wouldn't stand so close-"

The Warriors captain's grin turned to a smirk, and he growled like a dog. Before I knew it, he had me in a strong headlock.

"Hey!" I shouted through laughter, "Let me go, Billy!"

He gave me a noogie. "I can't let you have the last laugh here, Weston," he said, my head feeling like it was on fire, "You're my junior."

"Yeah, gotta give Billy some respect, Scott," added Lucas Colby, Billy's halfback who substituted for me yesterday.

"That's not fair!" I exclaimed through pain and laughter, "I got you!"

"Yeah, now you know how I felt at the lazy river," Jack joined in, folding his arms.

"Let him go, Billy," directed Calvin, placing a hand on his shoulder. "He knows you're his senior. Besides, he got you, and you know it."

"Yeah, yeah, I know," said Billy, releasing his grip. He mussed my hair and pinched my cheek, the one Jimmy had punched. A bolt of pain went through me, and I winced. "But it's such fun to play with this guy," he added.

Billy then gave my cheek a few light slaps and said with a wink, "Don't ever change, Weston."

I snarled at him, angry that he always had to be the winner, just like Jack. However, at that moment, Jack began squeezing my nape lightly. The tension in my body flowed out through my feet and into the ground.

"Ahh... Jack..." I whimpered, closing my eyes and sighing.

"That's his spot, Jack," said Ty.

"Oh, I know," Jack replied with a chuckle.

"You did that on Thursday too, Jack," said Billy, sitting on a nearby table, "Is he like a like a dog or something?"

Jack switched to patting me on the back. "Something like that, Billy," he replied.

Then, turning to me, he said, "That *was* awesome what you did, Scott."

I glanced at him and grinned, and Jack addressed our four team captains.

"Hey, guys," he started, "That is the kind of quick thinking that Scott brings to our team. He beat me today at the wave pool at White Water, even when he really had no chance of it." He went on to explain what had happened; Ty and Jaden confirmed it.

Calvin gave me a nod. "That explains his behavior yesterday at the pit against me," he stated.

"Now I *really* wish I had traded Adams instead," Billy mumbled to himself.

chapter twenty-two

We Panthers talked and horsed around with each other for about an hour more before our team captains took us to meet some of the other teams, to get a feel of their leadership. Most of the eighth grade players from Putnam knew a lot of the ones on the Eastland Razorbacks and the Pinedale Cobras; many of them had gone to the same elementary schools. I knew of a few seventh graders who went to Pinedale, but their team leaders didn't invite any of them to the party. In fact, Ty, Jaden, and I were the only seventh graders here who weren't squad leaders, and the ones who *were* squad leaders numbered only two – Jack Murphy and another kid from McClain.

After the introductions, we split up. Calvin Williams and his eighth grade teammates ended up chatting with Cameron Gunner and the guys from Riverwood; Mason Holden and the Jets hooked up with some players they knew from Eastland; and Damian Jackson and his Rams decided to play video games together.

Billy suggested that the rest of us should hit the bar and order snacks and drinks. Of course, the club didn't stock any alcohol, being strictly for teens. Damian had told us that when he was in Germany with his family last summer, the bars would serve beer to kids as young as fourteen if they were with their parents. That still

wouldn't have helped here, since no one was fourteen yet anyway, nor were any of our parents around.

We all ordered sodas; Billy said this was a special occasion, and it was Saturday night, anyway, so we could have as much sugar as we wanted. Instead of serving regular, popular brands of cola, the bar stocked over forty different sodas from around the country, each one poured out from their own taps set on a wall behind the bar. They had this thing they called The Cola Shots. For five dollars, they would serve you mini glasses of any flavor of cola you wanted to try, without limits. We each ordered around five different ones over a period of time before our food came. Ty, Jack, and I had ordered mini pepperoni pizzas, while Jaden wanted pretzel bites with cheese. Billy and most of the others ordered nachos or cheeseburger sliders. In the middle of our snacking, the music stopped, and a kid's voiceover came through the speakers.

"Hey, boys, welcome to the Edge of the World!" That voice sounded like Cameron Gunner's. "Tonight it's all about middle school football and us eighth – and some seventh – grade boys who lead the pack! Let's hear it for ourselves and our teams!" Loud whoops and hollers erupted, and Jack's cheer stood out. I looked over at him; he was sitting two seats down from me. He and Billy had an arm around each other's shoulders and held another kid's hand in the air; Jaden held Jack's, and Travis had Billy's. Jack then winked at Ty and me, motioning for us to join in. That reminded me that the two of us were a part of this as well, verifying us as among the best players on the Panthers. We, like Jack and Jaden, were *seventh graders*. We joined in, held hands, and shouted as loud as we could.

I looked around for the Riverwood team captain. He was standing in the middle of the club, under the triangular set of televisions, and holding a microphone.

"This is going to be the best fucking year!" he announced, "We are the best teams ever to play for our schools!"

All of us cheered again.

"The fully off-rails scrimmages start next week, and I can't wait! The most intense three-week training of our lives starts on Monday! Let's hear it for football!" Gunner raised his arm in the air, and everyone else, including me, followed suit and cheered, filling the room with our thrilled shouts. Ty and I mussed each other's hair, and then, Jaden and I exchanged high-fives. Billy glanced at us and gave us a thumbs up.

Cameron started laughing. "Speaking of off-rails," he continued, "It seems like that started a bit early this time, thanks to a kid in this very room. Take a look." He motioned to the televisions above him, and all three switched on as he sat down, showing our own Panther field during yesterday's practice; us Colts and Billy's Warriors going at it. Then, during a play, the screen showed me plowing into Jack and armpitting him. The entire room was filled with gasps first, and then, it erupted in laughter when Jack dropped to the ground. The video went on to show me trying to wake Jack up. The boys became hysterical as Jack's limp body was shown being carried off the field.

I wanted to laugh as well, but I didn't want to piss Jack off. I looked over at him; he was getting side hugged from Billy, laughing along with the rest. Jack flashed me a playful snarl, shaking his head as a smirk formed on his face. At least the camera didn't show our faces up close, and no one outside of our teams knew our jersey numbers. A wave of relief came over me. It was short lived, as Billy pointed me out and yelled, "That's Weston, the armpitter here!" before turning to Jack; "And that's Murphy, the kid he KO-ed!" he finished.

Everyone turned to look at us, and the room filled with cheers such as, "Way to go!" and "Awesome, man!" and "Just couldn't wait, huh?" A few of them walked up to me, patting my back. They also consoled Jack, patting him on the head and asking him how bad my body odor was.

Jack simply growled, giving me a nasty look; it didn't look very playful this time.

"Oh, you boys just keep watching," shouted Billy, "It ain't over."

The screen then showed Jack and me in the circle. I knew what was coming. Sure enough, it showed Jack plowing into me, knocking me down, and shoving his armpit in my facemask. I saw my body go limp immediately, my arms stretched out to my sides, and my eyes shut closed. The room exploded in cheers again, whoops and hollers filling every corner of the club. As the screen showed my body being carried off the field, someone started shouting, "Murphy! Murphy!" and the room resonated with the cheer as everyone joined in.

The guys who had consoled Jack before were now all over him, ruffling his hair, shaking his shoulder, and otherwise congratulating him. Jack's mood lifted, and I decided to join in the laughter too. When I did, the other kids started cheering for me as well.

"That's the spirit!" Billy shouted at me.

Once all that died down, Cameron took the stage again, motioning for Jack and me to join him. Once we were there, he shook our hands and wrapped his arms around our shoulders.

"We have some real boys here with us tonight!" he said, leaning into the microphone, "And they're only seventh graders!"

The other players gasped in disbelief, then cheered for us, curling fists and shaking them in the air. Jack and I grinned, and we fist bumped each other. But then, I had to ask something.

"How did you get the footage?" I asked, "Where'd the cameras come from?"

Cameron grinned. "Let's just say I have my sources," he replied, giving me a wink.

"Yeah, I wouldn't worry about it," Calvin added from behind us. We turned around to see him standing up, drinking soda from a glass. "We'll all be doing that to each other come next week anyway, so no need to be upset or embarrassed."

"Damn right!" shouted Cameron into the mic, evoking loud cheers.

Jack and I spent the rest of the time at the club like minor celebrities. Kids would come up to us and ask us what our first armpitting felt like, then they would congratulate us on becoming real middle school boy football players and tell us stories of their first time, both giving and receiving.

"Sounds like we're talking gay sex," Jaden quipped at one point, which made one Pinedale kid suggest that that was what Jaden had really wanted. Jaden, of course, threatened to kick the kid's ass in response.

"Save it for the gridiron, Jaden!" hissed Jack.

"Sorry," replied Jaden. The other kid, about as strong as Jaden, laughed at him and said, "See you on the field, Panther."

Eleven came around way too soon, and Ty and I weren't the only kids who had to go home at that time; dozens of others did too, including Jaden, although Jack's parents allowed him to stay till midnight. A bunch of kids high-fived me as we left, saying that they couldn't wait to meet me on the field. I left the club feeling

lighter than air, excited more than ever for the scrimmages that would start next week.

chapter twenty-three

The next day, Ty and I slept in till Mom woke us up around ten-thirty. The smell of pancakes wafting in from the kitchen lured us to go downstairs.

As we sat down at the table, Mom placed a pile of pancakes between us and said, "You two were absolutely glowing on the ride home last night."

"The party was a blast, Mrs. Weston," said Ty, helping himself to a few pancakes.

"Yeah," I added, grabbing a few for myself, "Like I said in the car, it was probably the best time I've ever had. I'd never felt so connected to so many people before."

"Same here," said Ty, drenching his pancakes in syrup and butter; I followed suit, allowing myself to some sweets today. I couldn't think of having pancakes without syrup.

"I am so happy to be a football player, Mom," I declared. My friend put three layers of pancake into his mouth, saying "Me, too," in a muffled voice.

My mom poured us some orange juice and sat down between us, taking food for herself. "Good to hear, Scott," she said, "And I'm glad you connected with the other boys."

"They treated Scott like a celebrity," said Ty.

My mom gave me with a puzzled expression; and I shot Ty a glare. I would have told him to stuff it, but my mouth was full of food. I wasn't about to explain armpitting to my mom. Ty just shrugged; it was as if he had no idea why I'd be upset.

"Oh?" she asked, "Why?"

At least having to swallow allowed me enough time to think of something that wasn't a lie. Luckily, my wonderful brain came up with the perfect answer. "Let's just say they saw an incredible play I made at practice on Friday," I said. Ty nodded vigorously as he continued to stuff his mouth.

"That's great, dear," she said, eating much more slowly than the two of us, "Tell me about it."

"I caught Jack off guard when he tried to blitz our quarterback," I laughed, "and I tackled him." I punched a fist onto my other hand for emphasis and said, "He didn't really see me coming until it was too late."

My mom just shook her head slowly. "I will never understand boys and their need for violence," she said.

"There's no better way to let out your aggression than on the gridiron, Mrs. Weston," explained Ty.

"That's how your dad convinced me to let you play, Scott," she said.

"Really?" I asked after I swallowed another heap of syrupy flapjacks.

"Yes. You had a lot of anger issues after we separated, remember?"

I wiped my mouth. "How could I forget?" I said, "It was only five years ago. Besides, why would you need to be convinced? Football is a great way for boys to bond."

She rolled her eyes. "That's a direct quote from your father."

"It's true, though!" I insisted before guzzling my orange juice, "Football is how I came to be friends with Ty and Jack!"

"And Jaden," Ty reminded me.

"Him, too!"

My mom held out her hand as a gesture for me to stop arguing. "Okay, okay, boys. I get it," she finally said.

After we finished breakfast, Mom took us shopping for a few hours and bought me a new pair of sneakers. Since the store had a "buy one, get one for half" sale, she bought a second pair for Ty. His face lit up when she offered. Then, she insisted I needed new T-shirts, socks, and underwear; so we hit a local clothes store.

She decided that I could only take one football related shirt, because she was sick of the sight of me wearing only those. Ty and I sifted through the boys' section and found one similar to what Billy had on at the mall; although, instead of an eight-bit football image from some really old video game, the image was of an eight-bit football *player* from some really old video game.

"Oh, perfect!" exclaimed Ty, holding it up.

"Yeah, I'm gonna get it!" I replied, snatching it from him.

"Man, I want one too!" frowned Ty.

Mom came around the corner with the cart; it had boys' underwear and socks inside, along with some clothes for herself. "Is there another one that's your size, Ty?" she asked.

Ty nodded excitedly, taking one off the rack and holding it up.

"Okay, I'll buy it for you," she told him.

My friend grinned from ear to ear. "Thanks, Mrs. Weston! You're the best!"

"My pleasure, Ty. Besides, your mom's bought stuff for Scott before. Not that I'm keeping score, but that it's just appreciated."

171

I wanted to try that shirt on right then; so, after scanning to make sure no one else was around, I took off the my own shirt and put on the new one.

"Scott!" my mom shouted, her mouth agape, "What are you doing?"

"Trying on my new shirt," I said.

"No one wants to see a bare-chested boy in here! That's what the changing rooms are for!"

Ty cackled.

"No one can see me," I insisted, but then, my mom pointed to the ceiling and a domed camera that was attached to it.

I started flexing my muscles, grinning at the camera. Ty laughed even harder, and my mom's brow started to furrow.

"Put on your shirt! NOW!" she yelled.

A man, his wife, and their little son riding in the cart, turned the corner and stopped dead in their tracks when they saw me.

"Oh, God!" my mom cried, holding palms to her face, "Scott!"

"That boy doesn't have his shirt on!" said the kid, pointing at me. The man burst out laughing, but his wife was less amused; she gave me a vexed stare instead. That only made Ty crack up even more, and my face felt hot with embarrassment. I quickly put my shirt back on.

"No! You put on the *wrong* shirt!" my mom exclaimed. I looked down and noticed that I had indeed put on the new shirt instead of the one I came in with.

"Oh my God!" Ty howled, "Bwahahaha!"

"Just go to the changing room and change into your old shirt!" Mom shrieked, her vocal chords straining, "Good God! *This* is why I wanted a daughter!" The man and Ty went on laughing hard, and my face became beet red.

As I walked off, I heard my mom apologize, "I am sorry you had to see my son act like an ape."

"I thought it was pretty funny, ma'am," said the man, "Something I definitely would have done at his age." That made me feel better, and I smiled to myself.

When I came back, wearing the right shirt, Mom snatched the new one and threw it in the basket, grunting at me. The other family had already left, but Ty couldn't help but snicker when he saw me. At least that was all over, and we could go back to picking out new shirts for me.

But then, the manager, a tall, thin man with a bushy mustache, suddenly appeared and came over to my mom. He had a big smile on his face. "Ma'am, your son made us all laugh like hyenas in the back room," he said.

"Oh, shit. Scott," Mom groaned.

Ty couldn't contain himself and fell on the ground in a frenzy. I could only shut my eyes.

"I want to thank you for lightening up our day. Those two shirts are on me," said the manager.

I looked up at Mom. She looked shocked as she glanced at the football tees Ty and I wanted. "Really?" she asked.

"Oh, yes. The entertainment was definitely worth the price of a few shirts." Then, he turned to look at me. "He even got some of the older girls saying how much they liked him."

"Oh, great," said Mom, shaking her head, "If my son flunks out of school, he can always make a living as a stripper." Ty rolled over on his side, clutching his stomach as he couldn't stop howling. Tears rolled down his face.

The manager burst out laughing at that. Patting me on the shoulder, he said, "You have a good mom, kid," before leaving.

173

My mom quickly picked out two random boys' shirts my size, threw them in the basket, and made a beeline for the cashiers. Ty and I had to practically run to catch up. We did get those two football shirts for free. As my mom paid for the rest of the stuff, the squat, pretty, brunette cashier smiled at me.

"You're funny," she said, "And kind of cute – both of you."

Ty and I blushed and gave each other a secret fist bump behind our backs.

That comment only made my mom grunt again. "They're only twelve," she said. The cashier just shrugged.

"We're never shopping here again," my mom declared, practically sprinting through the parking lot with Ty and me in tow pushing the cart. I thought for sure that one of the wheels was going to fly off due to how fast we were running.

She made me sit in the backseat of the car and asked Ty to sit in the front. On our way home, at first, she didn't say a word to us. She was blaring the radio instead, until she suddenly burst into a laugh, rubbing the wheel. Ty chuckled at her, and I asked, "What's so funny?"

"This song!" she said. I hadn't been paying attention to it, but as I listened closer, I heard the lyrics.

You've always been a wild boy
Strutting your own stuff
Smiling at all the girls
And always acting tough

"Grammy always called your dad a Wild Boy, and she absolutely loved him for it, even though he constantly did stupid shit and got into trouble." Mom explained.

"Grammy?" asked Ty.

"That's his father's mother."

When we got to a red light, she turned around to me, smiled, and said, "I guess, Scott, you are *my* Wild Boy."

I smiled back, relieved that she was in a better mood. "Yeah, I guess I am."

chapter twenty-four

We stopped to get some lunch, and when we got home, my mom got on the phone with my grammy; something that she always did when she needed to talk about me. I supposed she had spent enough time with boys for a while and needed some 'girl time'.

Ty and I went upstairs to my room, and after I shut the door to muffle the noise, we started playing *Alley Brawlers 5,* our favorite fighting game. We eventually threw off our shirts when it became warm in my room. After playing for a while, Ty started chuckling.

"What?" I asked, looking at him.

He shook his head. "I couldn't stop laughing at the thought of you," he started "a twelve-year-old kid stripping in front of a bunch of old ladies."

I broke in to a laugh at that as well.

"The guys are going to love this story," he said as he KO-ed my character.

"That's ten wins to your eight. I'm the champ!" he declared, dropping the controller and raising his arms in the air. I elbowed him in the gut. "Oomph!" he cried out and then, smacked me on

the side of my head. "Asshat," he cursed. I pounced on him, pinning him to ground and lying on top of him.

"Hey!" he shouted and laughed, "Get offa me!"

It felt good being close to Ty, in contact with his energy. I guessed he felt the same way that other day, and that's why he kissed me. I reciprocated the gesture, which surprised him.

"Hey!" he exclaimed, wiping his cheek. I wrapped my arms around him, put my head on his chest, and listened to his heart beat while focusing on his essence. Even though we hadn't been sweating, I could still detect a hint of his body odor. Ty chuckled and gently rubbed and squeezed the back of my neck. My body relaxed completely at his touch.

"Ty..." I whispered, feeling my eyes droop.

"Heh. Gotcha," he said, putting his other arm behind his head.

"I can't wait until tomorrow," I said, staring at his bare armpit.

He continued squeezing my neck lightly and yawned. "Me either, pal," he added, "Three weeks of overnight football camp. It's gonna be awesome."

The ceaseless, repetitive video game music became welcoming white noise to me, reminding me further of my bond with Ty, Jack, and Jaden. I found myself becoming so comfortable that I couldn't fight off the growing desire to drift off to sleep.

"You wanna keep playing?" he asked.

"Maybe later," I replied in a quiet tone, allowing my eyelids to shut. My friend's petting on my neck slowed down, and he gave it a final squeeze before stopping.

"Sounds good," agreed Ty, resting his arm on the floor. We were fast asleep in no time.

When I woke up, I noticed that the music had stopped. I lifted my head off Ty's chest and looked at my friend; his closed eyes and slow, deep breathing indicated he was still in dreamland. When I

saw my door open and the TV off, I figured my mom must have come in to check on us. I let Ty sleep while I donned my shirt and walked downstairs. My mom was on the couch with her eyes glued to the TV in the living room.

"Hi, Mom," I said when I got close to her.

She sprang up and put her hand on her heart.

"Jesus, Scott, you scared me!" she exclaimed.

I rubbed the back of my neck. "Sorry." She muted the TV and patted the cushion next to her. "Ty still napping?" she asked when I sat down.

I nodded and yawned, wiping the sleep from my eyes.

"You boys must have been exhausted," she continued, "I tried waking you up over an hour ago, but neither of your stirred. I also had to turn off your TV. That damn repetitive humdrum was driving me crazy." She laughed and took out her phone. "You two were so cute, with you asleep on top of Ty like that."

"How long *were* we asleep?" I asked, trying to change the subject.

"Two hours," she replied, "Look at this." She showed me the picture she clicked on her phone; I was sprawled out on top of Ty, both of us konked out.

"You are going to delete that, right?" I asked, reaching for the phone.

My mom moved it out of my reach. "No. I think it's cute," she said.

"Mom!" I cried.

"It's not like I'm going to post this on the internet, Sweetie."

I wasn't sure I could trust her. Besides, what if her phone got stolen and the thief posted it himself? When I voiced these concerns, she dismissed them, saying, "Don't be ridiculous. Like other boys your age don't sleep like that with each other. Grammy

had even said your dad and his friends would fall asleep against each other all the time, even through high school."

I grunted as she completely missed the point. "Yeah, but they didn't have cell phones with cameras back then," I protested, "Or the internet. And it doesn't matter what other boys do... only what we're seen doing."

"Are you ashamed of sleeping on him?" she asked, point blank.

I shook my head. "No, not at all. But, it's private, Mom."

She hugged me, pulling me close. "I understand," she assured me, "and it will stay that way. Please trust me." I resigned with a sigh and let her hold me for a while. "I love you, Scott," she said, kissing me on the head.

"I love you too, Mom," I replied.

"And I love you *just* the way you are."

She began listing off my traits, squeezing me as she listed each one: "Brave, strong, fearless, independent, needy, wild, even smelly."

She laughed at that last one, and I groaned, "Mom!"

"I am the luckiest mom in the world to have you," she said with a smile.

I smiled back as I felt her love for me. Then, she looked me in the eye. "I'm going to miss you these next few weeks," she said, "You're my baby boy, even if you're growing up."

"Thanks, Mom. But, I'll be home for the weekends, and I'll be only a few blocks away during the week."

"I know, but I'll still miss you."

"I'll miss you too."

The sound of footsteps coming down the stairs caught our attention, and we turned to see Ty leaning over the rails, rubbing his eyes.

"Got any more of those brownies, Mrs. Weston?" he asked, stifling a yawn.

My mom rubbed my hair, kissed me on the cheek, and then, stood up. "Sure do," she said, "You want some milk too?"

Ty bounded down the stairs, the pep back in the step. "Oh, yes, please!" he answered.

Then, turning to me, she asked, "You, too, Scott?"

"Of course," I nodded.

"Okay, but that should probably do it for the sweets. You two have practice tomorrow."

Ty and I followed her into the kitchen. As she put the brownies in the microwave, she said, "Oh. A boy named Calvin Williams called while you two were asleep."

I raised my eyebrows in surprise and looked at Ty, who had the same expression. "He did?" I asked.

"Yes. He said he's your – and Ty's – team captain."

Both of us nodded. "Yes, he is," I said.

"Is that the boy you were talking about Friday morning, Ty?" she asked.

Ty nodded again, saying, "Uh-huh."

The microwave dinged. My mom placed the plate of brownies between us on the table. I let Ty have the biggest piece before I grabbed the second one. I took a big bite, savoring the wonderful, sweet taste of the gooey chocolate chips.

"Why did he call?" I asked, my mouth full of brownie, allowing the crumbs to accumulate on the plate. I was saving those for later. My mom poured out our milk, and Ty slurped some of it in his mouth, letting it mix with the brownie inside, before he gulped it down and grinned.

"This is *so* good," he muttered.

My mom smiled at Ty and answered, "Just to introduce himself. Calvin explained that you seventh and eighth graders were pooled together, divided into four sub-teams, and each one has a captain and two squad leaders under him."

"That was all there in the handout you signed at the beginning of camp, Mom," I said, giving her an annoyed look.

"I might not have paid too much attention to that part, Scott," she admitted with a shrug.

Ty grinned, gulping down the rest of his milk. I took a few gulps myself. Nothing beats cold milk and a warm brownie – except for ice cream, maybe. Too bad we didn't have any of that.

"Well, what else did he say?" I asked.

My mom leaned against the counter and ate her brownie, cupping her free hand to catch the crumbs. In between bites, she said, "That starting this year, the team captains would have more day-to-day responsibility for the boys under them."

"Which means?"

"Your coach will be a lot more hands off, leaving it to the team captains to run the camp."

Ty shrugged. "The team captains and the squad leaders have basically been in charge of us the entire time up until now, anyway," he explained, "I don't know how much of a difference it'll be."

Brushing her hands over the sink, my mom confessed, "I wasn't too keen on that, but Calvin said Coach King still has the ultimate responsibility."

"Yes, he does," I said, hoping my confirmation would help ease her mind.

She wiped her mouth with a napkin, then continued, "He also said I could contact your coach if I had any concerns, but that he

would appreciate me calling him first. I have to admit, Calvin really does seem to be a responsible young man."

"Well," I started, letting out a surprising burp, "Coach Thimbleton did say all four of our team captains can put a lot of high school coaches to shame."

"Woah," cried Ty, "He did?"

"Yup."

My mom gave us a wide smile as she put the milk away. "You know what else he said?" she added.

We shook our heads.

"He really likes you two and thinks you're some of the best seventh grade players on the entire Panthers team." The doorbell rang, diverting our attention, but not before we gave each other wide grins. "Damn right we are," said Ty as my mom went to answer the door.

When she opened it, Ty and I could only stare in disbelief at the familiar woman, garbed in a red dress and high heels, standing at the front door. Her nine-year-old nephew stood next to her, holding her hand, and a purse dangled from her shoulder.

"Well, hi Max," my mom said with a smile.

chapter twenty-five

"Hi, Mrs. Weston!" greeted Max and pointed to the woman, "This is my Aunt Veronica. She's Scott's, Ty's, and Jack's nurse at the camp!"

Veronica and Mom shook hands.

"Nice to meet you, Miss...?"

"It's Lyon, but please call me Veronica," said Veronica, her voice bringing back memories of our incredible encounter.

"Dude!" Ty whispered to me.

My mom looked over Veronica's more business-like attire, and a curious expression formed on her face. Our guest picked up on it and pointed to her purse, explaining, "I'm not *just* a nurse. I had some other business today. Seems like I'm always working."

"Is Scott, Jack, and Ty here?" asked Max, peeking around my mom.

"Scott and Ty are. But not Jack."

Max's smile faded a little; his voice betrayed dejection as he said, "Oh." It lit up again when he saw the two of us. "Hi, Scott! Hi, Ty!" he exclaimed.

Veronica looked at us as well, and she gave us a big smile and a wink.

"Are you two boys *really* going to keep salivating," said my mom, putting her hands on her hips, "or are you going to show some manners and close your mouths?"

Veronica laughed again, brushing her brunette bangs away from her cheeks. "It's okay, Mrs. Weston..." she started.

"Call me Teresa, please," my mom insisted, "And, no, it isn't okay. Boys, learn some manners! Close your mouths!"

Ty and I did as instructed. As long as she didn't ask me to stand up, she wouldn't have anything else to complain about. I bet Ty was in the same predicament.

Max began jumping up and down like an over-excited puppy. "Can I come in?" he requested.

The two ladies laughed, and my mom ushered him inside. "Of course, you can!"

He let go of his aunt's hand and ran over to us, giving me a big hug and then one to Ty. Max started dancing around, shouting, "You'll never guess what I get to do, guys!"

Mom led Veronica over to the kitchen. My heart rate surged with her every step. Her heels clicked sharp on the hardwood floor. When she reached us, she shook our hands; her soft touch once again took me back to Thursday afternoon. She even smelt the same, lavender with whatever perfume she had on.

I spotted Ty from the corner of my eye; he was staring at her the same way I was. She told us not to bother standing up, like she instinctively knew we had massive boners. My mom didn't insist either; she probably figured it out as well. Regardless, I was relieved she kept her mouth shut about that.

Mom offered Max and Veronica a brownie and some milk, but Veronica politely refused. Max, however, snatched one off the plate and stuffed a huge bite in his mouth before Mom could even get to the fridge.

"Scott! Ty!" cried Max, his mouth full of brownie, "I have to tell you something! Something awesome!"

His barraging broke us out of Veronica's spell long enough to make us look over at him. Crumbs dropped from his mouth, which prompted his aunt to scold him for talking with his mouth full.

"What is it, Max?" I asked.

He forced himself to swallow, then bouncing up and down he said, "I'm going to be the Warriors' *teamboy*!"

Ty and I gave each other a bewildered look. "A what?" asked Ty. Veronica placed her hand on Max's shoulder and asked him to finish his brownie and drink his milk, and that she would explain things.

"Okay!" he agreed as Mom handed him his milk and asked him to sit down at the table. The young boy dropped himself down in-between the two of us, rocking in his chair and munching his snack.

My mom asked Veronica to join us at the table and offered some iced tea, which she accepted. She sat down on the opposite side, so she could face all of us.

"Starting this year," she began, "each middle school sub-team is allowed to have one elementary school boy football player as a team ball boy, called a *teamboy*. They get to assist the team at practice and scrimmages – outside of their own schedules, of course." Max nodded vigorously and took a few more bites of his brownie, washing it down with an equally large gulp of milk.

"For Putnam Middle," Veronica continued, "two were chosen from Gifford Elementary-"

"Me and Zach Montgomery!" Max interjected, swinging his legs.

"Yes," she said with a smile, and thanked my mom as she placed a glass of tea in front of her. My mom leaned against the small kitchen desk.

After taking a few sips of tea, our nurse continued, "And two others were chosen from a different school."

Max let out a loud burp and laughed. "Excuse me!"

Veronica rolled her eyes. "Max!" she chided.

"Hee!" he chuckled.

"Max is going to be assigned to Billy Thompson's Warriors," she carried on, "and Zach to Calvin Williams' Colts."

"And what about the Jets and the Rams?" asked Ty.

"Like I said, those two boys are from different elementary schools."

I scratched my head and asked, "How were they chosen?"

"By the team captains," she said, placing a finger on her lips and continued in a hushed voice, "Keep this a secret, but I sort of interfered and convinced Billy and Calvin to invite Max and Zach. I told them they already had good chemistry with many of the boys on their teams."

"I wish Jack was here," Max added, "so I could tell him today!" His face lit up as he got an idea. "Scott, you know his number, right? Would you call him so I can tell him? *Please*?" he pleaded.

"Fine with me," I shrugged, "My phone is my room. Go get it for me."

Before Max could jump out of his seat, Veronica cut in, "Wait, Max." Max looked at her, and Veronica looked at me. "You mind showing me your room, Scott?" she asked me, "I'd like to see what an older boy football player's room is like. I've seen Max's already."

Oh. My. God. Was she seriously coming on to me now, *in front of my mom*?

Ty's mouth dropped open.

"You and Ty look like she asked you out on a date, Scott," commented my mom with a chuckle. I sighed – If she only knew.

I looked suspiciously over at Veronica, and said, slowly, "Yeah. Sure. I don't mind."

"Great!" said Veronica, standing up.

With that, Max ran up the stairs and into my room. I had my mom lead Veronica so Ty and I could... calm down.

As we followed, my mom asked, "So are these teamboys going to stay the night too, with the players?"

Veronica shook her head. "Oh, no. But they'll be there for the night scrimmages for the bigger games, if their parents allow them."

When we got to my room, Max shoved my phone in my hands and asked me to dial Jack. When he answered, I handed the phone back to Max.

Max ran around my room, springing up and down, explaining everything to Jack. I heard Jack reply that he was really happy and looked forward to seeing him, but then, he asked Max what he was doing at my house.

"I'm with my Aunt Veronica, and Scott is showing her his room," was Max's reply. There was silence on the other end for what seemed like an eternity.

"I'll be there in ten minutes," said Jack finally, making my mom roll her eyes. With that, he hung up.

"Good God... Boys," my mom lamented, "At least mine isn't the only ill-mannered caveman."

Ty beat his chest and mimicked an ape, "Ooo Ooo Ooo."

That got Max to join in, "Ooo Ooo Ooo!"

I smiled and joined in too, "Ooo Ooo Ooo!"

"I said caveman, not ape," she said with a shake of her head, "but if the shoe fits..." Veronica laughed as the three of us walked around, beating our chests at each other.

"I like boys," said Veronica, running her fingers through Max's hair as we passed, "They're fun."

"Try raising one on your own," my mom shot back.

"What happened to your loving me just the way I am?" I asked, my voice quivering as I thumped my chest.

"You can stop that now," she said, placing her hand on my shoulder.

Veronica examined my room, looking at all of my belongings; Ty and I watched her while Max had ran downstairs to wait for Jack. She pointed to the numerous football posters I had on the walls along with the various football trophies on the top shelf of my dresser.

"You are really into sports," she remarked.

"Just football," I replied.

She glanced at my bookshelf and said, "You have a lot of the same types of books that Max has – Football ones, cartoon ones, adventure stories." When she noticed my gaming console, she asked, "You like video games too?"

"Yeah," I nodded.

She picked up the game case to *Alley Brawlers 5* – the one my friends and I played all the time. "What kind of game is this?" she asked, looking at the artwork and reading the title.

"It's a fighting game. Want Ty and me to show you?"

My mom shook her head and said, "I don't think she wants to see a bunch of guys beating each other up, and I don't think I do either."

"Well, there are girls in it too," added Ty, "but who'd want to play as a girl?"

I shrugged.

Veronica laughed and shook her head, but my mom grunted. She started to say something, but closed her mouth, let out another

sigh, and just said, "You two boys are in for a rude awakening." Then, turning to Veronica, she asked, "You have kids of your own?"

"No, I don't," she replied, "Not yet."

"May you be *blessed* with twin boys, then." The *blessed* in her words had sarcasm dripping from it.

Jack arrived quicker than I had expected, sweating from the bike ride over here. Max pounced on him the moment he opened the door.

"Hey, buddy!" smiled Jack, hugging him back. Max led Jack up the stairs to my room, where my friend stared with his mouth gaping at Veronica.

"My, aren't you the handsome, strong one," Veronica said to him, extending her hand, "You must be Jack."

Jack shook it, but his mouth stayed open and silent.

I felt a pang of envy, even though she had said the same to me on Thursday. It seemed like every girl that laid eyes on Jack had to comment on his good looks.

"I'm going to go to the grocery store for a while," said my mom through a long sigh, "You can come with me if you don't want to be overwhelmed with all the testosterone in this room, Veronica."

"I'll be fine, Teresa," she responded with a small chuckle, "I need to talk to them about their camp."

"Okay."

Veronica then turned to Max, who had grabbed on to Jack's leg, trying to tackle him down. "Hey, Max, it's time to go home now," she said.

Max's face fell. "Why?"

"I need to talk to these older boys, and then it'll be dinner time soon after that. Your mom is cooking for us."

"But Jack just got here! I want to be with them too!"

189

"You will be tomorrow!" she said, bending down and petting his shoulders, "You're Jack's teamboy, remember?"

"Yeah, so I should hear what you have to say!" he insisted.

"Max, don't argue with me."

"Max," my mom called back, "why don't you come with me to the grocery store, if Veronica doesn't mind? I'm sure Jack will still be here by the time we get back, and you can play with him and the other boys then?"

Veronica urged Max to go, and he looked over at my mom and tilted his head, letting out a noise that told us he was giving it a thought.

"Please, Max? I could use some help carrying groceries."

Jack looked down at Max and tousled his hair. "I'll still be here, pal," he urged, "Go help Scott's mom."

"Fine," he sighed, "But you *better* be here when I get back." Jack held out a V with his fingers. "Scout's honor," he promised.

"Okay," conceded Max.

"Do you want to stay back for dinner tonight, Jack?" asked Mom.

"I'd love to, Mrs. Weston," Jack shook his head, "but my mom wants me at home this evening."

"I don't blame her," she said with a smile, and motioned for Max to follow her downstairs.

When my mom's car had backed out of the driveway, Veronica shut the door.

chapter twenty-six

The three of us stood in silence, staring at our nurse and waiting for her to speak.

"You boys enjoyed your first week of football camp?" asked Veronica.

"Did you really have sex with Scott?" asked Ty, cutting right to the chase.

"Ty!" I hissed, elbowing him in the gut. He made a sore, guttural sound. If it actually *wasn't* her on Thursday, Veronica would be severely offended. Veronica glanced over at me, and I looked at the ground.

"You told them, huh?" she asked. I explained that I received the video when Ty, Jack, and Jaden came over.

"Jaden?" she asked.

"Yeah, Jaden Ludge, our other friend," I said, then turned to Jack, "I'm surprised you didn't invite him."

"I did, actually," replied Jack, "but he said his parents are making him spend the day with them and his sister. He sounded really pissed he was gonna miss meeting Veronica."

That made her smile. "I bet," she said.

"So why did you send the video to me?" I asked.

"I felt I owed it you, to prove to you that what you went through was real."

Jack rubbed his face. "Who was the old lady at the nurse's office," asked Jack, "when Billy and I brought Scott in?"

"Me," came the reply.

"Thought so," said Ty.

"Why the disguise?" asked Jack.

"I didn't want to reveal myself too early. But, I couldn't resist having a little bit of fun." She looked at me when she said that last part.

"I don't understand any of this, though," I shrugged, sitting down on my bed, "I feel like I'm missing something... a lot of things."

"Let's just say the *real* football camp begins tomorrow. Coach King and the team captains have been briefed. The schedules are lined up. And, you boys have been primed."

Jack leaned against the wall, opposite of my bed. "Primed?" he asked.

"Yes. You all have been exposed to chemicals that will greatly increase your strength and vitality... and provide you with enhanced sexual experiences."

The three of us blinked, and I stammered; I wanted to ask something, but I didn't even know where to begin.

"What-" Jack started, but Veronica interjected.

"Had any of you, or your fellow Panthers, suddenly passed out at any time this week?"

Ty and I glanced at each other and nodded; we both were shocked when Jack nodded as well.

"When?" asked Ty, sitting down next to me on the bed.

"Earlier this week," he explained, "I was playing video games with Jaden after practice, when all of a sudden, I passed out. It was only for a minute maybe. Jaden thought I had just fallen asleep."

"There you go," said Veronica.

"Well, when I told him I had passed out, he said the same thing happened to him when he was in the bathroom."

Ty then explained what happened to the two of us.

"So, this chemical... it'll make us stronger?" I asked.

Veronica nodded. Keeping her eyes on Jack, she added, "Yes."

Ty and I exchanged another worried glance before he asked, "Is it dangerous?"

"Of course not," she replied at once, placing her hand on Jack's cheek, "Nothing I do will harm you in any way." Jack gulped; his eyes widened at her touch. So, now she was coming on to Jack. Before things went too far between them, I wanted some more answers.

"But, why do this to us?" I asked.

"It's *for* you," she replied, stepping even closer to Jack, "Admittedly, not *just* for you. Let's keep it at that for now." Veronica put her hand over one of his biceps, feeling the muscles. Jack's mouth dropped open. Then, she leaned close to the boy's armpit and sniffed. "Your odor is pretty strong today," she remarked. The blond-haired boy rubbed his nape, but he didn't say anything. She backed away, and he stared at her.

"What's wrong?" she asked.

Jack stammered, "Um... are you... are you going to stop there?"

She laughed. After a moment of silence, she asked, "You want me to keep going?"

Jack immediately nodded and said, "Uh, uh, uh-huh."

"Well, do you promise to keep this between us?"

encounter with her on Thursday and the other weird things that were going on in the camp. Ty stared in complete disbelief as well, with an agitated expression and his mouth wide open.

Veronica breathed down on Jack's cock, which made it stretch. Jack's eyes were then as wide as they could possibly get; his head was bent down, so he could watch what she was going to do to him.

She gave his shaft a long stroke of her tongue, going over every inch and down his balls. Jack's jaw dropped open, his eyes rolled back, and after letting out a groan, he said, "Oh God, I'm... I'm not going to last... ooo..."

Veronica licked her lips, leaned her head forward, and wrapped her mouth around his unit. When she started sucking, Jack let out a long, drawn-out moan, closing his eyes and throwing his head back. He placed his hands on her forehead and scrunched up his face. His teeth gnashed together, and he began to spit as his breaths became labored.

"Ooohhh mmmyyy Goooodddddd!" he screamed, thrusting his pelvis. I noticed Veronica swallow as Jack ejaculated. He held his breath, and then, he let out a high-pitched, "oooohhhhhh".

Jack's breathing slowed down, and he leaned back against the wall. His eyes were still shut, and it was though he could hardly stand. Veronica licked his penis as it shrank, prompting more groans from Jack. Once it got to a size small enough, she pulled his underwear and shorts back up and rose to her feet.

She rubbed his cheek. "You liked that?" she asked.

A smile appeared on the kid's face. "Oh, yeah. Yeah, yeah," he whispered, opening his eyes and wobbling a bit.

"You are such a strong, smelly boy," she told him. The boy grinned.

She gave him a quick kiss on the lips. "And your breath smells like Doritos," she remarked.

"I, uh, had those for a snack earlier," he explained.

Veronica connected her lips with his, kissing him again and holding on to him. He felt her up as he kissed back, forcing her lips open with his tongue. She walked him toward the middle of the room as they made out, stopping only when they reached where her purse was lying on the floor. Jack grinned and cupped her face.

He smirked and said, "You really do like strong boys like me, doncha?"

"Very much so," she replied. Veronica kneeled down and lifted her purse, which was right next to them. As she rummaged through it, Jack looked over at Ty and me with a wide grin and a thumbs up. Veronica took a canister out of her purse and aimed it at Jack's face.

"Cologne or something?" he asked, looking at it inquisitively as she backed away a few inches.

My eyes widened; I recognized it as the same thing she used to gas me. I couldn't even warn my friend before she pressed the dispenser, and a soft hiss of gas hit the boy square in his face.

"Jack?" Ty and I shouted together.

"Urk!" Jack groaned, his eyes rolling around as he fought against the sudden urge to pass out. He didn't last long and finally gave in to the drug's effects, a soft sigh escaping his lips. His eyes closed, and his body slumped down on his belly like a sack of potatoes, making a loud thud as it hit the ground. One arm landed on his side, and the other landed outstretched.

"Jack!" we shouted again, standing up this time.

Veronica moaned in delight, kneeling down next to the unconscious Jack and turning him over on his back. She peeked under one of his eyelids; I could hardly see his pupil. They had rolled up to his skull, exactly what happened to me when I was

gassed. I knew he was out like a bulb. Then, she proceeded to kiss him on the lips and ruffling his hair.

"Dream strong boy dreams, Jack," she whispered in his ear.

I still couldn't wrap my head around this – this was just too surreal. Never in my life had I heard of an older woman doing this to boys our age. Ty and I gave each other quick glances, just to make sure we weren't hallucinating.

We watched Veronica place her head on Jack's chest, listening to his heartbeat and rubbing his chest. After about a half a minute, she stood back up, put the canister back in her purse, and faced us two conscious boys. We stared back at her with our mouths and eyes as wide as they could get.

"Suck me, too!" Ty insisted suddenly, rubbing his crotch. He apparently didn't seem to care that our friend had just gotten gassed out. I looked at Jack's unconscious form and finally managed to ask her, "Why did you gas him?"

Veronica didn't answer me. Although, she must have seen the worry on my face, because she said, "He'll be up in fifteen minutes at most – maybe even ten. Remember our agreement?" She stepped over Jack's body and walked over to us. She grabbed our units over our shorts and began rubbing them. It startled us, but then, we closed our eyes and groaned as the immense pleasure hit us. Ty must have come first, because he almost immediately shivered and let out an, "oooooh, yeessssss..." Her soft touch made me cum soon after, and I allowed my sperm to shoot right into my underwear. My mom had bought me plenty more, and I could give a new pair to Ty as well. Then, she kissed us both, rubbing our biceps.

"You aren't going to gas *us*, are you?" I asked, "I don't want to be knocked out."

"No need for all you boys to take a nap," she said.

197

Ty grabbed her arm. "When are you going to do me what you did to Jack? Or Scott?" he asked.

"Patience, Ty," she whispered in his ear, nibbling at it, "You'll get your turn."

"Oh..." he moaned in delight, closing his eyes, "You promise?"

"Yes. I'll be around." He let her go and grinned. "I need to get going," she said.

We followed her out of my room. On her way downstairs, she asked us to say goodbye to my mom for her and to tell Max to be home by six. The mundane change of subject and the normalcy of how she spoke made it seem as if nothing out of the ordinary had just happened. That was fine by me, actually; I needed the return to reality.

"Sure..." I replied.

"I'll see you boys next week," she said as she walked out the door, "You're going to have the time of your lives."

Ty and I headed back into my room, washed ourselves off, and changed into clean underwear. All the while, we whispered to each other how we couldn't believe what had just happened. We shook Jack a few times, but when he didn't respond, we moved him to my bed. That way, it wouldn't look weird when my mom and Max came home; we'd just tell them he was tired.

Ty dared me to smell Jack's armpit while he was out. While I didn't want a repeat of Friday, I did want to see his bare pit up close. I bent his arm behind his head and stared at it for a few seconds. The odor was strong, but not nearly as bad as it was the other day.

"Five bucks says you pass out if you smell it!" Ty said, laughing.

"You're on!" I replied, knowing I'd be able to take it.

"Okay, but you have to put your nose right up against his skin," he insisted.

A fit of coughing came over me as I did, the stench making me dizzy. I lost my balance and fell to my knees and then, to all fours.

Ty burst out laughing. "How is it?" he asked.

"Ugh... it's revolting, and it's only been one full day since he showered!" I replied, "Now you do it!"

"Okay, but if I don't pass out either, I don't owe you anything."

I leaned against my bed, holding the back of my head. "Okay," I accepted, "But if you do, you owe me ten bucks."

"Sure!" he said, and then, he began sniffing the unconscious boy's armpit. It knocked him down to the ground, and he began coughing as well.

"Ugh!" he said with a chuckle, "It's horrible!"

I laughed, lifted Jack's arm, and watched it drop back to the bed when I let go. I moved his head around and lifted his eyelid to look at his pupil, which was still rolled back.

"Man, he's out like a fucking light," said Ty.

Ty played around with Jack's body as well until we got bored and decided to play video games. Jack finally woke up about five minutes later.

"Oh, man, what hit me?" he groaned, rubbing his face.

Ty quipped in a low tone, keeping his eyes on the screen, "Hey, Blowjob Boy is awake!"

Jack sat up, shaking the cobwebs from his head. "Woah. I still feel dizzy," he said.

I paused the game and looked at him over my shoulder. "Yeah," I said, "that's how I felt when I first woke up from being gassed."

Jack leaned back against the wall, his eyes slowly blinking. "I... I've never felt anything like that before," he admitted.

"Being gassed or blown?" Ty asked, elbowing me softly in the ribs and waggling his eyebrows. I laughed.

"Both, actually," he said.

"You're a lucky bastard," Said Ty.

Jack looked around. "Did she leave?"

"Yup," I nodded.

Our friend, newly awakened, folded his arms, frowned, and asked, "Why did she gas me?"

I shrugged, answering, "She didn't say. But, it looks to me like she enjoyed watching you pass out."

"She kissed you while you were unconscious," Ty added, "just like she did with Scott."

"I didn't like being put to sleep like that," Jack grumbled.

Ty stood up and faced Jack, putting his hands on his hips. "Are you saying what she did to you wasn't worth it, Jack?" he asked.

Jack blinked, and then, he smiled and shrugged. "Well," he continued, "when you ask it like that, Ty, then no, it was totally worth it."

"That's what I thought."

"Did she do anything to you guys?"

Ty and I smiled at each other. "She gave Scott and me handjobs," Ty let him know.

"Nice."

We heard the garage door opening, which meant my mom and Max were back from the grocery store.

"Then Scott and I used you as an armpit challenge," said Ty, "to see if we could stand your stench."

"Seriously?" laughed Jack, "Did either of you pass out?"

"Nope," he answered, "but you stink, even after one day of not showering."

"Good," said Jack, standing up to put on his shirt, "That means you guys won't last during scrimmages." He then continued, "Jaden's gonna be *so* pissed he missed this."

Jack's phone alerted him of a new text message, and Ty waved his finger and reminded him, "Remember, we can't say anything to him." Jack's jaw dropped as he read the text. "Looks like we won't have to," he said, holding the phone up so we could read it for ourselves. It was from Jaden; he wrote, "Veronica said she couldn't find the chart of my physical and wants me to see her early tomorrow! Fuck yes!"

chapter twenty-seven

When Max joined us upstairs, Ty regaled him and Jack with my antics at the clothing store today, which made both of them break out in a fit of laughter. We horsed around with them for about half an hour before they left. Afterwards, I kept Ty company back at his house while he repacked for the coming camp week. When we got back, my mom had hamburgers and salad ready for us.

"You guys have a good talk with Veronica?" she asked as we ate dinner, "I hope you didn't make her feel uncomfortable."

Ty and I had planned to let me do the answering if Mom asked us about our 'talk' with Veronica, and he would just agree with me if she prompted him for information too.

"Why would you think we'd make her feel uncomfortable?" I asked, stabbing some carrot pieces with my fork, "We didn't hit on her or anything." That made Ty laugh.

"What's so funny, Ty?" asked Mom.

Ty immediately mouthed a fork full of spinach in his mouth, pointing to his orifice as he chewed. I picked up on what he was doing and answered, "The idea of us twelve-year-old boys hitting on a grown woman." The other boy nodded with a smile.

My mom didn't see the ruse and ate some salad. "Well, as long as you behaved yourselves," she said, "I felt a little guilty leaving her there with you by herself." I bit into my burger with a shrug. Oh, if she only knew. "Oh, I'm taking you boys tomorrow morning, remember," she continued, "so you don't have your bikes out all week."

"Yup," I said.

"I already put my bike back at my house," Ty said.

"And you're supposed to wear your Putnam practice tees to the school," reminded Mom.

"Okay," I said.

I decided to switch the subject to my grammy and avoid any more questions about Veronica or camp. My mom talked about how she was doing and how much she misses me. We ended the meal with my mom telling us that she had really enjoyed having Ty here and that she will miss us both. After dinner, we kept Mom company by watching TV with her, including the end of a really hokey sci-fi/western mishmash of a movie. Then, we went back upstairs, where I repacked, before we went to sleep. The alarm to wake us up seemed to ring almost immediately after.

We hopped out of bed full of energy and excitement. After a quick breakfast of ham and eggs, Mom drove us to the school. A bunch of our teammates had already arrived, but instead of walking toward the boys' lockers, they were heading to the gymnasium entrance.

My mom snapped her fingers. "That's right," she recalled, "Calvin asked me to tell you to use that entrance instead of going straight to the locker rooms. I knew I had forgotten to tell you boys something."

We both shrugged. "Eh, no worries, Mrs. Weston." said Ty. Then, he pantomimed tipping a cowboy hat and said in a bad

Southern drawl, "We can follow the herd," quoting from the horrid movie we watched the previous night.

The three of us uttered the next line in unison, "Toward our doom!"

We all laughed, and Mom kissed both of us goodbye. "I'll miss you, Scott," she said, "Call me!"

"I'll miss you too, Mom," I nodded, "See you Friday!"

We grabbed our stuff from the car and spotted Ryder Banks, our Colts tight end, walking with Jimmy Casten and a few others. When we shouted over to them, they waved back and waited for us to catch up. They, like us, were all wearing their Putnam Panthers shirts. Jimmy fist bumped Ty, and Ryder mussed my hair and said, "You and Jack were the life of the party on Saturday night."

"The way you flipped Billy over on his back was gold, my friend," added Jimmy.

Matt Manning, our seventh grade left guard and backup quarterback, glanced over at us with his dark blue eyes and frowned. He had a lean, muscular build with black hair, cropped like a soldier's. He seemed like a pretty cool kid, and I wished Ryder and Jimmy hadn't said anything about the party around him or other seventh graders. Sure, in reality, they'd all find out about it sooner or later; I just preferred it to have been later.

When we entered the large gymnasium, I caught a glimpse of four rows of perfectly aligned single-person capsules, about twenty-five in each row, that spanned the length of the gym. They looked like a cross between tanning beds and those small tubes from Japanese capsule hotels I'd seen on TV. Currently, all of them were open, revealing a soft material that must have been the mattress, along with a pillow on one end. They had some sort of controls on the inside, between the bed and the frame.

I also noticed that each capsule had a small, rectangular holder made of transparent plastic attached to its front. It had a white index card with a kid's name and jersey number on it. It didn't take a genius to figure out we were going to be sleeping inside them. They didn't look cheap; so, perhaps they'd be comfortable. A few of them had a luggage roller in front, although their owners were nowhere in sight.

"Wow," said Ty, gawking at the capsules.

"Yeah," added Ryder.

"Yo!" came Damian Jackson's voice, the Rams' team captain, as he tried to gain our attention. We looked to the side, in the direction of his voice.

All four team captains, dressed in shorts and Putnam Panthers Tees, were standing in front of a row of beds. None of us had noticed them or paid them any mind; our attention had obviously been on the strange beds that awaited us.

Damian, standing in front of the first row, and closest to us, asked, "Neat, huh?"

"We sleeping in those things?" asked Jimmy.

"Yup," answered Billy Thompson, calling from the second row down.

Ryder scratched his head and asked, "Since *when* did we get these?"

"Since today, Banks," he answered.

"No more sleeping on temporary bunks like last year," said Damian.

"Oh, that's sweet!" said Ryder.

"Thank God!" exclaimed Jimmy, "Those were really uncomfortable."

"I heard," said Billy.

"And the locker rooms, bathrooms, and showers have been upgraded too!" exclaimed Damian.

"Who showers during football camp?" asked another boy. A kid next to him shrugged.

"Were they upgraded from start to finish over the weekend?" asked Ryder in shock.

"Yup," answered Damian. Then, he told us to go to our team captains. A few boys headed toward Damian, some toward Billy, and some all the way down to the fourth row to Mason Holden, the Jets' captain. The rest of us walked over to the third row, where Calvin was standing.

"This is the Warriors' row," I heard Billy say to his teammates as we passed him by. He puffed out his chest and glanced at us, smirking. "The number one team here," he added. Billy then lightly slugged my shoulder.

"See you in the war room, Weston," he said.

"Hey, have you seen Jaden?" I asked, looking back at him.

"Yeah, he was here early. Said he had to see the nurse. Why?"

I had to dismiss his question. "Just curious," I said. I turned around and shared a grin with Ty.

Calvin smiled at us when we reached him. He pointed to the row of beds and said, "This is Colts territory. No need for me to boast, though. We'll have plenty of time for that after we win the Panther Cup on Friday." He gave a sidelong glance to Billy.

The Warriors' captain snickered, "We'll see about that."

Jimmy and Ryder grinned.

"Go find the capsule with your name on it," ordered Calvin, "Put your rollers in front, and then, meet everyone else at the upgraded boys' war room for overnight orientation. Put any football equipment you brought in your backpacks and bring them as well. Also, turn off any electronics."

"Upgraded?" asked Ryder.

Calvin nodded and continued, "The war room is now four separate areas that open into one. Each area has a colored wall: red, blue, purple, or green. As you know, we Colts are purple. So, go to the purple area and find a seat. Derek and Bryce are already there, so they can answer any more questions you have until the rest of us come."

I found my bed four spots from the other end, in between Derek Edwards and Ty. Next to Derek's was Bryce Winters', and next to Bryce, at the end, was Calvin's. The team captains' beds were all at the ends, with two belonging to the squad leaders next. We stationed our rollers at the front of our beds and put any football equipment we had brought with us inside our backpacks, just as Calvin directed. Then, Ty dropped down on his bed, and I saw the mattress form a small dent around his body.

"Holy shit," he exclaimed, closing his eyes, "This is so fucking comfortable."

"Ty!" came an annoyed shout from Calvin, "Get your ass up and into the war room!" Ryder and Jimmy snickered, and Ty reluctantly stood up.

I noticed two buttons on my bed labeled 'Canopy' – one on the outside frame and the other on the inside. Curiosity got the better of me, and I pressed the button. A thin, cylindrical top, made out of some type of opaque metal, came out of a slit on one side of the frame and made a dome a foot or so above the bed. It completely covered the mattress, stopping in a slit on the other side of the frame. The top hardly made any sound as it moved, except for a low, electric whine.

"Wow!" exclaimed Ty, "This is some futuristic shit!"

"No kidding!" I added.

"That is awesome!" said Jimmy.

207

"Uh-oh, Scott," warned Matt Manning, poking me on the shoulder, "Calvin is glaring hard at you."

Without acknowledging my team captain, I pressed the button again, and the dome retracted. It was only then that I looked over at Calvin. Sure enough, his eyes were shooting daggers at me. With my hands up, I shouted over to him, "We're leaving, Calvin! But you have to admit, these things are awesome!"

The five of us left the gymnasium and reached the door that used to be labeled '7th Grade War Room'. Now, it just said 'War Room'. Inside, we found that the wall separating the seventh and eighth grade war rooms was gone, making just one giant room, just as Calvin had told us. A large aisle split the room down the middle and another one across. Both of these aisles had small, one-inch rails running down from the ceiling, with a divider hidden in the walls.

Each side of the room had two different colored walls that joined at an angle, creating four different colored sections altogether. Each section had two rows of tabletops and about twenty-six chairs. In the back-right section, marked by a green wall, sat Damian Jackson's Rams. Opposite them, back by the blue wall, sat the players from Mason Holden's Jets. The two in the front had Billy Thompson's red Warriors on the right and us purple Colts on the left. It appeared that almost half of our team had beaten us there, with their backpacks on top of the table or resting on the ground next to them. All eight squad leaders were present as well, including Jack, who was yakking it up with Travis Bower and Lucas Colby, the halfback who had replaced me on Friday. The three of them sat in the front row, while Austin Miller, their center, sat directly behind Jack. Jaden was nowhere to be seen.

I spotted our squad leaders, Bryce Winters and Derek Edwards, sitting in the front row with an empty seat between them. When they noticed us, they waved us over. Jack turned and waved

as well. I sat at the end of the second row in our section, and Ty sat between me and Nicholas Schmidt, our tight end. He and Nicholas smacked hands and ended it in a handshake. Then, Nicholas reached over and did the same with me.

Ryder pointed to the seat between our two squad leaders in the front row. "That seat for Calvin?" he asked.

"Yup," answered Derek. "Seventh graders behind us, Matt," he added as our backup quarterback tried to move past Derek and sit next to Bryce. Matt frowned and pointed to Jack.

"Jack is a squad leader, Matt," Derek clarified, "Squad leaders sit in front. Team captains sit in front. Eighth graders sit in front. Everyone else, including you, sits at the back."

Bryce thumbed him over to an empty seat diagonal from him, next to a light blond-haired right guard named Brady McKee. "Sit there, Matt," he added, "We can still chat."

In a deep, raspy kid voice, Matt said to Ty and me, "I'm surprised you two aren't allowed to sit in the front, considering how special Calvin thinks you are."

"Because Calvin invited them to the party?" asked Bryce. That got a few other seventh graders to gasp at what they had just heard.

"Well, duh," voiced Matt.

Bryce nodded in understanding and looked through a stack of envelopes he had in front of him. I hadn't noticed those before, and I blinked in surprise as I looked around and found that every squad leader had at least one envelope in front of him.

"Here," said Bryce, holding one behind him for Matt.

"What is this?" Matt asked as he took it.

"You'll see," responded Bryce with a smirk.

Ty and I looked over and noticed that it had Matt's name on it, along with instructions only to open it when told. Matt made his

way to our row and sat down next to Brady, his eyes fixed at the mysterious envelope.

"I got one, too!" said Brady, showing it off to Matt.

Bryce then looked over at Ty and me and said, "They're only for seventh graders who didn't get to go to the party on Saturday, except for Jack. He's a squad leader and would get to go to the party anyway." Jack wiggled his eyebrows.

"So that means the only seventh graders who don't get an envelope are me, Scott, and Jaden," Ty correctly deduced.

"Yes," answered Bryce.

"Aw, man."

Matt licked his lips and felt the envelope with his fingers. Hopefully, whatever it contained would be enough to make it up to the rest of my fellow seventh graders, without making the three of us *too* jealous.

"Speaking of Jaden, you guys seen him yet?" Jack asked Ty and me. We shook our heads, but just then, the boy in question, wearing his backpack, walked into the War Room, his hair all disheveled and a glow about him. A wide smile was on his face when he saw us. He walked with an air of cockiness and a smug confidence, one which is usually only worn after some great achievement.

Jaden removed his backpack and plunked down next to Austin. Then, leaning back on his chair, putting his hands behind his head, he declared, "I'm in the club now, boys."

chapter twenty-eight

I took what Jaden's stated to mean Veronica had done more than just conduct a routine physical. I wondered whether she went all the way with him like she did with me, or did she just suck his dick, like she did with Jack?

"What do you mean, 'in the club'?" asked Austin, "Is this because you got to go to the party?"

Derek and Bryce turned around to face us and eyed each other, probably wondering if they should interfere.

"Nope," Jaden shook his head, "But those three know what I'm talking about." He pointed between Jack, Ty, and me. The three of us exchanged a glance, and I frowned at him. I wondered why Jaden couldn't keep his mouth shut. Did he have to point us out?

"Jaden!" hissed Jack.

"What? I'm not giving anything away!" said Jaden.

"Shut up!" Jack whispered, which made Jaden frown.

"Spill it, man," Nicholas elbowed Ty. Ty began to sweat, staring at the table.

"Don't ask," said Jack, but that didn't deter anybody, as Travis Bower and a few of the other kids began staring at us. I knew none

of them would let this go; so, I threw them a bone, a small one that would hopefully allow them to come to their own conclusions.

"Well, there's this girl..." I began, intentionally trailing off. I ignored the looks that Ty and Jack gave me.

"Of course there is," said Bryce with a chuckle, "Do we know her?"

"Maybe," I shrugged, "I dunno."

"Does she go to this school?" asked Travis.

"Yeah."

"Oh, you guys are probably making a big deal out of nothing," Matt joined in, "I bet Jaden just kissed his first girl and that's it. Who here isn't in *that* club?" Our backup quarterback emphasized on the word 'that'.

A bunch of guys laughed, which made Jaden smirk. "If only you knew," he finished.

Derek rolled his eyes and said, "Yeah, well, we don't know, and we don't care, actually. Matt has a point, anyway." He and Bryce turned back around. Once they did so, the other kids lost interest in this conversation as well and began to talk amongst themselves. I heaved a sigh of relief. That worked way better than I had thought it would.

Ty leaned close to me and whispered, "You're a fucking genius."

Jack gave me a wide smile and a few nods, probably amazed at my diversion. Jaden, however, looked upset that no one believed him. If Veronica did do something with him, wouldn't she had told him to keep quiet about it?

"Scott-" began Jaden, but I interrupted him, taking control of the conversation and not caring what he was going to say.

"Regardless of what happened, Jaden," I started in an attempt to hint for him to keep quiet about it, "Wouldn't she get upset if you

bragged about it in the open like this? She might not ever let you do it again."

"Scott's got a point, Jaden," added Derek without even looking back at us, "I've heard girls aren't that forgiving."

"Yeah, maybe," sighed Jaden, "Whatever. Never mind." I couldn't help but crack a very small grin. Mission accomplished.

The room filled pretty quickly after that, and soon, just about every seat was taken by seventh and eighth graders. Finally, the four team captains walked to the front of the room and stood by the podium, with Coach King standing behind them. Damian Jackson took the mic.

"Hey, fellow Panthers!" Damian began.

We all cheered.

"Welcome to what'll hopefully be the best weeks of your lives so far! It's gonna be a lot of hard work, but we team captains promise you it will be worth it. Of course, what you put into it will determine what you get out of it." Damian scanned the room as he continued, "This is the first year that we team captains will be calling most of the shots. As you know, Coach Thimbleton has retired," - he then pointed to Coach King behind him - "so Coach Sim King will be taking over as the sole coach for the camp and will have the final say on things."

Coach King nodded and approached the mic as Damian stepped out of the way.

"Boys," King began, breaking into a warm smile and looking between all of us, "I am very honored to be here with you. I can't express that enough."

His words carried an air of sincerity that made me grin.

"Your team captains have, so far, proved themselves to be amazing leaders," he went on to say, "and I feel you can trust them. Remember, you are autonomous players within one team. Be there

for each other. However, please know that I am here for each one of you, and that you can come to me with *any* problems."

The loving energy emanating from the coach enveloped the entire room, covering us like an umbrella. I felt instantly at ease.

Then, he concluded, speaking in a powerful, protective manner, "I will be overseeing everything from the sidelines, so to speak, making sure you boys are safe and, most of all, having fun. You are my life. And I am ever grateful to be here."

He spoke in such an authentic, enthusiastic manner that we all rose from our seats, clapping and cheering, with the team captains joining in as well.

Coach King placed a hand on his heart, bowed his head, and left the room, high-fiving the team captains on his way out.

When our cheers ebbed, Damian retook the mic, and we sat back down.

"Now, an important rule," the Rams' leader said, "When you're outside these walls during camp week, you have to be fully suited up, which includes wearing your football helmet. This means whether we're practicing on our fields, riding on the bus to another field, or playing in a scrimmage against another team; it helps remind ourselves, and tell others, that we aren't just individual boys anymore. We are, as Coach King said, autonomous players within one team, the Putnam Panthers."

"And when we're inside?" asked one of my fellow Colts.

"You can remove your helmet, but keep the rest of your uniform on until bedtime. You can sleep in it as well if you want. You'll find the beds pretty accommodating. We'll talk about those tonight."

Murmurs spread throughout the room about that. Some thought it'd be cool to try sleeping in our football uniforms; others,

not so much. Although, being able to wear my uniform all week sounded good to me.

Damian waved his finger in the air. "It's also possible," he continued, "that we'll have these four sub-teams when the season starts. So, no more separate seventh and eighth grade teams. And, no more A and B Teams. Just lots and lots of games so more of us can play."

That got another round of cheers, especially from us seventh graders.

"Calvin?" prompted Damian, giving him the floor.

My team captain walked up to the mic and said, "Some of you already know this, but the middle school End of the World party is supposed to be just for eighth graders and some guests who, with few exceptions, aren't football players." He pointed to Jack, saying, "Jack Murphy was an exception because he's a squad leader, and he was allowed to bring Jaden Ludge, his friend. However, this year, I invited Scott Weston for reasons of my own, and he asked me to include Ty Green, his own friend. I won't go into my reasons for inviting Scott right now, except to say I do not favor him, or Ty, over you."

Luckily, no one reacted, which hopefully meant they believed him. Calvin certainly sounded sincere.

Calvin coughed a few times before continuing, "Now, to make it up to you other seventh graders, open the envelopes in front of you."

The sound of paper ripping echoed throughout the room. Ty and I watched Brady and Matt open theirs. Inside, there was a ticket with their name on it, their jersey number, Calvin's signature, and some other signatures that I couldn't make out. The ticket read, "Saturday, July 28th. Maxium Entertainment Presents

'The Crew: Live at The End of the World'. Special Invite Only." My jaw hit the table.

"Holy shit!" yelped nearly all of the seventh graders.

"Are these for real? *The Crew? In concert?*" shouted a kid.

The four team captains were beaming at us and fist bumping each other. The eighth graders, of course, didn't sound pleased at all.

Calvin held up a hand to quiet everybody, and then, he continued, "Yes, those are real. Yes, *The Crew* is performing live just for you. And yes, you eighth graders are invited. Your envelopes will be handed out later." That got everyone else roaring with cheers, except for the three of us who were left out.

"Oh, man!" Ty exclaimed to me, "That means, out of the entire team, just you, me, and Jaden can't go!" One of the hottest bands was going to hold a private concert for our team, and I wasn't going. *Fuck.* So much for not being jealous. However, I found myself actually heaving a sigh of relief; now, the other seventh graders wouldn't have anything to hold against Ty, Jaden, me, Jack, or Calvin.

I couldn't blame Calvin and the other leaders for inviting the eighth graders either. And, I told myself I wouldn't hold anything against anyone for going. I hoped Ty and Jaden would feel the same way.

"Ty?" I called.

"Oh, that is so not fair!" my friend grunted.

"Yeah, I know," I continued, "but we had so much fun ourselves, didn't we?"

"Yeah, yeah. Although, I wish we could have had both."

I fist bumped him. "Me too, but we'll have each other. And Jaden too." I looked over at our other friend, just in time to hear

him whine to Calvin, "No way I have to miss that! You gotta be fucking kidding me!" So much for Jaden understanding.

"How the fuck did you manage this?" asked one of the kids.

"Connections," replied Calvin, "Thanks to Coach King and our nurse, who we'll introduce later." He then looked at Jaden and said, "I understand you're upset, Jaden, but we have to even things out here. We hoped you three would understand."

"Or learn to," added Billy with a growl.

Jaden rested an elbow on the table, cupped his face in his hand, and shook his head in resentment.

"How do you two feel?" Calvin asked Ty and me. All the other boys looked at us as well.

"Disappointed," I said, "But I understand. It's cool."

"Yeah," said Ty, nodding his head. I saw a few boys grin at us, including Brady and Matt.

Jack turned to face Jaden. "Don't worry, buddy," he started, "Even though I'm invited, I'm not gonna go."

Jaden raised his head, and his face lit up as he replied in disbelief, "You *aren't*?"

"Nope. As much as I want to, I want to be with my buddies more." Jack looked over at Ty and me as he said that and winked at us. I thought Jaden was going to leap out and kiss him.

"Oh *really*? Thanks, Jack!" he said.

Ty and I smiled and echoed our own gratitude. That made the team captains smile at him as well, especially Billy. The Warriors' team captain curled his thumb and index finger together into a circle and gave him a 'good job' sign.

Then, I saw Max's face peek out from the front entrance, while another little hand grabbed his shirt and pulled him back. A bunch of us snickered.

"Well," said Billy, looking over at the entrance and laughing, "I guess it's time we introduced our teamboys."

"Come on out, boys," Damian called out to them, "And stand by your team leaders."

Four nine-year-old boys entered the room, wearing kid-sized Putnam Middle School Panther tees. I didn't even know they made them that small. As Veronica mentioned, Max and Zach were among them, with Max walking to Billy and high-fiving him, and Zach doing the same with Calvin. Another kid, a stocky, short, black-haired boy with blue eyes, walked over to Mason. The fourth kid looked like a younger version of Damian, with the same short, black hair and hazel eyes. He must have been Damian's younger brother.

"These fourth graders have the privilege, or rather, *we* have the privilege, of them being our helpers," explained Damian, "They will help communicate between our teams and coaches, bring us gatorade, help with plays and practice, and be our support during our scrimmages."

"Just like the pros have!" added Lucas Colby.

"Exactly!"

The four boys beamed with pride. Once Max saw Jack, he started making a beeline for him. Billy grabbed Max's shirt, making the kid run in place. "Woah there, cowboy! Wait until the introductions are done." A bunch of us, including Jack, chuckled, and Max rubbed the back of his neck. "Heeee..." he grinned.

The team captains introduced our little helpers. The Rams' teamboy actually was Damian's younger brother - Jeremy, a center and left tackle for his elementary school. The Jets' teamboy, an all-star quarterback for his school, turned out to be one of the Jets' player's little cousin, Nate Harrison.

"Give it up for our teamboys!" shouted Damian.

With that, the room erupted in whoops, hollers, and cheers for the kids. They blushed and waved back. Damian then asked them to take a seat in their team's section.

Billy pointed Max toward Jack and said, "Go get 'em, tiger." Max sprinted to Jack, gave him a high-five, and sat down on his lap.

"Oomph," groaned Jack, "I wasn't expecting that."

"Hee!" Max chuckled, and Jack patted his head.

Jeremy and Nate sat on empty seats in their sections, and Zach walked over to Ty and me. He smelled like he hadn't showered in a week.

"You have a head start on us stinking like a football player, Zach," said Ty with a grin. Zach smiled and sat on Ty's lap. I give him a slap-shake combo.

Jack pointed to Max and said, "I think this kid would give Zach a run for his money in the stink division." Max laughed.

"In a few hours, Murphy, their odor won't compare to ours," said Billy.

"Yeah, that's true," Jack agreed.

"Speaking of odor," began Billy as Damian stepped down to let him have the mic, "As a middle school boy football player who has been primed, the more you sweat and the stronger you get, the more powerful your body odor becomes. One good sniff of another boy's sweaty armpit, and you'll be out for a good while. Just ask Murphy and Weston." Jack and I smirked at each other as most of the other boys looked over at us. "So, during a play, if you can armpit another player, good. But, you're only allowed to do it during games or what's called off-rails practice. Otherwise, you'll be running laps until the other kid wakes up. We need to be conscious to build up our athletic and football skills. Got it?" A round of yeses filled the room. "And, armpitting only works on

other boys," he continued, "And only primed football players. So, don't go trying it on others, or you'll probably get punched or slapped."

"Primed?" asked some kid.

"Yep," Billy nodded, "If you're here, you're primed. Same goes for the other boys at other middle school football camps."

He went to explain what Nurse Veronica had told him, which mirrored what she had said yesterday in my room, except he left off the part about enhanced sexual experiences. I wondered if that was on purpose or if he hadn't been told.

"Any other questions," the Warriors' leader then asked, "before we talk about our lovely nurse?"

"So, we don't really need to shower, then," said another kid.

"Only if you want to," came the answer, "But, it'll be harder armpitting someone when you smell like soap. Besides, you'll just be around other stinky boys, so it won't matter – at least until Friday afternoon before you go home. Then, showering is mandatory. Gotta leave the dirt and the stench here."

A seventh grade Rams player raised his hand.

"What's up, Colton?" asked Damian.

"What's this about a lovely nurse?"

"Good question, Kipper," said Billy, referring to the boy's last name. Then, he called out toward the front entrance, "Nurse Veronica? You still there?"

"Sure am!" answered Veronica's familiar voice.

Veronica entered the room, wearing the same skimpy nurse's outfit she was wearing the previous Thursday. Every boy, including the team captains and the nine-year-olds, stared in awe as the gorgeous woman walked across the front of the room. If getting a boner made a noise, there'd be about one-hundred deep springy

sounds plus four higher pitched ones. A lot of the boys whistled, including Jack and Jaden.

Veronica reached the podium, and when Billy stepped down, she gently rubbed his face with back of her hand. "Thanks, Sweetie," she said.

Billy gulped, for once not being able to say anything. Instead, he just nodded.

"My name is Veronica Lyon, but just call me Nurse Veronica." She continued, "I will be your aide for the duration of this camp. If you need anything, please come see me in the new athletic nurse's station located across from the coaches' offices, near your lockers."

"*Anything?*" asked Ryder with a grin, earning chuckles from his fellow eighth graders.

"Yes," replied Veronica, staring at the boy.

Ryder's grin faded, stunned by her simple, dead-pan answer.

chapter twenty-nine

Ty, Jack, Jaden, and I smirked at Veronica's response, giving each other an insider's nod.

"I will also need to run some examinations on you Putnam boys from time to time," Veronica said, then added with a smile, "But just remember, I will never hurt you. Everything I do is for something very special."

I wondered if the things she had done to me and my friends counted as some of those 'examinations'.

Veronica concluded with, "I can't wait to watch you wonderful boys play."

The nurse left, but you could have still heard a pin drop. Finally, Damian Jackson said, "Time to get suited up, boys. Don't forget to leave your backpacks in your lockers, and meet back here. We'll have a quick individual team meeting, then head outside for warmups. Teamboys, stick with your team captains."

As we all made our way to the locker rooms, Ty, Jack, and I confronted Jaden.

"Well?" said Jack, "What happened earlier?"

"Oh, so *now* you want to know, huh?" replied Jaden with a smirk.

"Don't be a fucktard."

"Fine, fine," Jaden began, "Let's go to the equipment storage area behind the locker rooms."

We headed to the locker rooms and then through the door to the equipment room, where we stored all our training gear. Once we were inside, I heard my phone's distinct ring going off in my backpack.

"Scott, is that your phone?" asked Jack as he closed the door behind us.

Ty elbowed Jack and commented, "Who else has a ring tone of an old 1980s video game start music?"

I removed my backpack and brought it up to my ear. The ring got louder.

"Yeah, it is," I answered and retrieved my phone.

"Who'd be calling you now?" asked Ty, "Your mom?"

I looked at the caller ID and read it out loud. "Unknown caller."

"Didn't you know you were supposed to turn your phone off before our orientation meeting, Scott?" asked Jack, with a not-so-subtle hint of annoyance.

"Oops," I said, "I completely forgot about that."

"Mine's been off since this morning," said Ty, with Jaden adding, "Same here."

Jack let out a grunt. "You're lucky it didn't go off during orientation, or you'd be off running laps."

Since the phone was on and was ringing, curiosity got the better of me, and I answered the call.

"Scott!" Jack hissed, reaching for the phone, but I side-stepped him.

"Hello?" I said. As soon as I did that, the other line disconnected.

"Whoever it was, just hung up," I said.

Jack frowned. "Well, that was fucking anti-climactic," he said, "Turn it off. Now."

A text alert went off on my phone. It was from the same unknown four-digit number as last week, but this time with a hyperlink that had the phrase 'veron_jaden'.

"Look, guys!" I yelped, showing them the phone, "This must be a video from Veronica!"

"Woah!" said Ty.

Jaden just smiled.

"Click on the link, Scott!" demanded Ty.

"Why would she send it to me, and not you, Jaden?" I asked.

"Who cares?" said Ty, reaching for my phone. I side-stepped him as well, but I bumped into Jack, who yanked the phone away from my hand.

"Hey!" I protested, reaching back for it.

Jack held it out away from me, and pressed down on the off button. I grabbed his arm, but he shoved me *hard* against the wall with his other arm, stunning me. His lip curled into a snarl. When he came a few inches from my face, the smell of eggs and hot sauce wafted out from his breath. What I wouldn't give to be stronger than Jack for once, I thought.

"Woah!" said Jaden.

"Scott!" seethed Jack.

"*What*?" I seethed back.

"I told you to turn off your phone!" he growled with his eyes narrowed, "What the fuck do you think would happen if we were caught in here watching this?"

Ty grabbed Jack's shoulder and forced him back. "Ease up on him, Jack!" Ty demanded, "Don't you want to watch the video?"

Jack pushed Ty away and spat back at him, "You guys might not care about running laps if you get caught, but I'm a fucking squad leader. And Billy can easily replace me if he thinks I'm just fucking around!"

I hadn't thought of that. As if on cue, the door opened, and in stepped Max and Billy, along with a few other eighth graders, who were still in their practice tees. They didn't see us at first, focusing instead on what Billy was saying. "We're going to use the practice dummies, sleds, and agility ladders," we heard him say, "So, after our meeting, grab a few seventh graders to help you-"

He stopped when he saw the four of us, then, turning his attention to his squad leader, he asked, "What's going on, Murphy?"

"I was just taking care of something," said Jack, shoving the phone in my hands and snarling at me with a glaring look of 'I told you so'.

Billy folded his arms and asked, "Was it that important? Were you guys, like, sucking each other's dicks or something?" Billy must not have caught Jack's bad mood, which was actually a good thing. That meant he wouldn't press for details. The other eighth graders snickered at Billy's remark, and Max's eyes grew as wide as they could. He covered his mouth through a snort.

"We know you'd want in on that, Billy," said Ty, giving me a grin. Those same boys oohed, but I knew that wasn't the best time to be giving lip back to a team captain; so, I didn't smile back.

"Ty!" snapped Jack, glaring at him.

"What?" shrugged Ty.

"This isn't the time!"

Billy stepped closer to my fellow Colt. "Green?" he began.

"Yeah?"

"I'm going to let that one slide."

"What do you mean?"

"Normally, you talk to me like that, you do laps."

Ty's mouth dropped open. "What!" he cried out, "You can't insult us and then make me do laps when I insult you back!"

"Was I even fucking talking to you in the first place, Green?" asked Billy, narrowing his eyes.

Ty threw up his hands. "What does that matter?" he answered, "You can't say shit about us like that and not have us diss you back! Isn't that right, Scott?" Our safety looked at me, and everyone else followed, including Billy. The eighth grader folded his arms and waited for me to answer.

"I don't think this was the right situation for that, Ty," I said, making a quick side-long glance at Billy. "We should just get going."

"Waddya mean?" Ty demanded.

I sighed at having to further this conversation, risking us having to run laps, or even worse for Jack. "I think Billy was irritated that we were in here," I explained, "And not getting suited up. When it comes to football, he doesn't fuck around much."

"No team captain here does," added Billy, "And neither should you. And what pisses me off more than anything is when I see guys fucking around when it's time to get serious... or they do stupid shit like Weston and Casten did when they got into that fight on Thursday. Got that, Green?"

Jack gave Ty and me an extended glare for emphasis.

"Yeah," replied Ty, looking back at Jack, "I get it."

"Good," said Billy. Then, turning to Jack, he asked, "You okay? You look upset."

"Yes, I'm fine," said Jack curtly, keeping his eyes on me, "Nothing I couldn't handle."

"Good. Because our team is on equipment duty for the next few days, and I need your help organizing this."

Jack broke his gaze on me and looked back at his team captain. "Sure thing," He nodded.

Billy then turned to Ty, Jaden, and me. "You three go get suited up and meet at the war room, like Jackson said. Quit wasting time."

I gave Jack a look of remorse and held out my hand, my way of apologizing without having to say anything in front of Billy. Jack accepted and slapped it, ending it in a handshake. On our way out, Jack whispered to me, "We'll watch the video later together."

With the tension having left us, I entered the locker room in a much better mood.

"I gotta see what Veronica did to me while I was knocked out!" said Jaden.

"Knocked out?" asked Ty, swallowing.

"Yeah," he replied, "She gassed me just like she gassed Scott."

Ty's eyes widened, and he unconsciously rubbed his crotch. "How'd it feel?" he asked.

"Passed right out," Jaden answered with a shrug.

"Well, hopefully, the link is still active," I said.

"Hope so," replied Jaden, turning to me with a frown, "But yeah, like you said, Scott, I wonder why the video was sent to your phone and not mine."

"Maybe Nurse Veronica didn't have you number?" suggested Ty.

Jaden nodded, saying, "Oh, yeah. Probably not. She did talk to my mom yesterday, and not me. Ah, well, at least one of us got it.

You can forward it to me later." Then, he waved goodbye and walked over to his locker, saying, "See ya'll out there."

When Ty and I reached ours, Ty asked, with concern in his voice, "You think the link might not work?"

"I don't know," I answered as I opened my locker. My football equipment was still sitting there exactly how I had left it, waiting for its master to don it again. The smell of my sweat still clung to it, which filled the locker with my scent. I took out the uniform and kept it on the bench next to me. I stripped down to my underwear and football socks, and after fetching my cleats and athletic cup from my backpack, I stowed it along with my street clothes into the locker.

As Ty was putting on his shoulder pads, he remarked, "Jack certainly switched to squad leader mode on a dime back there."

"Yeah, that surprised me at first too," I replied, "But lucky for us that he did, or else, we'd all have gotten into serious trouble."

I slid the cup into my underwear. "Gotta protect the family jewels," I chuckled.

Ty grinned and knocked on his crotch; his cup made a thunk sound. "Yup, me too!" he said.

Just like the previous Friday, I took my time putting on the uniform.

"You going slow for a reason, Scott?" asked Ty as Jaden came over to us, both of them fully suited up and clutching their helmets by the facemasks.

"I like taking my time to put on my uniform," I explained, "I like relishing my transformation from just an ordinary boy into a warrior. It makes me feel... I dunno... masculine and strong."

"I guess I can understand that," said Ty, lifting his helmet in the air.

"Me too," Jaden joined in.

I finished putting on my uniform and stood up with my helmet. I held it out to my two friends and proposed, "To being a warrior."

"To being a warrior!" they chorused, and we banged our helmets together.

A few boys passing us by joined in as well, and then, we headed back to the War Room together.

chapter thirty

Someone had pulled the curtains to section the War Room off into separate team areas. They must have had some kind of sound dampening quality to them, because we could barely hear the voices from the other sections.

Ty and I sat in the same chairs as before, and soon, our area filled with suited up Colts players, each boy carrying his helmet and placing it on the table in front of him after sitting down. Zach, our teamboy, stood proudly next to Calvin, hounding him about Calvin's youth football championship win.

"Ty! Scott!" Zach shouted out to us, "Did you know Calvin won the Southwest Youth championship a few years ago?"

"Yup," we said together.

"I'm going to as well!"

We smiled at the confident little football player.

When we all got settled in, Calvin announced, "Okay, Colts, today is just mostly practice and drills, and tonight's scrimmage is going to be against Mason's Jets."

"We're up against the previous team I was on," Ty said to me.

"Yeah," I replied, "but I hope we'll play against Damian's team soon."

Calvin pointed to a few empty buckets next to him. "Put your Gatorade bottles in these buckets," he instructed, "And Zach is going to do us a favor and fill them up." Calvin patted Zach's head, and the boy grinned. "One more thing," he continued, "Our fields now have spray misters. So, if you start feeling really hot, stand under them. They'll cool you off pretty quickly." We all cheered. "Now let's get out there and start warming up. Stretches first, as usual."

Then, he held up his helmet and shouted, "Colts!" We followed suit, yelling as loud as we could.

Our team meeting must have been really short, because it wasn't until about five minutes later that the other sub-teams showed up. Billy's players positioned themselves on our opposite side, and Mason's team walked over to the high school field, where Damian's team soon joined them.

We did our normal warm-ups and stretches, which included pushups and sit-ups. Even Zach participated, and we were surprised at how well he could keep up with us. Then, Calvin had us run two miles, with the Jets joining us. He and Mason had their teamboys fill up our Gatorade bottles and said they could join us when they were finished.

By the time we were done running, any freshness left on our bodies from the weekend was replaced with pools of sweat and odor. It felt good, especially after I stood under the mister for a few minutes and guzzled down an entire bottle of Gatorade that Zach had filled up for me. Those misters had little fans that blew cool air and water on us. Maybe it had something else mixed in there too, because my body cooled off quicker than I had expected, especially considering I still had my helmet on. I couldn't help but feel we were being treated like pro athletes, and that made me smile.

"Oh man, these things are great," said Jimmy Casten, standing next to me. All of us had positioned ourselves in a row under the fans that dotted the overhead pipes. "Nice job, little guy," Jimmy said as our teamboy handed him his bottle.

"Thanks," smiled Zach.

After that, we broke into individual team offensive and defensive drills. Calvin went over some plays he wanted Matt Manning to try as quarterback, while our team captain joined the defense himself.

I was on offense as halfback. In our huddle, Matt made some mistakes calling out plays, prompting Bryce Winters, our squad leader and running back, to grab Matt's helmet and order him to slow down and think. Adding to that, our defense was ruthless, with Derek Edwards and Jimmy seeing through many of his signals, leaving our safeties, including Ty, with not much to do.

Finally, Matt got the hang of things, and we tricked the defense into thinking he would throw the ball to Bryce, when in fact he threw it to me. I made a quick forty-five-degree angle cut across the middle of the field. The ball landed right in my hands and gave me enough time to brace myself for Ty's oncoming tackle. It took all of his strength to tackle me to the ground.

"Fuck!" spat Ty, angry at the completed pass, "I can't believe I didn't see that coming!"

"Hehe!" I laughed and slapped him on the shoulder pads.

Derek Edwards, Ty's squad leader and our defense coordinator, chuckled. "Yeah, Matt got us good there," he said.

Ty then pointed to his armpit. "You're lucky we weren't off-rails, Scott," he jeered.

I bent my arm up by the elbow and retorted, "I can only use one arm to carry the ball, you know. Don't think you can't get pitted by me."

"Let's go again!" he demanded, thumping his chest with a fist and pointing at me, "You're mine!"

"Man, Ty's really fired up," said Jimmy.

"He hates when someone gets the best of him," I said.

"No," said Calvin, "It's break time."

"Fuck!" cried Ty, "Come on, Calvin! One more time!"

"Yeah!" a bunch of us shouted, including me.

"I want to get past Ty again!" I said, smiling at him.

"Fuck you!" swore Ty, slamming into me and knocking me off balance.

"*I'm* heading inside," said Calvin, "If you want to stay out here, you might as well run laps." As Calvin said that, I hurled myself back at Ty, tackling him to the ground. He belted out a loud grunt.

"Get offa me!" he demanded.

"Haha!" I sneered, standing up and helping Ty up as well.

He got into my face and challenged, "You are *so* mine after the break."

I took a deep breath and just soaked in the moment – being in my full football uniform, standing on the field with Ty and my other teammates as the smell of our perspiration hung in the air, and all the while having to let loose a whole lot of masculine aggression. Life couldn't have gotten much better than this.

I noticed our other Colts members, including Calvin, heading toward the benches. Zach began handing out Gatorade bottles again.

As Ty and I followed our team captain, Derek came over to me and said, "Calvin asked me to work with you one-on-one on his tackling after our break."

"Aw, man," frowned Ty. "Your ass beating will have to wait, then, Scott."

233

"I'm a better halfback than a defensive tackle," I admitted to Derek, then said to Ty, "Keep dreaming."

"No, you're an excellent defensive tackle," said Derek, patting me on the shoulder. I blushed. "But, Calvin thinks I can help you improve," Derek continued, "I'm good at that sort of thing."

Ty agreed, "Yeah, you *are* our defense coordinator."

"Have you ever beaten Calvin in the pit?" I asked.

"Yup," Derek replied, making Ty's mouth drop, "That's partly why he wants me to help you."

"Sounds good to me," I laughed.

Billy's team shared the break with us, with our teamboys already having filled our Gatorade bottles. When Zach spotted Ty coming toward him, the kid ran up to him and personally handed his bottle to him.

"You were awesome out there, Ty!" the kid commented, his shirt drenched in sweat, "You have such awesome moves!"

"Aw," said Ty, patting his head, "Thanks, Zach."

"That was such a cool play, Scott," he added as I grabbed mine, "But, I think Ty's stronger than you."

"By far," agreed Ty.

I opened my helmet just enough to bring the bottle up to my lips. "Keep dreaming," I repeated after gulping down my drink.

We stood under the misters for a few minutes and chatted with Billy's team as the two team captains spoke among themselves. After our bodies cooled off, we continued practice. As Calvin asked, Derek Edwards worked with me on my tackling skills, putting me up against the tackling dummies and tackling sleds first, before I went up against him and some of the other guys on the defensive line, most of them eighth graders. It was then that *I* became the tackling dummy, being knocked off my feet and thrown to the ground like a rag doll. Each time that happened, though, it pissed

me off more and more, which pleased Derek, as he could see the fire in my eyes. Soon, it was time for lunch, so we all headed inside and removed our helmets, sighing with pleasure as the refreshing cool air hit us.

The cafeteria served pasta with chicken or beef, grilled veggies, and warm, buttered bread. Everyone at my table scarfed their food down, and even Zach didn't leave enough for Jeremy or Ryder to finish up.

We still had a half an hour after lunch to relax before resuming practice, and we were permitted to use our electronics at that time. I grabbed my phone from my locker and met Jack, Jaden, and Ty in the equipment room again.

We sat down in a semi-circle, so we could all see the screen. When I switched on the phone, the text message with the link was still there, waiting for me.

"You want me to forward it to you first, Jaden?" I asked.

"No," he replied, "Just play it."

"Okay, you guys ready?"

"Oh, fuck yes," said Ty.

Jack placed a hand on Jaden's shoulder pads and nodded at me.

With that, I pressed the link, and the video started rolling.

chapter thirty-one

The video showed Jaden, dressed in his Putnam practice tee and shorts, walking into the new nurse's office. It was twice as big as the old one and held several more beds.

He stared open-mouthed at Veronica, dressed in her nurse's outfit, as she approached him. Veronica asked him to strip down to his underwear and sit on one of the beds. The boy rested a palm over his crotch and blushed.

"Oh, sweetie," said Veronica, touching his cheek with the back of one of her hands, "We've seen plenty of boys' boners. No need to be shy."

She then asked, "Why don't you let me take off your clothes?"

Jaden froze in his place as Veronica lifted his shirt up, feeling his abs during the process. Jaden's breathing became heavy as she raised his arms, one at a time, to remove them from the sleeves. Veronica then took off his shoes and socks.

"You are strong, Jaden," remarked Veronica, feeling the boy's muscles and rubbing his chest. Jaden swallowed hard and gritted his teeth.

"You okay?" she asked him.

Jaden shut his eyes and only gave a nod.

back up and left the boy alone, walking out of the frame. The camera focused on Jaden's form for a few more seconds before it shut off.

chapter thirty-two

We stared at the screen stunned – exactly like we had on Thursday. Just like the previous time, a "Footage has been deleted" message appeared for a few seconds on the screen before disappearing.

"That was some physical Veronica gave you," commented Jack through a chuckle, placing a hand on Jaden's shoulder, "She didn't even make an effort to check your vitals."

"Except one," said Jaden, pointing to his dick and raising his eyebrows. That made the rest of us laugh.

"Wow, yeah," said Ty, "And you passed right out when she gassed you."

"So, how was it?" asked Jack.

Jaden smiled and replied, "I'd never felt so good in my life. It was incredible."

"Well, congratulations, man," said Jack, giving him a light noogie.

"Hey, it's my turn next," said Ty, "Not fair she sucked your dick too, Jack. And she had full on sex with you, Scott."

Jaden's eyes widened. "Woah, she sucked you off, Jack?" he asked in amazement.

Jack nodded.

"When?"

Jack explained what had happened to him the previous day, and the events Ty and I had informed Jack of after she had gassed him.

"So, she did the same things to you after she knocked you out, Jack," Jaden summarized.

"Yeah. Scott thinks she gets off on that sort of thing."

"I think it's fairly obvious," I added.

"I don't understand that, though," Jack admitted.

The rest of us added our own bewilderment.

Ty pointed to my phone. "Is the link dead, too? Lemme see!" he insisted.

I handed my phone over to the kid to try, but just like Thursday, the link went dead.

"Shit!" Ty grumbled, tossing the phone back onto my lap.

I put my arms behind me and leaned back against them, asking, "So, what did you do after you woke up, Jaden?"

"I went straight to the war room, like Billy had asked me to."

"Wait," said Jack, "Billy knew you were going to see the nurse?"

Jaden wrapped his arms around his knees and replied, "Yeah. Billy was already at the gymnasium when I had arrived. I let him know that the nurse wanted to see me. So, he showed me my assigned bed and told me to meet at the orientation room after I was finished."

"You think the nurse will have sex with our other teammates?" asked Ty.

"Maybe she already has," said Jack, rubbing his neck, "Like with Billy. He told me the team captains met Veronica on Saturday. I'd like to see her suck his dick."

The three of us stared back at him. "Really? Why?" I asked.

"It'd be fun," shrugged Jack, "You and Ty got to watch her do me. I saw how hard you guys were."

"Yeah," I admitted.

"It is like a secret club right now, though," Ty observed with a grin, "Just the four of us." Ty held out his fist in the middle of our circle, and the rest of us extended ours so that they touched each other's. We only had a few minutes left until practice began again, so we headed back to the cafeteria to grab our helmets from the racks where we had stored them. Then, we headed to the war room for our team meetings.

There, Calvin said we would spend the following hour hitting the new weight room before heading back outside. Each team got a turn every day to use the new workout facilities, which had weight machines that could be adjusted for working out in full pads, minus the helmets.

Calvin correctly figured most of us seventh graders hadn't had proper weight training before, so he demonstrated the do's and the don'ts, emphasizing on the *why*'s of the don'ts. He concluded by stressing on the importance of proper breathing. His explanations proved extremely helpful, and I found myself, and Ty as well, able to do more reps than ever before. Ty thought that perhaps it was more due to whatever strength enhancing chemical that we had been primed with, but I gave most of the credit to Calvin.

After our workout, we went back outside and practiced our usual drills. About forty-five minutes into it, Damian's and Mason's teams had an impromptu scrimmage against each other on the high school field, with Billy acting as the ref. It marked the first full-on off-rails game, which meant armpitting was allowed. The rest of us had wanted to watch, but Calvin and Billy insisted that we

continue practice, promising us that we would have our own match against each other after our afternoon break.

Billy had left his squad leaders, Jack and Travis, to guide the team's practice while he was away. After about another forty-five minutes of drills, we took a break under the misters and chomped on our protein bars that our teamboys doled out. The conscious players from the Jets and the Rams game joined us, which included Damian and Mason. They said that fifteen boys, mostly seventh graders, ended up taking a B.O. nap, and some hadn't even woken up by the time the game was over. Mason added that the nurse had wanted the unconscious football players to be put in the gymnasium.

"Yeah, she had some of the knocked out Rams and Jets players transferred to examination rooms for observation and testing," said Damian.

"Just like she said would happen," Ty said.

"So, what were these tests for?" asked Calvin, furrowing his brow.

"She wouldn't say," shrugged Damian, "But she did say they'd be perfectly fine once they recovered. She eventually asked us to bring them back to the gymnasium."

"But they haven't even woken up yet," Mason noted with a frown, "They should have by now. It's been more than an hour since they've been pitted."

Jaden motioned Jack, Ty, and me over and whispered, "You think Veronica did to them what she did to us?"

"And gassed them out afterwards?" added Ty.

Jaden nodded.

"Possibly," I answered, "But, I wonder what kind of testing?"

Jack smacked me on the shoulder pads, his face smeared with dirt, "You'll find out once you wake up from *my* armpitting, Scott." Jaden laughed.

After we warmed up, Calvin had us form a circle and take a knee. He paced around in the middle, with Zach standing next to him, and said, "With off-rails games, if a team runs out of conscious players, the game's over. The other team wins, no matter what the score is."

"What if both teams lose enough players at the same time?" asked Brady Mckee, wearing number thirty-one.

"Then, the team with the highest score wins."

Then, Brady asked, "What happens if all of our team leaders get knocked out? How will we know what to do?"

"That's what tests how well we act as a team. We have to spread out the knowledge and authority. Someone will have to step up, or we'll lose."

"Um, we have Coach King," said another kid.

"For before and after the game," replied Calvin, "During the game, he wants it all on us."

"Who's going to ref?" asked Nicholas, who then pointed to Zach, our teamboy. "Him?"

A bunch of us, including Zach, laughed. "Yeah!" the nine-year-old said.

"No. Damian will," Calvin replied. "This is just a friendly scrimmage."

"No adults?"

"Not unless we really need them. This is about us boys and football. Got it?"

Nicholas and Brady exchanged worried looks. It didn't bother me, though. I loved being with just us boys... and Nurse Veronica, of course.

Calvin scratched his neck and said, "I know I'm forgetting something here."

Bryce shouted out, reminding him, "The play is over once the whistle blows, Calvin."

"Oh, yeah! Thanks, Bryce."

Bryce gave a thumbs up, and then, Calvin continued, "Once the whistle blows, the play is over, and no armpitting is allowed. That means, if you tackle someone and can't armpit them before the whistle blows, too bad. There's always next time."

After our war cry of "Colts!" we lined up against Billy's team. Calvin placed me on defense at first, with Matt Manning as quarterback. About twenty minutes in, five boys, three from Billy's team and two from ours, had been pitted and carried out to the gymnasium. Then, we lost Nicholas Schmidt, our tight end, to Jack, followed by Bryce Winters, my squad leader and our running back, to Billy.

After that, Calvin took over as quarterback and positioned me as halfback. In the huddle, he called a play where he would fake a pass to one of our wide receivers, throwing the ball to me instead. As soon as he finished the cadence, Jack blitzed, running straight for him. Calvin passed the ball in my direction, and Jack, turning on a dime, barreled straight for me. He, or more likely Billy, had seen that play coming. I caught the ball, though, while Jack lowered his shoulder pads, going for a tackle instead of an armpitting. I figured he was going to try to tackle me to the ground and then, pit me like he did in the circle on Friday. All I had to do was evade him long enough to raise my armpit up to his facemask. Although, if he caught me, it'd be all over.

As he lunged toward me, I tucked the ball under one arm and pivoted, lowered my torso just enough so that I could cover part of his face with my armpit. Hopefully, that'd do it.

"Urk!" he gurgled as his head snapped backward. I thought I heard him moan, "Nooooo..." as his body sank to the ground on his back, his eyes shut tight. "Jaaaackkk!" I heard Max, his teamboy, cry out, "No!" I held my arms high in victory, completely forgetting that the play wasn't over.

"Scott, don't just fucking stand there!" I heard Calvin shout at me. But, it was too late.

"You're mine!" I heard Billy shout from the side. I turned to see Billy's raised armpit come crashing down on my face; the sight of his stained pit was the last thing I saw, as the horrid stench made me squeak out a groan, drop the ball, and crash down unconscious on top of Jack.

chapter thirty-three

I slowly regained consciousness, but the smell of Billy's armpit hadn't completely dissipated. I could barely open my eyes before I passed right back out. When I woke up again, the first sound I heard was of a boy moaning in pleasure, merged with the noise of some machine moving up and down.

After a few seconds, my eyes opened to a bright light shining down on me and making me squint. I found myself facing up in a large room, with one of those old, tube-style monitors hanging over me. I was still completely suited up in my football uniform, including my helmet. I lifted my head to see that I was lying on a hard table, my wrists and ankles shackled to it. My football pants and cupped underwear were down to my knees, and my eyes widened when I saw my penis exposed, a wire attached to the base, and leading to the monitor. I also noticed wires attached to my biceps and armpits, all of which led back to it as well. The monitor showed three lines of text:

B.O. Level: 31

Strength: 24

Testosterone: 31

I looked to the left and saw another table. There was an unconscious football player strapped to it as well. He had on a

Panther jersey with the number four. I looked into the kid's facemask and knew right away – it was Billy Thompson. His eyes were closed, and his pants had been pulled down as well. I shouted out to him a few times, but he didn't respond. He had wires attached to his dick, biceps, and armpits as well, and they all led to the monitor above him, reading:

B.O. Level: 41

Strength: 32

Testosterone: 39

It was the moans coming from my right that carried my attention away from the unconscious team captain. I looked over and saw another football player in the same predicament as Billy and me. His jersey had the number sixty-four. I was about to look into his facemask to confirm whether it was Jack, but then, I noticed that same long, transparent tube had been placed over his penis, and some soft human-looking tissue gyrating around it, rubbing up against his hardened dick. The monitor had his B.O. level increasing, from 28 to 29 to 30. His strength kept steady at 28, but his testosterone continued to skyrocket, from 39 to 42 to 49.

"Ooooo," came the voice of a young woman from some speakers near him, "I can't resist such a strong boy, Jack! Give your huge boy cock to me!" It sounded just like Veronica! I found myself getting a boner just by her moaning, but I had enough will to break free and look at the player's face.

"Jack?" I beckoned.

The boy turned his head toward me; his muddy face was dripping with sweat. His gnashed his teeth together, and instead of saying anything, he just moaned real loud and turned his head back to the center.

The gyrations got faster, and Veronica's voice got louder, saying, "Oh, Jack! You strong, dirty boy!"

Jack tilted his head back and rolled his eyes up. He clenched his fists, lifted his waist, and closed his eyes as a cry of rapture escaped his mouth. Sperm shot out of his penis and got sucked up into the tube.

"AAAHHH!" he cried.

"Yes! Your hot boy sperm is just what I need!" the woman shouted.

"Oh my God..." moaned Jack and continued to do so for a full five seconds.

After that, a stony computerized male voice announced, "Seventh Grade Panther football player Number Sixty-Four's sperm has been collected. Time to orgasm: forty seconds. Eight CCs collected."

Sperm collection? What was that all about?

The gyrations stopped, and the tube retracted into some machine hanging in the middle of the three of us, leaving the boy's penis to slowly shrink back. His testosterone levels dropped back to 39, but his B.O. level remained at 31.

Jack kept his eyes closed, breathing heavily as sweat ran down his face.

"Jack, you okay?" I asked, struggling against my straps.

The lineman waited a few seconds for his breathing to slow down before turning his head to me and answer, "Yeah."

"When did you wake up?"

"About five minutes ago," he answered through labored breaths, "You and your fucking pit. How'd you end up here?"

"I don't know. Billy pitted me right after I pitted you."

"Good," laughed Jack.

Then, he motioned with his head to the right, and I looked beyond him to see another one of our teammates lying unconscious on the table. It was Number Eighteen, Nicholas Schmidt. The four

of us appeared to be lined up in a circle around that machine in the center of the room. All of our penises were exposed. I lifted my head again and tilted it to see around the bright light to check if anyone else was here. Sure enough, another kid was strapped to a table, motionless, almost directly across from me. His facemask prevented me from recognizing him, but the number twenty-one on his jersey meant it must have been Lucas Colby, one of Billy's halfbacks.

"I saw you and Nicholas unconscious, Scott," continued Jack, "And yelled to try and wake you up. Then, I heard that computer voice say that I had awakened, and it was going to collect my sperm."

I squinted my eyes. "What? Really?" I asked in amazement.

"Yep. Then, that tube thing lowered itself over my dick, and those tissue things began jerking me off. That woman's voice – I swear it must be Veronica's – started moaning." He sighed, and then, his tongue licked away some of the sweat from his mouth. He added, "It felt just as good as when she gave me a blowjob the other day."

"By the way, Billy's here too," I said, jerking my head over at Number Four.

"No way!" shouted Jack, "I didn't see him. Billy!"

"He's out cold, man." As if just to contradict me, Billy awoke. "Ugh," he groaned as he opened his eyes, "Fucking Calvin and his pit." He shuddered in panic when he found himself strapped down. "What the hell?" he yelled.

"Billy!" I shouted back.

The kid looked over at me. "Weston?" Then he looked over at Jack. "Murphy?"

He must have noticed our exposed penises, because he looked at their general direction. Then, he noticed his own and repeated, "The hell?"

We heard a beep, and a hose attached to the ceiling lowered and aimed itself at Jack's face. I hadn't noticed that contraption before. "Seventh Grade Panther football player Number Sixty-Four will now be gassed unconscious," it announced.

Jack peered straight at the hose. "Hey, wait a-"

I watched a stream of gas escape and envelope Jack's face.

"Agh!!" exclaimed my blond-haired friend, his body immediately going limp. It was as if a puppet's strings had been severed. The twelve-year-old's eyelids closed shut as his head struck the table and turned toward me. His mouthguard dangled from his helmet's facemask, and his lips were pursed together.

"Jack!" I cried out, but there came no answer.

"What just happened?" Billy shouted back.

"Jack!" I yelled again.

"Seventh Grade Panther football player Number Sixty-Four has been successfully gassed unconscious," the computer voice announced once more.

"What?" asked Billy, "What the hell is going on, Weston?" That meant he obviously had no idea. He looked to his left and shouted, "Colby! Hey! Lucas Colby is next to me!"

The same stony voice announced, "Eighth Grade Panther football player Number Four and Seventh Grade Panther football player Number Fifty-Five have awakened. Sperm collection will now commence. Randomly choosing..."

Then, after a few seconds' pause, "Number Four." The tube emerged out of the machine and positioned itself over Billy's limp dick.

"What the fuck is this?" the boy demanded to know.

"Oh, Billy, you are such a strong player," Veronica said, "Such big muscles and strong body odor." Number Four's mouth dropped open as the soft tissues began gyrating around the boy's dick; it instantly got hard. He certainly didn't have a small sausage dick like I had teased him about the other day.

Billy's throat made guttural sounds, and just like Jack, his B.O. and testosterone levels began to spike, enough so that even I could smell him. My own penis began to throb, and I so wanted to jerk off. I cursed, not able to free my hands.

"Such a huge penis for a boy your age, Billy!" announced the woman, "I love strong, dirty boys to have their way with me. Oh, Billy! This feels wonderful!"

"Oh YEAH!" he moaned, sweat dripping down his face. The intense sensation must have taken away all his cares about being shackled.

"Take my big boy cock!" Billy demanded, "Aaahhh!"

The gyrations began to pace faster than with Jack, and Billy couldn't hold out. He closed his eyes as he orgasmed; sperm shooting out of his rock-hard penis. Just like with Jack's, it got sucked up into the tube. The woman moaned in delight.

"Gggrrrahhh!" the kid bellowed, continuing to spit out sperm as he repeatedly banged his head against the metal table, the sound echoing throughout the room.

"Yes, yes, yes!" she moaned, "This is wonderful, Billy! You strong, smelly boy!"

"Holy shit!" exclaimed Billy.

The gyrations continued for a few more seconds, and then, the woman said, "That was so fast! Maybe we'll do this for real next time and go slower!"

Billy had the biggest grin on his face. "Oh, fuck yes!" he shouted out.

He looked over at me, sweat spurting from just about every pore. "Now *that* was awesome. I don't know what all this is for, but..." his voice trailed off.

"Eighth Grade Panther football player Number Four's sperm has been collected," ringed the computerized voice, "Time to orgasm: Twenty seconds. Seven point five CCs collected."

The tube retracted into the machine, and Billy's breathing stayed heavy for several seconds after. He watched his dick shrink back and opened his mouth to speak again, but a moan next to him diverted his attention.

"Colby!"

The newly awake boy, Lucas Colby, moaned again, opening his eyes slowly. Just like Billy and me, Lucas began to panic the moment he found himself bound to the table and struggled against his straps. We were able to calm him down a bit, but then, we heard a beep – the hose that knocked Jack out began to move toward Billy, who could only watch helplessly as it came closer.

"That thing has some sort of knock out gas, Billy!" I warned him, "It gassed Jack out, and now it's-"

"Eighth Grade Panther football player Number Four will now be gassed unconscious," announced that familiar voice.

"Oh, hell no!" he grunted, moving his head away from the hose and struggling against his straps, growling. "I'm not going to be knocked-"

The hose had merely adjusted its aim and a puff of gas sprayed into Billy's face.

"Blargh!" the boy struggled, his fists uncurling while his eyes rolled up before rapidly closing shut. Then, he went still, the sweat ceaselessly dripping down his face.

"Billy!" Lucas shouted, "Hey, dude! Wake up!" I called out his name as well, but just like when Jack was gassed out, the boy didn't react.

"Eighth Grade Panther football player Number Four has been successfully gassed unconscious," announced the computer voice as the tube retracted again.

"How did we get here, Scott?" asked Lucas.

I told him what Damian had said.

"Well, why are my football pants down?" he asked.

"Hey, hey!" a pre-pubescent voice called out, "Someone get me out of here!" It was Nicholas.

"Sperm will now be collected from Seventh Grade Panther football player Number Fifty-Five," came the announcement again.

"What?" shouted the other two boys at once.

My eyes widened. The machine set the tube over my large boner. I almost lost it as soon as I felt the tissues wrap around my penis.

"Ooooo! Scott!!" moaned Veronica, "Such a large dick for a twelve-year-old! And so sweaty!" The gyrations began, and the most incredible feeling hit me.

"Look what a strong boy you are! What big muscles you have! And how strong a body odor you have to match!"

"Aaahhh..." I groaned, looking at my muscles bulge and noticing my body odor intensify as sweat pooled in my armpits. My B.O. And testosterone levels spiked, just like Jack's and Billy's had.

"Holy shit!" I heard both my teammates exclaim, again at the same time.

Veronica carried on the dirty talk. "Oh my God, Scott!" her voice came to me, "Take me with that big boy cock! I love a dirty boy in a sweaty football uniform!"

The gyrations intensified, and I felt myself losing it. It didn't matter if she was really there or not. The most incredible sensation engulfed me, and I shouted as I felt semen jet out of my dick like bullets, glob and after glob. Sweat streamed down my face as the woman moaned louder and louder, "Yes! Take me! Take me!"

"Oh God!" I moaned, my teeth gnashed together and my entire body tightening up. When it was over, I could only take short, shallow breaths, and my heart nearly beat out of my chest. I knew then why Billy and Jack had enjoyed it so much. I could barely even keep my eyes open.

"Maybe you, Billy, and I can have a threesome, Scott," the woman suggested, "And maybe Jack too. Would you like that?"

"Yes," I whispered.

I heard the woman chuckle, and the computerized voice announce, "Seventh Grade Panther football player Number Fifty-Five's sperm has been collected. Time to orgasm: Thirty-five seconds. Eight CCs collected."

The tube pulled back into the ceiling, and my dick began to shrink.

"Is that going to happen to us too?" asked Nick.

"I sure hope so!" replied Lucas.

They apparently didn't care anymore about being restrained.

Lucas added, "I'm sure as hell ready."

I looked over at them, and I could make out that both of them had massive boners. The familiar beep was heard again, and the hose that knocked out the other two boys came close to me, adjusting its aim at my face.

"What is that?" asked Nicholas.

"Seventh Grade Panther football player Number Fifty-Five will now be gassed unconscious."

"No way!" exclaimed Lucas, "Not you too, Scott! You gotta resist it!"

I thought maybe I'd be able to, but whatever it was, it sure knocked Jack and Billy out pretty damn quick.

The hose sprayed out a puff of gas onto my face, and the foulest odor hit me. It was as if my nose had been shoved into a dozen sweaty, middle school boys' armpits at once. That explained why Jack and Billy lost consciousness so quickly, and I wasn't an exception.

"Argh!" I cried out as the overpowering odor knocked me out instantly. I could hear Lucas shouting "No!" It was the last thing I had sensed before I joined my two fellow football players in dreamland.

chapter thirty-four

My head felt as though it was spinning, and it took me a few seconds before I was able to open my eyes. Whatever had come out of that nozzle did quite a number on me. I could hear voices near me, but I couldn't figure out who it was. It felt as though my body was leaning against a wall. My head was drooping down, and when I opened my eyes, I saw my lower torso and what looked like the gymnasium floor. I still had my helmet on.

A strong odor wafted in from my immediate left, and I turned my head to see Jack's unconscious form leaning against the wall as well; his head drooped and eyes shut tight. I shook Jack's shoulder pads, but all it did was bob his head around.

"Looks like Weston's finally coming out of it," I heard a voice near me.

It sounded like Billy. I lifted my head to see him, Max, and Calvin standing near us. The two middle school players were carrying their helmets in their hands. Calvin was drenched in sweat from head to toe, but Billy's had dried.

"Jack hasn't woken up yet," Max said with a frown, "I've been trying for ten minutes."

"I just woke up a few minutes ago myself," said Billy as he reached down to help me up. I quickly found out the dizziness hadn't dissipated yet. I wobbled on my feet and might have fallen back down if Billy and Calvin hadn't supported me.

"Take it easy," said Calvin.

"Lucas and Nicholas are still out as well," said Billy, pointing to Number Twenty-One and Number Eighteen. Lucas was lying unconscious next to Jack, and Nicholas was lying next to him.

I rubbed my face and asked, "Did... did we go through what I think we went through?"

Billy folded his arms. "You mean having our sperm sucked out of our dicks?"

I nodded.

"Yep. Felt fucking amazing. But I'll tell ya, that gas knocked me out quicker than any armpitting ever had." He then placed a hand on Calvin's shoulder pads. "Like I told Williams here," he continued, "even *his* pits didn't stink that bad."

Calvin grinned.

"Did you get pitted or something, Billy?" I asked.

The boy looked at me with a scowl, then nodded over at Calvin.

"Way to go, Captain," I smiled, "Thanks for taking revenge for me."

Calvin's smile faded.

"What?" I asked.

He let out only a soft growl as an answer.

"So, you got gassed too, Weston?" asked the Warriors' team captain.

"Yeah," I replied, removing my helmet, "It smelled horrible. How long was I out?"

"I don't know," said Billy with a shrug, "Our game ended about five minutes back. So, I guess, we were unconscious for about an hour in total, including the armpitting."

A groan escaped Jack's lips, and the kid slowly opened his eyes. "What the fuck hit me?" he asked.

"Jack!" exclaimed Max, jumping on him and giving him a hug.

"Urk!" grunted the linebacker, "Max, please not now."

Billy pulled the kid off of him and, in Billy's usual fashion, addressed the nine-year-old by his last name. "Hey, Walker," he said, "Let him recover." As Billy and I helped Jack on his feet, the other two boys started coming out of the daze. They also confirmed that same thing had happened to them.

Calvin said, "Damian and Mason both told me their players went through the same experience as well."

"So none of this happened to you eighth graders last year?" Jack asked Calvin.

My team captain shook his head. "No. This is all new."

"Must be one of those examinations that our nurse talked about today," Billy figured, then winked at Calvin and jeered, "Bet you wish you'd have gotten knocked out instead of me, huh, Williams?"

"I'll just take your word for it, for now," replied Calvin, "You can't help your team win if you're not there." Calvin looked back at me when he said that. Was I in trouble or something? Just for being knocked out?

Billy shoved Calvin with his shoulder. "It wasn't like I asked for this to happen, fuckwad," he replied, "I'll beat you next time."

"You guys should have seen it," Lucas said to Nicholas, Jack, and me. "Calvin and Billy hit each other straight on, and it was a

fight to see if they could pit each other before the play ended. Your boy won!"

Calvin grinned, and then, he frowned as he looked at me again. I grunted in irritation at the silent, but angry, treatment. "Okay, Calvin, why the hell are you upset with me?" I finally asked.

"You could have made the yardage yourself if you had kept running after pitting Jack, instead of celebrating like an idiot," he replied.

"Sorry," I apologized, looking at Jack, "I got lost in the moment of my victory over Jack." My pitted victim growled and pushed me, harder than Billy had shoved Calvin. I shoved him back. "Don't push me, Jack!"

"Take it easy!" Billy snapped at Jack.

Jack snorted, gave Billy a look of anger, and then, stood inches from me. He breathed into my face and stared me straight in the eyes. I wasn't going to allow him to scare me, and I forced myself not to flinch.

Eventually, Jack said, "I'll get back at you for that, Scott."

I coughed as his odor hit me again. "Yeah," I retorted, "With the way you stink now, I don't doubt you could." That got a chuckle from Billy.

"I see why you passed out so quickly on Friday, Scott," Nicholas nodded, "Jack's pits reek."

Jack's mood lightened, and he turned to our tight end. "I got ya good, didn't I, Nicholas?"

Lucas nudged me, and asked quietly, "What's with Jack's mood swings?"

"He's a hothead," I said in a volume that Jack could hear, "Most of it is just intimidation, but if you push him over the line, you're fucked."

Max laughed at that, and Jack puffed out his chest. "Damn right you are," reiterated Jack.

"Like what happened to you and Ryder on Friday?" asked Lucas.

"Yeah," I answered, grinning over at Jack. He smiled back.

Calvin cleared his throat to get our attention. "You don't think what you did is serious, Scott?" he asked, "Your fuck up cost us yardage that could have gotten us a score."

My face fell. "Who won the game?" I asked.

"That doesn't matter right now."

"But-"

His eyes narrowed. "No buts! Drop and give me thirty for your attitude."

"Fuck," I shouted. Then, throwing my helmet on the floor, I started the punishment.

"Count them out loud too!"

"What did Scott do?" asked Jack as he watched me do my pushups.

"Murphy, you should have seen it," Billy burst out laughing, "Once he pitted you, Weston started celebrating, completely forgetting the play wasn't over."

"No shit?" asked Jack, chuckling, "What happened then?"

"I barreled into him. Shoved my pit right into his face. He fell like a stone on top of you, dropping the ball." I looked up to see him stick his tongue out and roll his eyes back, mimicking my falling down.

"That's awesome!" laughed Jack.

I sighed and put my head back down.

"Yeah, Billy got him good!" said Max.

Lucas grinned and said, "Then, Billy jumped on Scott's body and put his facemask up against his, staring at him until Calvin made him get off."

Billy rubbed his crotch, saying, "I love to look at my victim's unconscious face and watch my victory sweat drip all over them."

I was on my last few pushups when he had said that, and the visual of that made me gag and pause to stare up at him. Jack stared at him as well.

"Ew!" exclaimed Max through a laugh, "That's so gross!"

"Not to me," shrugged Billy.

"Yuck," I said, finishing my last few pushups with some strain. When I stood back up, I wiped my face with my towel, running it over a few times just to make sure I was rid of Billy's sweat, even if it had already dried by then.

"Who pitted *you*?" Jack asked Lucas.

"Fuck if I remember," Lucas replied, "I got tackled by a bunch of guys, and one of them shoved his armpit in my face. Woke up on the examination table."

"That would be Ty Green, Number Forty-Two," answered Calvin.

"Really?" Jack and I asked.

"Yeah," replied Calvin, "Jimmy made an awesome hit on Lucas, then Ty brought him down."

"Good for him," said Jack.

"Yeah," I agreed.

Calvin then pointed to the exit and said to me, "Go run four laps."

My eyes widened. *"Seriously?"*

"Yes. It's for your fuck up. I have to set an example."

I groaned.

"Oh, no," muttered Nicholas, wincing at me, "Sorry, buddy."

"Make sure you hydrate," added Calvin, "And when you're done, meet us in the war room. We're going to go over plays as a single Panthers team before dinner."

As I was heading for the door, Billy called after me, "Put your helmet on before you walk out of that door."

I had half a mind to flick him off. He wasn't my team captain, but I knew doing that would only get me into more trouble. So, I just strapped on my helmet without a word. A thought made me stop in my tracks. I turned and asked, "Is everybody else inside?"

Calvin nodded.

A memory from my childhood of a friend being kidnapped while he was alone came flashing back. I opened my mouth to tell him there was no way in hell I was going out there by myself, but he snapped his fingers.

"Shit. I completely forgot about that. No, I won't let you go out there by yourself."

I sighed in relief.

"Scared of being alone, are we?" Billy asked with a smirk.

Jack told him about my friend, which made Billy shake his head and reach out in compassion. "Sorry, man," he apologized, "I was only joking."

"Did they ever find the kid?" asked Nicholas.

"Yeah, eventually," I said.

"Well, the coaches actually told us never to let a player go outside alone," said Billy, "Although, no one is going to try to kidnap a smelly, twelve-year old boy."

"True that," said Calvin as he put on his helmet and followed me out the door.

chapter thirty-five

Calvin stood on the sidelines and watched me run laps. I found myself having the energy, and surprisingly the will, to run, despite the heat and the pads making me sweat constantly. Maybe this was all part of being primed. I actually didn't mind being out here alone with Calvin's presence as solace. I could hear the birds in the trees, my cleats hitting the dirt, and the sound of my own breathing. Even the distant vroom of an occasional car became welcome background noise. I must have entered some kind of trance as I ran; I felt one with myself, my uniform becoming one with my body. I pushed myself to become stronger and faster, and I trusted my unconscious mind to steer my body as I focused on the moment – every step and every breath. When Calvin was out of sight, my faux solitude connected me to the earth and nature around me, and when Calvin came back into view, I felt a wave of gratitude and relief for his vigilance.

My team captain had to call out a few times to stop me after my fourth lap; I wasn't even paying attention. When he walked over and handed me some Gatorade, an incredibly strong urge to hug him overcame any reservation I would normally have about doing that. He edged back in surprise when I wrapped my arms around him as much as my shoulder pads would allow.

His energy was amazing. I felt so cared for, so appreciated by him. I found myself transmitting that energy back to him.

"Woah. Scott, you okay?" he asked, looking puzzled.

When I stepped back, I looked into his eyes and grinned, "Yeah, I'm great!"

"Really?"

"Yup."

That made him chuckle. "I've never seen a guy so joyful after running laps," he said, "What happened to you out there? You seemed like you were in a different world."

I removed my helmet just enough to drink straight from the bottle, downing all of the refreshing liquid. "Yeah," I replied, wiping my mouth, "I felt really good out there alone for some reason. And having you watching me just made me feel... safe, I guess."

Calvin didn't say anything at first. He just banked his head and gave me that expression he usually used when he tried to figure me out. Eventually, he said, "You really are a mystery to me sometimes." We started heading back, and when we passed the pit circle, a little idea struck me.

"Can we... can we try something?" I asked.

"What?"

I thumbed over to the pit. "Can we go a round in the pit?"

Calvin looked at me, bewildered. "*Now?*" he asked, "You just got through running laps and doing push-ups."

"I know."

My team captain rubbed his chin and reminded me, "We have our team meeting, Scott."

"I know, Calvin. Just once. Please."

The other boy let out a sigh, and then, he shrugged and relented. "Okay, if you want."

A surge of excitement flowed through me as we stepped into the circle. We bit down on our mouthguards and got into position. My earlier beatings from Derek Edwards and his linesmen came flashing back into my mind, kindling the fire within me, and as soon as Calvin finished counting down, I felt my body plunge forward with a speed and force I had never experienced. When we crashed, I sent him backward to the edge of the circle. He caught his footing, and letting out a primal roar, he suddenly turned the tide, pushing me back. I had, however, dug my cleats into the dirt with such force that I didn't go down. My legs held, but I couldn't resist enough to prevent myself from being pushed out of bounds. Calvin let go of my jersey.

I couldn't believe I almost had him. I *almost* beat Calvin! So fucking close!

"Man, I almost got you this time, Calvin," I said through labored breaths. He didn't respond. He was just staring at me, his mouth agape, his breaths heavy, and his sweat dripping down his face and arms.

"Calvin?" I asked.

"How the *fuck* did you do that?" he asked in a high-pitched tone as he sized me up.

"Huh?" I asked.

He looked utterly perplexed. "How the *fuck* did you get that strength and speed?"

I thought about that for a moment and said, "I don't really know, Calvin. It just sorta came out of me."

"Fuck me, man," he shook his head, "I can't believe a kid your size knocked me back so quickly."

"Well, if it's any consolation, I still lost."

"No, you did *not*," Calvin insisted.

Suddenly, he reached out and hugged me. This time it was my turn to edge back in shock. However, it made me smile, even though I was confused about his words and actions.

He backed away, and I asked, "What do you mean I didn't lose?"

"You stopped me, Scott," He continued, "Yeah, I was able to push you out of the circle *eventually*, but I wasn't able to knock you down. In a game with you on defense like that, the time you bought would have stopped me from catching a runner."

"Really? Are you serious?" I asked. I felt such elation at that statement that I could hardly believe my ears.

"Fuck yes, I am," he said, "I don't know what happened while you were running, but you tapped into something fierce."

"Thanks, Calvin," I grinned.

"Good job, man. And, not that you should get into trouble more often, but if you can get back to that state, you'll be practically unstoppable." He wrapped an arm around my shoulder and walked me inside.

"So, who really won our game against The Warriors?" I asked.

"We did," he said, sounding proud, "Seventeen to ten."

We reached the war room, and he was glowing as he told our team what had happened, me standing next to him. My teammates' mouths dropped open. Jimmy even exclaimed, "Nuh-uh!" Ryder Banks doubted that as well, exclaiming, "No fucking way he did that! I don't believe it!"

"It's true, Ryder," said Calvin, an irritation in his voice at his teammate's skepticism.

Ty beamed at me, giving me a thumbs up.

"Fuck yeah, dude!" Derek Edwards smiled, "Way to go!"

"Yeah!" said Bryce Winters, clapping for me. The other guys – even Ryder – joined in; Everyone did, except Jimmy. His expression of disbelief stayed put.

"Come on, Calvin!" Jimmy prodded, "You must have been going easy on him or something."

Derek, Jimmy's squad leader seated next to him, smacked the other boy's head with a growl.

"Ow! What was that for?" he asked, frowning at Derek. Calvin's mood instantly dropped, a snarl forming on his face. He glared at the cornerback and yelled, practically spitting at him, "No I was *not*, Jimmy! I can't believe you'd even fucking *say* that!" I knew every kid on the other three teams must have heard his outburst. Zach, in my seat next to Ty, dropped his jaw.

Jimmy's eyes widened and he held out his palms, waving them from side to side in surrender. "Woah, woah, man. Okay, okay. I'm sorry. It's just that you're a fucking wrecking ball in the pit, and Scott's like half your size."

I had to defend myself. "I'm not *that* small, Jimmy!"

Calvin's eyes burned a hole through Jimmy's head. He didn't let up, saying, "We've played together for five years, and now you accuse me of going easy on a teammate? The fuck is wrong with you?"

"Yeah, Jimmy!" added Derek, "You know Calvin would never do that!"

Jimmy maintained his submissive tone as he tried to backpedal. "Yeah yeah, I know!" he insisted, "Forget I said that! Really. I'm sorry, Calvin. That came out all wrong."

Calvin took a few deep breaths, keeping his glare on Jimmy. "How about apologizing to Scott?" he suggested not-so-subtly, "That was very disrespectful to him."

Jimmy looked at me and said, "Hey, I'm sorry. Guess I got a bit envious, to be honest."

"That's okay," I said, "It didn't bother me that much, except the part about me being half Calvin's size."

That made Bryce and Derek laugh. "Buddy," Bryce said to me, "every guy here compares his strength to Calvin, and everybody overestimates themselves – except for a few." He pointed to Derek as an exception.

Just then, the curtain behind us, separating us from the Rams, slid open enough for Damian to peek his head in.

The kid looked around, glanced at Calvin, and asked, "You okay? Mason said it's time to start the Riverwood film."

Calvin opened his mouth to speak, when the curtain to our right opened enough for Billy to peek in as well.

"Yo, Calvin!" he shouted, chewing on some gum.

Billy saw me standing next to Calvin and shook his head. "Weston," he started, "Please don't tell me you're the reason why Calvin was yelling at Casten."

"Yes," I responded, before Calvin could even get a word in, "but I'm also the reason why everyone was clapping and cheering for me."

"I'll fill you guys in later," Calvin said to the other two team captains and motioned for me to go and sit down.

"You better, Williams," said Billy.

Zach stood up from my seat and walked over to Calvin, high-fiving me as we passed and saying, "Good job, Scott!"

"Thanks, kid!"

Billy glanced at me with a puzzled expression, his jaw moving back and forth as he chewed on his gum. I sat down next to Ty, who patted me on the shoulder pads and congratulated me again. The

curtain next to Damian opened up a bit more, and Mason appeared next to him.

"World War Three over in here, Calvin?" asked Mason.

"Yeah," Calvin grunted back.

"Riverwood time," said Mason, tapping an invisible watch on his wrist.

"Yeah, yeah."

Damian, Mason, and Billy retracted the curtains so that the room opened up, and we all whistled, waved, and said hey to the other teams. The four team captains stood on the podium steps, and even Coach King came in to join us.

Jaden leaned over the aisle and whispered to Ty and me, "What happened? What got Calvin so mad?"

"Tell ya after the meeting," I replied.

We watched last year's film on the games against Riverwood Junior High. The team captains, along with input from Coach, guided us through what offensive and defensive patterns they all had observed, and what we would need to be looking out for.

Afterward, the teamboys handed out binders with plays that we were supposed to memorize, based on our positions. They looked solid to me. One kid asked if we would have the chance to do a scouting scrimmage before the game tomorrow.

"Yes," replied Damian, "During tomorrow's morning practice, our individual teams will do an offensive scout team first, and then a defensive one."

Billy, the gum still in his mouth, said, "But after dinner's all about our first inner-Panther scrimmage – fully off-rails, of course."

"Yep!" nodded Damian, "So, everyone relax and enjoy dinner so we can have an awesome game tonight! It's the Colts versus the Jets and the Rams versus the Warriors! May the best team win!"

Damian held up a fist and we all cheered. Then, he dismissed us for dinner break, with Coach King saying he'd switch between watching both games.

The four teamboys had their own football practice, so they had to leave early. Zach wished us Colts well before he left and said he looked forward to being with us all day and night tomorrow. Ty, Jaden, Jack, and I congregated in the back and waited for everyone else to leave before I told Jack and Jaden what I did in the circle against Calvin.

Jack smiled and gave me a light noogie. "That's fucking awesome!" he exclaimed.

Jaden did the same, except his noogie wasn't so light. He repeated his question from earlier. "But what got Calvin so upset, then?"

"You guys heard all that, huh?" I asked, rubbing my head. Jack rolled his eyes at my stupid question.

"The *dead* heard all that," Jack quipped back.

I explained what Jimmy had said, which made Jack snarl. "If that fucker on *my* squad," he blurted out, "He would be out running laps. What you did was incredible, Scott."

Ty had remained quiet throughout our entire conversation, his expression stoic. A frown eventually formed on his face.

"What's the matter, Ty?" asked Jack.

"You and Scott had sex twice, Jaden once, and nothing for me."

"Twice?" I asked, glancing over at Jack, who just shrugged, "I don't remember the second time."

"In the experiment room, Scott. Jack said you guys had your sperm collected by those machines."

"If you count that as sex," added Jack.

"I would," grunted Ty. He started heading toward the exit.

"Where are you going?" asked Jack.

Not turning around, Ty replied, "To see the nurse. It's *my* turn now."

With that, Ty was gone.

chapter thirty-six

Jack, Jaden, and I washed our hands to get ready for dinner. The reflection on the mirror showed that I still had dirt smeared on my face left over from practice; I felt like leaving it on. It matched the grittiness of my uniform. Besides, Jack and Jaden didn't wash their faces either.

When we entered the cafeteria, the aroma of lamb gyro made our mouths water. I prepared myself a plate and walked over to my usual table. As I passed my fellow Panthers, most of them congratulated me on my victory over Calvin. Both Damian and Mason shouted out to me as well. Elation filled me, making me smile and feel light on my feet, although a nagging thought made me doubt whether I'd be able to conjure up those super-human abilities on the field again. I told myself I wouldn't worry about that until later. Right now, I'd just soak in all the positive attention.

Before I could get to my seat, though, Billy shouted out to me from his table. "Yo, Weston!" When I looked over at the eighth grader, he pointed to an empty seat directly across from him. "Have a seat," said Billy, taking a big bite of his gyro.

I glanced over at Calvin, seated in his usual spot at our table. He had his mouth full of food as well, so he just nodded to me as an indication that I should join Billy. It had been a few days since I ate

with Jack and Jaden, and since Ty had decided to postpone dinner for a chance with Veronica, he wouldn't feel left out. Knowing Veronica, Ty probably wasn't feeling much of anything at the moment, except maybe the blackness of unconsciousness.

I sat down between Austin Miller and Logan Adams, a hulking eighth grade linesman who Billy had traded from Calvin.

"Hey," said Logan in a twangy accent. We shook hands. His grip was tight, and his body odor was stronger than that of just about everyone's. The number fifty-three on his jersey was still soaked in sweat. Jack sat down in his usual seat next to Billy, and Jaden sat next to Jack. Billy swallowed his food and then said, "I wanted to hang out with the seventh grade kid who beat Calvin, a boy twice his size." Of course, he had to add that stinger at the end. He extended his hand, which I shook with a smile. "Congratulations," he said.

"Thanks," I said, "But I wouldn't say Calvin is twice my size."

"I would," came the predictable response.

"Yeah, good going there, Scott," echoed Travis Bower, sitting on the other side of Billy.

I got congratulations from the other Warriors as well. I dug into my food, hardly even tasting it as I gobbled it down. I hadn't realized I was that hungry.

"Of course," started Billy, "If Calvin hadn't told me himself, I'd never have believed it."

"Me neither," I quipped, which elicited a laugh from him and the other guys. "Seriously, though," I continued, "I didn't think I won, since I didn't push him out of the circle."

Billy nodded his head, wiping his face with his napkin. The leftover dirt on Billy's and many of my fellow teammates' faces showed that they didn't fully wash up either.

"If Calvin says you won, you won. Leave it at that."

"Let me ask you something then," I said.

"Okay..."

"If it was you in the pit instead of Calvin, and I managed to do the same to you, would you have considered me the winner?"

Jack glanced over at Billy as well; he wanted to know the answer too. Billy took another bite of his food, looked up, and furrowed his brows in thought while he chewed. Finally, he swallowed and said, "I'll answer that with this: If you would have applied the same speed and force on me that you had with Calvin, you would have pushed me out of the circle without a problem."

Billy's answer made Jack freeze mid-bite, and his eyes widened. He took his sandwich temporarily out of his mouth and exclaimed, "No way, Billy!"

"Oh, you better fucking believe it, Jack," he answered as my friend started chewing.

Jack didn't bother swallowing, before adding, "Wow." Many of the guys on our table echoed that sentiment, including me. I certainly didn't expect that answer.

"Calvin told me something happened to you when you were running laps," Billy continued, "That he felt your energy change. What happened out there?" The other Warriors stopped eating to listen to my response.

The connection I felt with these other guys prompted me to just lay it all out on the table, figuratively speaking. "I connected to myself," I replied, "I fell in love with my body, with football, and being a football player, being right there and then, outside running laps in my uniform with Calvin watching my back."

No one said a word, the curious expressions on my fellow players' faces indicated that they wanted to know more.

"Deeper than that, though," I finished, "I think I fell in love with myself, of what I created by being here. And being with you guys."

I expected laughs and gay jokes, especially from Jaden, and maybe even some smart-ass comment from Billy. But, I got none of that. Jaden did look at Jack, who had on a small grin of approval, and Jaden decided to mirror that expression. Billy folded his arms, picked food from his teeth with his tongue, and stared at me like I was some kind of a mysterious alien. The other guys watched Billy and waited for his reaction.

"Fuck," he finally declared, "Now I really, *really* wish I hadn't traded you for Adams, Weston."

I couldn't gauge the seriousness of what he just said. Still, I felt horrible for Logan Adams; that was a very dick thing to say, especially because Logan was sitting right here. Many of his fellow Warriors dropped their jaw in shock. However, Logan himself burst out laughing. The rest of us, except for Billy, Travis, and a few others, raised our eyebrows. Billy and the others just chuckled along with him.

"Yeah, the feeling is mutual, boss," said Logan, "You took me away from Calvin. I'm stuck defending your scrawny hide instead of beating it like last year."

Billy? Scrawny? Logan was big, but not bigger than Calvin, and he was certainly not that much stronger than Billy.

"Scrawny, huh?" replied Billy, "Who knocked whose ass out of the pit earlier?"

Logan shrugged. "You obviously used one of your three wishes today. Knowing you, you better save the other two for money and a boyfriend."

Jaden snorted, the milk he was drinking came out of his nose. I couldn't help but laugh out loud either, and everybody joined in at our table. Even Jack chuckled. Logan elbowed me and grinned.

Billy nodded through a smile and wrapped an arm around Jack's shoulder pads. "You're just jealous of us," he said.

Jack pushed Billy's hand away with a grin of his own. "Hey, we're not *that* close, Billy!" he played along.

"That hurts, Murphy."

Jack and Travis Bower just shook their heads, and I laughed. Jaden didn't seem that amused. Billy noticed Jaden's mood and pointed a finger at him. "Don't be jealous, Ludge," he addressed him, "You can have Miller." He then pointed to Austin Miller. Austin nearly spit out his water.

"Leave me out of this!" Austin shouted back.

Jaden folded his arm. "Yeah, I don't want him!" I waited for Billy to slip in a joke about me and Ty.

Logan looked at Austin and Jaden. "Don't you two let what Billy says bother you none," said Logan, "He just has a small dick." Now *that* had our whole table bursting out in laughter, even though I already knew, from our 'examination' earlier, that Billy's penis wasn't really that small. Logan winked and scarfed down two huge bites of his gyro, nearly stuffing the entire thing in his mouth.

"That's not what I was told today in the examination room," replied Billy, "Or on Saturday."

I stared at Billy and noticed Jack and Jaden doing the same thing. Did Billy have sex with Veronica over the weekend?

"Saturday?" one of the guys asked, "What happened on Saturday?"

"None of your business right now," Billy barked back, and then, he peered between Jack, Jaden, and me, "Something only a few of us have experienced."

Logan dismissed that. "Yeah, whatever, Billy,"

The team captain turned around and glanced at our table. I figured he was also going to include Calvin. When he turned back around, he asked me, "Where's your boyfriend, Weston?" Yep. There was the joke. I had to roll my eyes at his continued insistence of my relationship with Ty.

"He's gone to have an experience," I simply said, figuring he'd pick up on what I meant. Although, if he played dumb, I would too.

Billy raised his eyebrows.

"Who?" asked Logan.

"Ty Green, Logan," said Jack, "Number Forty-Two."

"Oh. He's your boyfriend, Scott?" Logan asked in surprise. He sounded serious, which only made Billy, Jack, and Jaden snort.

I gave Logan an irritated, dumbfounded look. "No, dude."

Logan just shrugged. "Okay. Not like it matters none." After the laughter died down, Billy pushed his tray aside so he could rest his arms on the table and lean against them.

"When did Ty go for this 'experience'?" he asked.

Suddenly, Ty appeared from the entrance of the cafeteria, looking disoriented. Jaden and Jack called out and waved to him.

"Guess you can ask him now," I said.

Ty stumbled over to us, a huge smile on his face and a glow about him, pretty much like Jaden this morning. Except, unlike Jaden, Ty moved like the drunkards I'd seen in the movies. He placed both his hands on my shoulder pads and leaned onto me.

"Hey, buddy," he said, sounding out of sorts.

"Um, you okay?" I asked, looking over my shoulder at him.

"Never felt better..." Right then, Ty fell down unconscious.

chapter thirty-seven

"Ty!" we all yelled, and I jumped up. The boys from the other tables stood up to see what was going on. Ty had landed on his back. I bent down and jerked his shoulder as Jack, Jaden, and the other three team captains ran over.

"Give him some air!" ordered Calvin, preventing anyone else from coming near us. After a few seconds, Ty let out a moan, opening his eyes and saying, "Oh, man." Ty sat up and blinked.

"You okay?" asked Jack, kneeling in front of him. Our safety stared at Jack, put a hand on his cheek, and gently slapped it.

A wide smile appeared on Ty's face as he repeated what he had said to me, "Never felt better in my life, my friend." Then, he reached out for Jack's hand, who helped him stand up, keeping his eye on our friend.

"What happened to you?" asked Calvin.

Ty placed his hand on mine and Jack's shoulders, and flashed a wide smile.

"Just had to see the nurse about something," said Ty, "I'm good now." Jack, Jaden, and I exchanged a glance.

"But you passed out," said Calvin.

"Yeah, I should have waited a few minutes to get my energy back before I came in here," Ty admitted, "That visit took a lot out of me."

Jaden nodded. "Yeah, I bet! Tell us about it!"

"All in good time," replied Ty, "Right now, I'm starving."

"You sure you're okay now, though?" asked Calvin. Ty nodded, winked at me, and walked over to the counter and grabbed a tray. Billy and Calvin looked over in my direction.

"Experience, huh?" asked Billy.

"I guess so," I said.

Billy smirked at Calvin. "Okay," shrugged our captain, "As long as he's good to play in tonight's scrimmage."

I was surprised the team captains, especially Calvin, didn't press Ty for details; a bunch of other guys certainly did. However, Ty just kept the grin on his face and told them he was a man now.

It didn't take them too long to figure out Ty was probably hinting at some sexual experience, but many of them still wouldn't believe it. A few of the guys, however, said they'd have to see the nurse sometime as well. I wondered if they'd actually go through with it, or if they had just said that to stroke their egos.

After dinner, the team captains stood up, and Damian began to speak.

"Before our scrimmages, we're going to do our oneness meditation, which is what we did last Friday in our big circle. Now that we're together, it's important that we do this every day from now on – to feel the connection we have for each other."

"It also strengthens our bond as a single team," added Calvin, "No matter if we're playing against each other or another school."

I certainly felt that way after Friday's session and looked forward to it again. We donned our helmets and headed outside to our middle school field. Instead of standing in the middle of the

circle like last time, Coach King positioned himself to the side, saying he would just witness.

"This time, either switch positions or sit next to two different boys from Friday," instructed Billy, "Weston, you're with me." He motioned me over to where he and Calvin had positioned themselves on the field. I sat between them, with Calvin to my left and Billy to my right. I rested the back of my left hand on Calvin's right knee, which he grasped tight. Billy placed his left hand on my right knee. Once I held it, I instinctively closed my eyes and started breathing consciously, allowing the flow of energy to take its natural course. An incredible, powerful energy came from Calvin, lifting my spirits and filling me with confidence. I gladly mixed that with my own energy - my sense of self-worth - and passed it on to Billy, receiving, in return, gratitude and joy from him. We repeated this process, each time feeling the amalgamated energies of my fellow teammates with every breath, and each time feeling more at one with them in my heart.

No instructions came from Coach King this time, except when it was time to open our eyes. Once again, I found my hands placed over my crotch, feeling Calvin's, Billy's, and everyone else's energies mixing with mine. That began another powerful mini-orgasm through my body and made me moan and close my eyes. When I opened them, I saw Calvin move his hand from his crotch and place it on my shoulder, shaking my pads with a smile on his face.

Billy started to squeeze the back of my neck. My eyes closed as I couldn't help but relax. I leaned my helmet against his.

"Billy," I whispered.

"That's right," said Billy, "You like that, huh?"

I found myself drifting off to sleep. "Yeah..."

Calvin grabbed my facemask and pulled me toward him, jerking me awake. "Hey, Billy!" spat Calvin, "Stop messing with my player!"

Billy stuck his tongue out at him. "He's fun to play with, though."

Calvin grunted and shot Billy a glare.

"Okay, okay! Relax, Williams. It's not like I was going to let him sleep through the game. Sheesh."

Damian had us all stand up and remove our helmets, citing the oneness meditation as an exception to the helmet rule. "Just like on Friday," Damian instructed, his voice amplified by the megaphone Coach had handed him, "On three, we will shout 'Panthers! Panthers! All as one!'"

"One! Two! Three!"

We filled the sky again with the one hundred shouts in unison, *"PANTHERS! PANTHERS! ALL AS one!"*

Damian had us repeat it twice this time, with Coach King looking on, smiling. Once the echo faded, Damian continued, "Okay boys, please welcome the two refs for our scrimmages. From Gunner high school, Denton Cryer and Elliott Grossfield!"

The two high school football players I had met at the mall on Saturday entered our circle, both fully suited up in their blue and gold Gunner uniforms. One had number eighty-two and the other number twenty on their jerseys. Very much like ours, their jerseys and pants were covered in dirt and sweat stains. From what I could remember, it looked like Denton was the kid wearing number eighty-two and Elliott wore number twenty. Our team captains gave both of them manly hugs. Murmurs spread throughout my seventh grade teammates, mostly out of disbelief that a high school kid was going to ref.

"What's the matter?" shouted Mason, "These guys are some of the best players on the Gunners side. It's an honor to have them."

"It sure is!" Denton replied with a grin.

"Don't worry," added Elliott, "We'll be fair. Plus, we had the same issues about high schoolers as refs on our own middle school camp. But, it turned out great."

That didn't bother me, as long as they were truly impartial. The Warriors and the Rams were to face off on the middle school field, where Elliott would referee, while we Colts and the Jets were to play on the high school field with Denton as the ref.

Calvin positioned me first on offense as halfback. The energy I felt earlier only got stronger during the game, and I loved every minute of it. Every time I charged into another player, I relished the contact, the hit, the grunt, the explosive masculine energy I shared with him. I was a force to be reckoned with, plowing through the defensive line and evading tackles to gain massive yardage, and on defense, breaking through the offensive line. Although I didn't score, I managed to intercept the ball twice. I also managed to armpit three Jets, including one of Mason's squad leaders, Number Seventeen Noah Talan, who was also the Jets' best running back. That gave us an advantage; however, Mason's team won twenty-one to twenty, thanks to an amazing, last second, thirty-yard field goal by their kicker, Number Fifty-One, seventh grader Jacob Gatton. The kid also played cornerback on defense, managing to tackle Bryce Winters more than once and armpit a wide receiver. I felt the same incredible force that I had, the love of life, flowing through Jacob. We relished the times whenever we came up against each other, me running with the ball and him trying to stop me. It was like a dance, and in the end, he tackled me about as much as I had managed to evade him, and neither of us were able to armpit the other.

Time flew by, and none of us wanted to quit when Denton called time. As Elliott had said, Denton was a terrific ref. He praised us whenever one of us made an amazing play, whether it was a pass, a block, a tackle, or a score. He had no bias over who won. We shook hands and high-fived each other as we marched down the line after the game. The guys who had known each other well even hugged after the game. Jacob was the first kid on Mason's team I truly connected with, and we hugged after we shook hands.

"We definitely need to play more often," he said.

"Yeah," I replied, "Maybe we can practice against each other more during the day."

He grinned.

A few kids on Billy's team got armpitted, including Jaden, Logan Adams, and Austin Miller. On the Rams' side, Damian got pitted by Jack, which meant Hayton Rendal and Cody Kula, his squad leaders, had to take over. Billy's team smoked them, twenty-five to seven.

We all thanked Denton and Elliott for refereeing. "It's something we high school football players do for middle schoolers during camp," Denton said as they were leaving, "It's actually an honor for us as well. We will ref whenever you need us."

With that, we were asked to head back inside and brush our teeth or whatever we needed to do before turning in. Calvin asked me to return the bag of spare footballs to the equipment room before going to sleep.

Yawning, I made my way inside, starting to feel really tired. It was as though the bed in the gymnasium kept calling out to me. When I was walking through the locker room toward the equipment room, I noticed that the back door had been left slit open. I heard strange noises coming from inside. Curiosity got the better of me, and when I pushed it open, I beheld Jack and Billy

kissing each other on the lips; the blond-haired seventh grader feeling Billy's arms, and the team captain's hand on Jack's face. My jaw dropped in shock.

chapter thirty-eight

I watched as the two sweaty boys backed away from each other, breathing heavily.

"Billy..." whispered Jack.

A smirk appeared on his captain's face as he began to untie Jack's football pants.

"Wait, Billy," panted Jack.

"Nah," replied Billy, "You ain't gonna stop me either." Jack's eyes widened as Billy pulled his pants and cupped underwear down, exposing Jack's large boner. He nodded his head. "Nice size, Murphy," remarked Billy, "All that energy waiting for me."

Jack began to unlace Billy's football pants hurriedly, as if to beat him to the punch. The older boy watched with glee, and after Jack switched to unbuckling the pants, the eighth grader grasped Jack's penis with his dirty hand and began stroking up and down its length.

Jack's arms immediately fell by his side, and his head fell back. His eyes were shut, and his mouth open, letting out moans of pleasure.

"Thought you were gonna get *me*, huh?" laughed Billy, "Yeah, right."

"Oh... Billy..." Jack sighed and moaned as sweat dripped down his mud-smeared face.

"'Oh, Billy...'" his captain repeated, mocking Jack, "Yeah, you are *so* mine." Billy kneeled down and took a long lick of Jack's penis.

"Ooohhhhhh..." Jack groaned, and held on to Billy's head, kneading his scalp.

I felt myself getting a boner watching this. A part of me wanted to leave; I wasn't sure they would be happy with someone knowing they had done this. But, I was so turned on that I caught myself unconsciously rubbing my crotch. Did I want to be Jack or Billy? Or both?

Jack opened his eyes and turned his head. His eyes widened again when he noticed me. He took a breath, probably to call me out, but right then, Billy took his whole cock in his mouth and began sucking on it in a corkscrew motion.

"Oh God!" the boy yelled, his eyes closing again, "Billy! Aaahhh..." That was it for Jack. I saw Billy start swallowing as Jack's face scrunched up, his throat making loud raspy sounds.

After a few seconds of heavy breathing, Jack's body began to wobble. As soon as Billy took his dick out of his mouth, Jack let out a final moan before dropping to the ground. His eyes caught mine for a moment before they rolled up and closed. Billy wiped his mouth and lightly slapped Jack on the cheek. "Thanks, buddy," he whispered, "I needed that energy." Then, he pulled Jack's pants back up and retied them.

"I smell another kid's body odor," Billy said out loud, turning his head in my direction. I backed away instantly.

"Hey, Weston," he said, nonchalantly, "How long have you been standing there?"

I didn't answer.

"Well, it doesn't matter. What are you doing here anyway?"

I ignored his question again. "Jack?" I called out to my friend. Billy patted his head, feeling the hair moved between his fingers. "Oh, this boy's not waking up until morning," he said, "After a hard day of football with our meditation thrown in there, sex will put your ass out for the evening."

"I didn't know you had a thing for Jack," I mumbled.

"More like he has a thing for me," Billy corrected, staring at Jack's face, "But, I wasn't about to let him suck me off."

"Why not?"

"Because I didn't want him taking my energy tonight," he replied, "I wanted his."

"Huh?"

Billy rolled his eyes and looked back at me. "Really, Weston? What are you doing here, anyway?"

I held up the bag of footballs.

"Well, unless you're going to teleport them with your mind, move your ass."

I pointed to Jack's body, which was blocking my path. Billy leaned the boy against a wall and watched as I entered the room and placed the bag under a shelf that read "Footballs".

"Will you help me carry him to his bed?" asked Billy.

I leaned down next to Jack and shook his shoulders. Of course, he didn't react.

"What are you doing?"

I didn't answer, putting my face next to Jack's instead, taking in the smell of lamb coming from his breath, mixed with the odor of his sweat from the rest of his body. Then, I peeked under his eyelid, staring at the visible part of his pupil. When I bent one of his arms, his biceps bulged out, and I lifted it enough to peek at the

jersey's sweat stains under his arms. The strong stench made me cough and back away.

"You getting off on this or something?"

My large boner felt like it would burst out from my pants. I must have unconsciously stroked my cup, because I heard Billy chuckle and say, "You *are* getting off on this." The thought of Jack's lips around my penis, or better yet, mine around his, made me close my eyes and groan.

"Hey, Weston, snap out of it!" Billy wrapped a hand around my biceps and pulled me up. We stared at each other for a few seconds; his eyes were slitted.

"You have a thing for Murphy, don't you?" he asked. My heart started pounding. "Yeah," he smirked, "you have the same look I've seen Ludge give him." The revelation about Jaden didn't surprise me.

"Well, I didn't think *I* did," I replied, "I mean, I don't want to be his boyfriend or anything."

Billy burst out laughing. "Wow, Weston. I thought you were more secure than that. Are you telling me you haven't done anything like this with him yet?"

I shook my head.

He gave me another one of his playful grins and asked, "With Green?"

I looked away.

"Hah! I thought so."

"Billy, I-"

"Then, you know what I'm talking about. The energy you received when you sucked him. How awesome it was to feel one with him like that."

I simply nodded.

Billy pointed down at Jack. "And now you want *his* energy, don't you?" I recalled what Ty had told me on Thursday – him wanting my energy. I began to understand. "I don't blame you," said Billy, "He has amazing energy." Then, he added, "Like you."

"Huh?" I exclaimed. Before I knew it, Billy reached out his hand and began squeezing the back of my neck lightly. A warm, relaxing feeling came over me and made my eyes droop.

"Oooohh," I moaned as my forehead leaned against his brown hair, and I inhaled his strong odor, "Billy."

"'Billy'," he mimicked my voice, "Yeah. Yer mine tonight, you smelly kid." He unbuckled my pants and began to untie the laces. The thought of him sucking my dick made my heart nearly burst out of my chest, but something inside me wasn't all that excited about it. It felt... not necessarily *wrong*... but not the right time. I didn't want him to take my energy. In fact, quite the opposite. I realized I wanted *his*. Nevertheless, his gentle massage and the thought of an incredible orgasm that he would give me was rapidly zapping any will to fight back. If I didn't act quickly, and he managed to start playing with my dick, it'd be all over for me.

I forced my eyes open and found that I was staring at Billy's crotch. Fortunately for me, Billy hadn't thought to retying and re-belting his football pants. I thanked Jack in my mind for providing me with a way out. After summoning the energy I needed in a single breath, I made one downward pull, and Billy's football pants, along with his cupped underwear, fell down his knees; his hard, bare penis stretched out as far as it could go.

"What do you think you're doing, Weston?" Billy shouted through a snarl, tightening his grip on my neck and making me yelp, "You aren't-"

I turned around to leave. Suddenly, I came face to face with Veronica standing in the doorway.

"Nicely done, Scott."

chapter thirty-nine

I could only stare in awe as she walked over to the two downed boys and peeked under their eyelids. My penis began to harden again and push against my cup.

"Incredible," she said, "You are such strong boys, and Billy is such an amazing lover. Like you."

"W-What are you doing in here?" I stammered, making a mental note to come back to that Billy statement later.

She stood back up and walked over to me, and after that, she swiped her fingers down my face. "So sweaty and dirty," she grinned, looking at her fingers before rubbing them together and sniffing them. If my penis had teeth, it'd be chewing its way out by now. "I bet you enjoyed the sperm collection today, Scott," she suggested.

I licked my lips and asked, "Why did you do that to us?"

She stroked my cheek. "Every boy football player gets his sperm collected, at least once," she replied, "It's not important for you to know why at the moment. But, I will say I was serious in what I said to you during your collection."

I could feel the sweat pouring again.

She placed a finger on my chest and moved it toward my biceps. "I've watched you boys practice and play and eat and armpit each other," she continued, "The masculine energy you boys produce – the bond you create – is incredible."

I gulped, having no idea what to say. All I could think about now was sticking my dick into her.

Rubbing my muscles, Veronica said, "I paid attention to you after you beat Calvin in the pit."

"How did you know about that?"

"I saw it through some cameras we have," she said. "You should have lost against him. But you didn't. Whatever came over you during your run, you used that again at tonight's game, didn't you? Armpitting those three other players?"

"Yeah," I nodded.

She put her lips against mine and gave me a slow kiss, saying, "And then I saw what you did here with Billy. He had you, but you took advantage of a weakness he failed to see."

I just stared at her.

"You are so incredible, Scott. Something powerful is waiting to bust out of you. This is why you are here. Why *I* am here."

"I don't understand."

"Let me show you." She put her lips against mine, and we started making out. The enticing feminine aroma of lavender emanating from her made me grab her arms and force my tongue into her mouth. She moaned and rubbed my crotch with her knee. The intense pleasure made me stop, and I sighed as I leaned my head back. Then, she pulled down my football pants. A few drops of sperm, still attached to my underwear, broke free and started dripping from my penis. My cock had grown bigger than I had ever imagined, and it had large veins popping out.

294

My mouth dropped open, my eyes widened in excitement, and my breathing became erratic. I gulped as she lifted her skirt with one hand and guided my penis into her.

"Take me," she insisted through a soft whisper.

I thrusted my cock the rest of the way in, and I let out a moan as the most intense pleasure struck me. All the built-up masculine energy from me and all the other boys that I had taken in began to swirl around, focusing on a single point above my crotch. Veronica shouted my name, and I thrust my pelvis back and forth, moaning and groaning.

Suddenly, I became one with a larger part of myself – a pure, young masculine soul. Powerful. Joyful. Playful. I let out a fierce, howling bellow as the oneness within me orgasmed, sending waves of the purest bliss I had ever felt in my entire life throughout my entire body. This feeling, the pure, youthful, masculine energy, gushed out into Veronica. She let out a shriek, yelling out, "Thank you! Oh, Scott! Thank you!"

The oneness within me filled my heart with love and gratitude for my being alive. For being here. For being me. I fell into its calm, relaxing presence willingly and peacefully. As the orgasm ebbed, I sunk into a deep slumber, without care if I would ever wake out of it.

chapter forty

I woke up with a start, not with vigor, but with a sharp pang of pain shooting down the right side of my face, droplets of sweat lining my forehead. "Ow," I winced.

"Oh my God!" I heard Jack's shout boom through my ears, "He's coming to!"

I brought my fingers up to my cheek and opened my eyes wide open in shock, feeling a bandage. I found myself lying in our old nurse's office. I was in the same bed where I had woken up after being knocked out by Jimmy that first scrimmage. In fact, I was dressed not in my football uniform, but in my practice tee and shorts. What the hell was even going on?

I turned my head to catch Jack dressed in his practice tee and shorts as well, his face hanging above me. He leapt for a hug, his odor smack in my nostrils.

"Dude!" he exclaimed, "I thought we'd have to take you to the hospital!"

"Yeah, no kidding!" said Ty, emerging from nowhere. I spotted Jaden sitting on the bed across from me. He jumped up and came right next to Ty.

An short old lady, wearing a white smock and sporting a wrinkled face and gray hair tied up in a bun, stood up from the nurse's desk and walked over to me. Where was Veronica?

"Give us some room, boys," she told them, her voice raspy from what was probably a smoking habit. "How are you feeling, Scott?" she asked, as she checked my pulse.

I opened my mouth to speak, but the fuzzy bewilderment over where I was prevented me from voicing anything at all. This wasn't right. I had already woken up, perhaps in that very bed, days ago.

"What day is it?" I asked.

"Day?" the nurse asked gently.

"Day?" Jack repeated, "Dude, it's Thursday. You were only knocked out for about two hours."

"That's impossible!" I said, panic beginning to consume me. I sat up and yelled out, "I woke up five days ago! It should be Tuesday! And... where's my football uniform?"

"What the hell?" exclaimed Ty, turning to the nurse, "What's wrong with him, Nurse Lowe?"

The nurse frowned and shined a flashlight right into my pupils, making me squint. The door swung open, and my mom, dressed in her work clothes, came rushing in. When she saw me awake, she exclaimed, "Thank God!" and rushed over to me, nearly shoving my friends and the nurse out of the way.

"Be careful, Mrs. Weston," warned the nurse as my mom gave me a squeeze, "I don't think he's fully come out of it yet."

"Come out of *what*?" I yelled, demanding an answer.

"What do you mean?" my mom asked, backing away and staring at me.

"I don't know exactly," was the nurse's reply.

This couldn't be right! All the experiences I had over the past five days... what the fuck had happened to all of that?

My ability to think dissipated. I couldn't focus. I couldn't conjure a fucking thought. My heart began to pound faster. My breath stuck somewhere in the lump forming in my throat. I started to cry out, as I felt dizzy and my hands and feet began to lose all sensation. The nurse bent me forward and held me tight. A wail escaped my mouth, and tears started gushing down my face.

"Jesus, what's wrong with him?" my mom too started crying in panic.

Every breath I tried to take reinforced the notion that something was gravely wrong. My heart was racing out of control.

I shut my eyes and shouted, "I FEEL DIZZY! I CAN'T BREATHE! I'M DYING!" My mom held me close to her. But I didn't want her. I wanted Jack. Or Ty. Or Calvin. Or Billy... Hell, I'd even take Jimmy in this desperate moment.

"Jack!" I shouted out.

I felt a warm, strong grip on my hand. "I'm here, buddy!" he said. Was that really Jack's hand? It felt the same, but there was something different about it.

"Call 911!" my mom barked.

The nurse checked my pulse. "His heart rate has skyrocketed," she said, "Is he prone to panic attacks?"

"NO HE'S NOT! CALL 911!" she bawled. I had never seen my mother get that intense.

A man's voice interrupted the chaos. "He's just having a panic attack!" he said, "Calm down!"

"Coach King!" shouted Ty.

Thank God Coach was here.

"What's a panic attack?" asked Jack, pressing on my hand.

"How do you know that?" my mom asked, her voice loud and distressed.

"Trust me," he assured my mom, his voice much calmer, "I know one when I see one."

"No!" I insisted, barely able to get the words out, "Something's not right!"

"Tell me what's wrong," my mom pleaded.

I couldn't muster enough strength to put together even a few words, let alone a sentence. All I could mumble was a feeble, "No... Coach!"

I could hear my mom sobbing.

"Oh, man," exclaimed Jaden, "What's wrong with him?" His question made me cry out again.

"There's nothing wrong with him," the coach answered, "He's just been through an ordeal that needs sorting out. I know first-hand."

I sensed that the nurse was standing up and someone else was taking her place. Someone's large hand landed on my shoulder. I felt calmness radiating from it.

"Scott?" the coach said, standing right next to me.

"Y-yeah?"

"You're okay."

"No."

"Yes. I will help you sort everything out. What you're going through is perfectly normal. You are *not* dying. You are going through an intense shock. It will pass. No need to talk right now. No need to think. Can you feel the energy from my hand?"

I nodded.

"From your friend's hand?"

I could feel Jack squeeze, and I nodded again.

"Does it feel like it's really his?"

It didn't. Despite it physically feeling like Jack's hand, there was something different – a different energy altogether. I shook my head, and Jack, offended by that, let go of me.

"Dude, it's *me*," he insisted.

"How about mine?" Coach asked.

I nodded. It was definitely King.

"Okay," said Coach King, "That's fine. Focus on the energy from my hand, and take it into your heart. You can do that for me, eh Scott?"

"What..." my mom started, but she suddenly stopped. Maybe the coach had motioned her to do so.

A strong, calming energy flowed into me from his hand, and when it reached my heart, I felt a small tingle of warmth there. As I focused on that, I found that it was slowly getting easier to breathe.

"Good," said King, "Just concentrate on that feeling. Let it take you if you can."

Sensation began to return to my fingers and toes, and the dizziness began to wane away. After a few minutes of silence, I opened my eyes. I could feel my mom's squeeze. "Oh Scott!" I heard her say.

The nurse checked my pulse. "Coming back down to normal now," she said. My friends collectively heaved a sigh of relief.

I turned to look at Coach King. He still had this twinkle in his eyes, which made me trust his intentions.

He grinned and patted my shoulder. "Are you feeling better," he asked, "Physically?"

I nodded.

"Okay, good. The next step will be to tell us exactly what you've experienced. Can you do that?"

I had no desire to tell anything to the women there. My mom didn't need to know all that, and the old nurse certainly did not either.

I looked at the older lady, and then, at my mom, and finally, at Coach King.

"Go ahead, buddy," he urged, "What's on your mind?"

"I... I only want to tell you and the guys," I said, not able to look Mom in the eye.

"Scott!" my mom frowned.

"Mom, I'm sorry. But it's a man thing."

"You're twelve, Scott!" she grunted. I knew she was going to say that.

"A boy thing, then. Please," I insisted, "I appreciate your being here and holding me." She started to cry. "Mom..."

"Trust him, Mrs. Weston," Nurse Lowe suggested, handing her a tissue, "He isn't rejecting you. He needs the trust and bond of males right now."

My mom blew her nose into the tissue. "I know," she nodded, "It just makes me sad that his dad isn't here either."

The nurse patted her shoulder. "I understand."

"I'll tell you afterward, Mom. I promise," I said, leaning onto her.

"You don't have to, actually," she said, kissing me on the forehead, "I'm just glad you're okay. You can tell me whatever you want, whenever you feel like you should."

My mom stood up. "Call me when you are ready to go home."

"I don't want to go home," I told her, "I want to go back to my life as I had just lived it."

"You *sure* he doesn't need to go to the hospital?" my mom asked the nurse.

"He doesn't look like he's suffered any physical injury," the nurse replied, "But he's obviously gone through something while he was unconscious."

"Maybe I can come over and stay with him for a bit," suggested Ty.

I shot a quizzical look at him. "Weren't you staying over through the weekend, since the rest of your family is out of town?"

"Scott..." my mom cut in.

"No, buddy," said Ty, looking equally confused, "They're home."

"Let's go grab a coffee, Mrs. Weston," suggested Nurse Lowe.

"Where?"

"The cafeteria."

"Is it open?"

The nurse smirked. "It will be for us."

She led my mom out the door, and when it shut, all four pairs of eyes were staring at me. Jaden scooted toward me on a stool, and Jack and Ty sat down on the bed opposite me.

"So, what did you dream about?" asked Jaden.

"It wasn't a dream, Jaden!" I shouted back.

Jaden looked at the coach. "Please tell him it was a dream," he told him.

"Jaden!" chided Jack.

"Well, it obviously was. We're here. It's Thursday."

I shook my head as panic started to overcome me again.

Coach took my hand again.

"Take a deep breath and calm down, Scott, then tell us everything you can, or at least, what you desire to," he prompted, "And Jaden, be supportive. You don't know what he's gone through."

I took a breath, then started with what happened after I woke up, about my experience with Veronica.

"Wow, you had sex with a hot chick!" Ty exclaimed, "No wonder you've been bawling for this to be real."

"She turned out to be Max's aunt," I added.

"Does he even have an aunt?" asked Ty.

I ignored that question; instead, I explained the part where Ty and I were traded out to Calvin's team.

"Yeah, that was going to happen," nodded Jack, "How did you know?"

The coach hushed him.

Then, I moved on to Thursday night, where we all watched the video Veronica had recorded. That made the guys grin.

I looked at Ty, and almost blurted out that he and I had sex with each other, but I wasn't sure I wanted anyone else but Ty to know about that, maybe not even him.

I then told them about Friday's practice, and how Jack and I armpitted each other. That made the other boys cringe, but King chuckled.

"I'm not laughing at you, buddy," he said, noticing my frown.

"Yours and Jack's armpits could definitely knock any kid out," Ty said, managing a grin.

When I mentioned our being invited to the Edge of the World party, Jack said, "There's no such thing at the middle school level, dude. Just at the high school."

"Yeah," added Ty, "Remember we talked about wanting one for us middle schoolers?"

I shook my head again. "No... this isn't right," I insisted.

"Boys, let him speak," the coach said, "Take another deep breath, Scott, then continue."

Maybe this was the dream, I told myself. Maybe, I'd wake up at any moment. I closed my eyes, took a deep breath, and wished myself to wake up, back in the reality, the real one this time. But, that didn't happen.

After letting out a sigh, I went on to tell them about the high schoolers we met at the mall on Friday, Saturday's jaunt to White Water, the awesome party afterward, and Veronica's visit and her sex with Jack.

Jack's eyes widened. "Holy shit!" he exclaimed.

"Did she do us too?" asked Jaden, pointing between him and Ty.

I nodded, telling them about Monday, but I left out all the stuff at the end between Jack, Billy, and me. I didn't want to embarrass them, or myself for that matter. I made sure I mentioned the close bond we all had and the amazing meditation we did on Friday and Monday. I also told them of the incredible feats I had accomplished, which included beating Calvin in the pit and the sex I had with Veronica again, along with how that had been the most incredible experience of my life.

"Wait, so the last three weeks of camp were overnight?" asked Ty.

"Yeah," I said, "I guess that isn't true either?"

Jack and Jaden simply shook their heads.

Ty went on to ask, "And there were, like, no adults? No coaches?"

"Thimbleton retired, so it was just Coach King," I said, "but he was pretty much hands off. The team captains acted like coaches, and the high school football players were refs."

"And you thought *that* was really real?" Jaden rebuked, unable to contain himself.

"Yes!" I shouted back, glaring at him.

Coach King addressed Jaden. "Have you ever had a dream, Jaden," he asked, "That felt so real? And in your dream, everything made sense?" I frowned at his hint that all my experiences were just in my head. Jaden admitted with a nod of his head.

"Me, too," said Ty.

"Same here," added Jack.

"But then, I woke up and knew I was back in reality," said Jaden.

"The mind is very powerful, boys," the coach continued, "Once it gets used to something, it rebels easily against anything that contradicts that comfortable reality." The coach looked at me as he said, "It even comes up with rationalizations as to why certain things can't be real."

"Well, I don't know anything other than this reality at the moment," said Jaden, "I mean, sorry, but women don't have sex with young boys like us. Football camp is only during the day. We players don't coach. And we don't knock each other out with our armpits, even though Ty is right. Scott, you and Jack could easily do it."

"Have you smelled yourself lately?" Jack asked him with a glare.

"I'm not saying I couldn't either," replied Jaden, looking at him, "Or Ty. Phew." Ty laughed. "And I wish I had White Water tickets," he added, "I'd totally invite you guys."

Coach King asked Ty and Jack, "Do you two boys feel the same as Jaden about Scott's experiences?"

Ty grabbed Jack's hand, curled it into a fist, and hit himself with it. "Dude, knock me out," he joked.

Jack laughed, and then, his face turned quite serious.

"No wonder you are so depressed," he said, "I would have had a fit as well. Oh, man. I'm sorry."

I looked at Jack and Ty. "So, you guys do think it was all in my head."

They nodded.

"You were only out for two hours," said Jack, "That's it."

"But, how could two hours turn into five long days?" I asked, "Five real days with sleep and everything? No time skip. No nothing."

My three friends shrugged.

I looked over at Coach King. "How about this," he said, "Give it the weekend and see if things start to make more sense."

"I don't want to," I argued back, "I want to wake up."

"I know," King patted my head, "But you can't do anything about it until you accept where you are now."

"And if things don't make more sense?"

"Then come see me on Monday. Okay? But right now, just take it easy!"

"Okay," I mumbled, my voice low and dejected.

"If you start to slip, take a few deep breaths and remember that Monday's just around the corner," the coach advised, "And until then, don't forget, you aren't alone. You have your friends here to help you." Then, he turned around to ask them, "Isn't that right?"

"Uh huh!" agreed Ty. Jaden nodded, and Jack stood up, walked over to me, and gave me a tight hug.

I so desperately wanted to get lost in his energy, to feel the oneness with him in my heart, but I couldn't. His energy was too strange to me, which just distanced me from him. He even smelled different. I didn't want this false Jack touching me. I pushed him

away, and he frowned. His voice was sharp and curt as he hissed, "Dude, I'm just trying to show you my support!"

"I'm sorry, Jack!" I said, looking at him.

"Give him some more time," King urged him.

"Fine, whatever."

"Can you stand?" Coach asked me.

I stood up.

"Good. If you want, you can go to the locker room and get your stuff. Camp's about to wrap up, so you'll probably get to see the other boys. I'm sure they'll be happy to know you're okay."

The coach had my friends escort me to the seventh grade locker room. The other football players were grabbing their stuff from their lockers. I didn't notice anyone new or different from the ones I'd just been with in the other reality.

"Hey, Scott's back!" said Austin Miller, and everyone clapped.

"Jimmy clocked you good!" said Nicholas Schmidt, looking at my cheek.

"Did Calvin make him run laps for the rest of the day?" I asked.

"Run laps?" laughed Austin, "The dude got sent home. He may not be allowed to come back to camp."

My heart sank.

"Weston!" shouted a familiar voice rather angrily. Billy's head peered from the entrance of the eighth grade locker room. "Get your ass in here now!"

chapter forty-one

The other seventh graders watched as I started walking toward Billy.

"You too, Murphy!" Billy ordered.

Jack followed me in. Most of the eighth graders were still in the locker room, and even they all were the same as in that world I had just gotten out of.

Billy stood, arms folded, along with the other three team captains in the middle of the room. Calvin was shirtless; he had the same amazing physique as his counterpart. I wondered if he was an all-star in this reality too.

"I was going to have you transferred to Williams' team to even things out. But now, thanks to you, he doesn't want you on his team."

I looked at Calvin. "Why not?" I asked.

Calvin narrowed his eyes at me and replied, "Because you hurt one of my players, and his retaliation got him suspended." I took a deep breath and tried to apply what I had learned from my previous experiences.

"I over-reacted, Calvin," I began to apologize, "I admit it. I let Jimmy get the best of me because I was angry at him. I'm sorry."

Calvin and Billy didn't respond, so I continued, "Not only did he stop me from scoring, he pushed me down so hard. It was like he was rubbing defeat in my face." I hoped that would pacify them.

"You poor baby," Billy spat, "Your feelings get hurt so easily?" My eyes widened in disbelief at his cutting words, and then, I clenched my teeth as pure rage surged through me. My breathing became heavy. How *dare* he say that to me! What the fuck happened to the Billy who I had come to know? The one that had intuitive understanding and empathy?

"You have a problem with me?" asked Billy.

I blew up, letting loose my rage. "Yes! You asshole!" I barked. The room went dead silent, and all eyes were glued to me.

"Scott!" hissed Jack.

Billy's mouth dropped open. He blinked, looking between the team captains as if he couldn't believe what I had just said.

Billy pushed me against a locker. "What did you just call me?" he growled.

"This isn't you! " I shouted back, getting back in his face, "You help people understand teamwork! You help them learn about themselves and learn from their mistakes!"

Billy stared at me and screamed loudly, "WHAT THE FUCK DO YOU KNOW ABOUT ME?"

I couldn't connect with this Billy at all. All I felt from him was scorn and contempt, but I tried again anyway.

"I know you! You-"

Billy pushed me against the locker again, and pain ran down my spine, pouring forth from my head. "The *fuck* you do!" he snarled.

"Billy," started Jack, wrapping his hand around his biceps, "He's acting really weird right now and hasn't fully recovered yet. He just needs to go home."

The eighth grader continued to glare for about five more seconds before turning around to Jack and saying, pointing to me, "Good. Get this little shithead away from me!"

"How hard were you *hit*, dude?" asked Mason.

Would I have to start all the way over with these guys? With Calvin? I glanced at the Colts' team captain. His cold, blank stare offered me no solace.

"I even managed to beat Calvin in the pit," I said. Billy, Damian, and Mason burst out laughing.

"In hell, Weston," said Billy, "You can't even beat me or Murphy." Calvin didn't say anything. He slowly shook his head at me before turning away and going back to his locker.

I looked at the ground and repeated to myself, "This isn't real. This can't be real."

"Dude, he's freaking out," said Mason.

Jack turned beet red. He jerked my shoulders and whispered through clenched teeth, "Scott, snap out of it! Remember what Coach King said! Take deep breaths!"

I did what Jack said, but it only calmed me down a teeny bit. I needed to get out of there.

As I started to leave, Damian said, "We all hope you get better."

"Yeah," added Mason.

Appreciation and relief flowed through me. At least Damian seemed to act like the one I had come to know; the one who rallied everyone together and made us all act as one team.

"Thanks," I said.

I took a mental note to try and get to know Mason. Out of all the team captains, he was the one I knew the least about, and I had never given him much attention.

Jack walked me back to my locker. I grabbed my stuff and called my mom. Ty and Jaden were waiting for me as well, and I told the three of them goodbye and headed outside to meet her. Mom asked me to leave my bike, stating that I could ride it home tomorrow.

I didn't say anything on the way home, ignoring my mom's questions, and only ate a little bit of my dinner up in my room, even though I felt like I was starving. I played video games, which didn't seem much different from the ones in the other reality.

That night, I laid awake in my bed, praying to wake up to the other world, the real world. I felt utterly disheartened when, after waking up, I found that I was still in my room. I welled up. Was it cemented? Was this reality *really* going to be my reality now?

My mom asked me how I was feeling. I lied and told her I was better. I could tell by her face she didn't believe me, but she didn't push it. When she dropped me off at football camp, no one said a word to me, except for Jack, Jaden, and Ty. Jaden only really said hello and said he hoped I felt better. Other than that, he stayed clear of me. So much for being a friend.

Many of the other guys, especially the eighth graders, sniggered and said that Jimmy Casten had *literally* knocked the sense out of me, but that it was bullshit that he got suspended for a week, whereas *I* wasn't going to be punished at all for pushing him down initially. They warned that I better watch my back when Jimmy returned.

Even Jack told me to stop with all this 'other world' bullshit, and that it had totally humiliated him yesterday. I apologized to him and then lied, saying that everything was back to normal with me. I wasn't sure whether or not he had caught on to my lie, but he accepted what I said with relief.

Ty was the only one who kept real conversation with me. I apologized to him for the previous day as well and told him the

truth about the energy differences I had felt, and that it was okay if he didn't understand. I said I would just go along with everything as it was, and that I wouldn't bring it up with the other guys ever again. He seemed relieved to hear that. Although, he did tell me that Mason had traded him to Calvin's team, just like I had predicted.

We were given our football equipment, but unlike the other Friday, I wasn't asked to suit up early to meet Calvin outside. That was fine actually, because I just stared at the box like it didn't belong to me. I ended up being the last one to get out of the locker room. I eventually forced myself to don everything, but I felt alien in it.

Practice sucked too. Billy must have not wanted to deal with me; he never put me in to play until the coaches made him, and that was only on defense. At lunch, all the guys were joking around amongst themselves – it was as if I wasn't even there. Jack didn't say anything to me either, except only afterward, when he asked how I was doing. I lied again and left it at, "Better."

We ended up playing a scrimmage against Calvin's team, and I did implement what I had learned in the other reality to improve my game, but that went completely unnoticed by Billy. Jack noticed that and, to his credit, tried a few times to get Billy to notice it as well. But Billy paid no attention. Not only that, but Calvin's whole team ganged up on me, piling on top of me time and time again. They didn't seem to care, stupidly enough, that all that attention on me made our team score more and eventually win the game. That victory felt hollow though, and I shared no joy with my so-called teammates.

When practice finally ended, Ty asked if he could stay over, which I was grateful for. I invited Jack and even Jaden, but they said they were busy. Ty let it slip that Jaden had invited both him and Jack to watch a flick, leaving me out intentionally. He also said

that Jaden guilted Jack into going for the movie, but that Ty had said he'd rather stay with me. That elevated my mood, at least a little.

My mom took us out for pizza, and afterward, we watched a movie on TV with her. Then, we played video games up in my room. The relief I felt with Ty around me was a silver lining, and I relished every bit of the comfort his company brought me – and even though he wasn't the real Ty to me, he acted like that.

At the end of one round, he turned to me and said, "You know, I think I understand what you've been talking about."

I banked my head. "What do you mean?" I asked.

"You know, being from an alternate reality and all that."

"Huh? Are you fucking with me?"

"No. There's a different energy about you as well. I noticed it all day today. Something is definitely off." I didn't want to think about it anymore, so I started the next round.

"I guess that means you aren't going to kiss me then," I joked, completely forgetting that I hadn't mentioned anything about that. I felt the energy within Ty swirl and morph into a cloud of darkness. He paused the game and stared at me. "What? Why would I ever do that?" he asked, confused.

Oh, shit. I had to recover from this. "Never mind," I said, "Just joking. Let's continue."

Ty shook his head. "No. You're not 'just joking'. I can tell."

"Does it matter?" I shrugged.

"If I'm going to kiss you? Of course it matters! Are you saying that I actually kissed you in this dream of yours?"

I frowned at his use of the word 'dream'. I told him, "It wasn't a dream, Ty."

He had a disgusted look on his face. "Then that's even *worse!*" he hissed back, "Did you kiss me back?"

"A few days later, yeah, but-"

Ty dropped his controller and stood up. "Not doing this," he said, a pained expression taking over his face, "I feel sick."

As he grabbed his backpack, I begged, "Hey, wait! Please don't go! That was that reality, and this is this one! And in this one, I don't want to kiss you!"

Ty threw up his hands, backed away from me, and said, "Get away from me, faggot."

My heart broke.

He then hurriedly trotted down the stairs.

"What's wrong, Ty?" I heard my mom ask him from the living room.

"Sorry, I'm not feeling well," he replied, before hurrying past her. I saw him throw open the door and run out, not bothering to even shut it. My mom hopped up, shut the door, and then, looked up at me.

"Scott?" she called out.

I ran back into my room, slammed the door, and crashed onto my bed, sobbing. My mom eventually tried to console me, but I wouldn't tell her what the matter was, I just kept asking her what was wrong with me. That made her try to hug me again, but I didn't want that.

"GET AWAY FROM ME!" I screamed. She started sobbing as well and left my room. A pain crept up in my heart, filling it with a void, a darkness that began to separate me from my own self; the boy I was, from the boy I had loved being. The next few days marked the longest, loneliest weekend since the time my dad had left. Neither Ty nor Jack would answer my calls. I even tried to speak to Jaden against my gut feeling, but even he didn't answer.

Dark, frightening thoughts invaded my mind: Ty must have told Jack and Jaden what I had said, and now, they were all avoiding me. These thoughts told me how wrong I was. How fucked up I was. How crazy I was. How gay I was. I started avoiding looking at myself in the mirror. I couldn't face the faggot I had obviously become.

I spent the weekend up in my room, lying in bed and only coming downstairs once in a while to eat. My mom spent a lot of time talking on the phone with Grammy. On Sunday night, she said Grammy was flying in the next day, and that I would see her after football practice. For the first time in my life, the words 'football practice' filled me with absolute trepidation; I dreaded having to go. The sport I had once cherished as the greatest thing in my life had now become the thing I most hated and feared. The only thing that prevented me from making some excuse not to go was the prospect of seeing Coach King. His was the only presence that made me feel good. I told myself that I would go see him if things hit rock bottom.

Something inside me told me they would.

chapter forty-two

When I reached my locker the next morning, Ty was nowhere in sight. Jack and Jaden were almost through suiting up, and when they saw me, Jaden turned away.

"Some friend, Jaden," I called out.

"Faggot," he taunted back.

I closed my eyes as I felt the word sting. I then remembered Billy mentioning how much Jaden wanted Jack, and his behavior over the last few days certainly mirrored that. Hell, the last few years. I hadn't realized until then just how clingy Jaden had been to Jack. Okay, so Jaden wanted to throw stones? He'd get a huge one back.

I snarled, "Faggot? Me? Who's the one with the hots for Jack, huh?" I pointed to Jaden as I uttered that last bit.

His eyes widened in shock, like he'd just been outed. He glared at me, saying, "I do *not*!" The other kids stopped what they were doing and stared at us.

"Your face tells everyone otherwise!" I said. Jack began to heave.

"Fuck you!" spat Jaden.

"Fuck *me*?" I said, chuckling. I pointed to Jack. "There's your dream fuck buddy."

"Scott!" Jack snarled, "Watch your *fucking* mouth!"

Pain seared through me. "Traitor!" I cried out.

"Oh!" cried a few seventh graders, "Fight! Fight!" they started chanting.

Jaden came running over to me, cocking back his fist. I pulled back my own fist, ready to pound the ever-loving *fuck* out of that asshole.

"*THAT'S ENOUGH!*" bellowed Coach Thimbleton's voice, echoing throughout the locker room, stopping Jaden in his tracks. We all stared at the coach, standing in the doorway, his mirrored sunglasses hanging from the neck of his shirt.

"I cannot believe this!" he continued, hands by his side, "You are supposed to be a team!" He then pointed to Jack. "Murphy, aren't you their squad leader?"

Jack's face turned red, and he lowered his eyes. "Yes," he answered.

"And you let this escalate... why?"

"I-"

"I'm beginning to think Thompson made a huge mistake, making a seventh grader a squad leader." Jack's worst nightmare was beginning to come true.

"No, Coach!" Jack pleaded, looking up at him.

"Is Thompson still in the eighth grade locker room?" asked Thimbleton.

A kid went to check, and a moment later, he re-emerged, Billy in tow, fully suited up except for his helmet.

"What happened, Coach?" asked Billy. He had a worried expression on his face.

"Thompson, I want to see you and Murphy in my office. Now."

He then addressed Jaden and me. "You two get suited up," he ordered, "Then head outside immediately and start running laps. I don't want you corrupting the rest of the team with your attitudes."

Jaden grunted.

"The rest of you suit up and meet in the seventh grade war room. I want no more talking." With that, he motioned for Jack and Billy to follow him into his office, which was adjacent to our locker room. He must have heard everything that went on.

Billy and Jack passed Jaden, who said, "I'm sorry, Jack."

Jack snarled back at him. "You just had to start something with Scott, huh?"

"I didn't start it!" Jaden protested, but Jack just mouthed something to him that I couldn't hear. Whatever it was, it just about made Jaden well up.

I walked to my locker and sat down on the bench. The other players suited up in silence as fast as they could, including Jaden, while I just stared at my locker.

I could hear Jack's desperate cry from the coach's office. "No, Coach! I can handle it!"

"It doesn't appear that way to me!" I heard Coach Thimbleton yell back. Billy said something, but I couldn't make out what it was. Some of the kids glared at me; the others, at Jaden. Jack stormed out of the office, tears streaming down his cheeks. I knew what had happened. My heart sank, and I couldn't bear to look Jack in the eye. I had managed to separate myself from all of my friends there, cause all of them pain – even my own mother. The realization shot through me like a stab right in the chest, swelling my heart.

I barely had enough will to open my locker, and when I did, the uniform reeked of sweat, but not the sweat I had grown used to. It disgusted me... it belonged to some other smelly boy. It was like he and I had switched places. I was in hell. The isolation, the

separation, the sheer agony of being alive overwhelmed me to the point that I simply wanted to die. When I grasped that it wasn't an exaggeration, that I literally had no will to live, the pain in my soul cried out. I could no longer hold it in. A loud wail escaped me, and I collapsed in a heap on the floor, sobbing uncontrollably. The other kids cried out in shock too, and someone shouted to go fetch the coaches.

I heard the sound of cleats surrounding me, which meant some of the other players had approached me, but they didn't know what to do.

"Coach King's here!" I heard a kid shout.

A few seconds later, King ordered, "Get away from him! All of you!"

Then, I felt a large set of arms wrapping themselves around me and pulling me close. It must have been King; the warmth that emanated from this person's chest reminded me of him.

"Let it go, Scott. Let it all go," King whispered to me, "It's over."

I carried on sobbing as Coach Thimbleton asked everyone to leave immediately and carry their uniforms with them. The loud clanks of the numerous cleats running for the door finally died down, replaced with just the sound of the air conditioner and my sobs.

Coach King finally spoke. "I got this, Coach Thimbleton."

"You sure, Sim?" he asked, "I've seen this before when my sister's kid died a few years ago. I could be of help."

"Very much appreciated, Coach, but this is something between Scott and me. If you wouldn't mind, please let me handle this alone."

"Okay. I'll be in the eighth grade war room if you need me."

"Thanks."

After about another minute, I had purged myself of the despair, leaving only fatigue and a large pit of sadness behind. King must have sensed that I had calmed down.

"You are such a brave kid," he said, "I am so, *so* proud of you and *so* thankful for you." That made no sense to me. I opened my eyes and wiped my nose, looking up at him.

"Huh?" I grunted, "Why?"

He chuckled. "You have put yourself through such hardship over these past few days. Talk about jumping into the deep end of the pool." He let me go and sat on the bench, patting the spot next to him. I sat down.

"I don't get it," I said.

"I know. You will, though," he said, "First, tell me what happened over the last few days that led to this fight with your friend."

I passed on the urge to correct him on the status of my friendship with Jaden. Instead, I told him what I had been through since Thursday afternoon. I felt comfortable enough with him to go into every detail, including what had happened with Ty, how had I treated my mom, and how I felt about myself.

When I was done, Coach King nodded, the twinkle in his eyes back again. "So," he began, "If you had to wrap up this whole experience in one word or one short phrase, what would it be?"

The answer came quickly. "Hell."

He smiled.

"I like that. Not your experience, but the word. Seems apropos."

His good cheer made me both laugh and grunt in irritation. I didn't understand how he could be so happy and so seemingly detached from my situation.

"You know, people go through years, or entire *lifetimes*, with your level of pain and suffering," he said. I couldn't imagine that. I didn't think I'd be able to survive another day of this, let alone years.

"Really?" I asked.

"Yes." I felt a wave of compassion swell from my heart for those people, and I leaned onto Coach King.

"I feel sorry for them," I mumbled, wiping my nose again.

He wrapped an arm around my shoulder and pulled me close, saying, "I'm so relieved to hear that."

"Yeah?"

"Yes. It's because of them, of what *they* went through, that your time here gets to be so short." A million thoughts raced through my mind, trying to make sense of what he had just said, but I couldn't fathom an understanding.

"I don't understand that at all," I admitted.

He pulled me closer, and looking into my eyes, he said, "That's perfectly okay. One day, I promise, you will fully realize what that means." We then stared at each other in silence. Was he going to leave it at that? Surely not.

"You ready to go home?" he finally asked, "To go back where you belong?"

My eyes lit up. "I can?" I asked.

"Yes. All you have to do is snap my fingers."

I raised my eyebrows. "Um... huh?"

"I'm being serious."

I could have called him crazy, but that would be the very definition of hypocrisy. Besides, he didn't sound like he was joking. I reached out to his hand to snap his fingers together, but he waved his index finger at me and let out another chuckle.

"No," he said, "It won't work like that, I'm afraid."

"What am I supposed to do then?" I grumbled.

"Close your eyes."

When I did so, he said, "Now, take a few deep breaths and focus on your heart again. Call upon the oneness you felt, up until you awoke in this reality. Let me know when that's done."

The connection came after only a few deep inhales. I felt my soul, the football player I knew myself to me, envelope me in love and understanding. This self told me everything would be okay, and then, he allowed me to rest in him. I felt calm. Peaceful. At home.

"Okay," I whispered, "Done."

"That's my boy. Now, this pain. This experience. You will need to call upon it later. It will serve you well in ways you'd never thought were possible. Think of it as an invaluable tool that you'll be able to use at a moment's notice. So, take all the pain and suffering you've experienced these last few days into your heart and bless them."

The pain swirled in my heart, becoming a ball of darkness in its depths. Once again, I held two completely polar opposite emotions. Except this time, the joy enveloped the pain. I saw myself in a round, golden room, with a single shelf that had many different objects. Then, I saw myself placing this ball on that shelf, and pure joy surged through me as I gazed upon its beauty. Something inside of me became ecstatic that I now possessed this.

Coach King let out a laugh. "You have a different perspective on this pain now, don't you?"

"It feels that way, yeah," I said.

I felt something, some energy, appear at the top of my head. It pulsed, connecting to a point on my forehead, right above the bridge of my nose, exactly where I had seen people from India wear

a dot. I felt the power from my heart, and this pulsing on top of my head, meet at this point, making it tingle.

As Coach King spoke, a deep, resounding power resonated from his voice, which transferred to me. It felt as if the very fabric of this reality kneeled to our every word.

"What do you feel?" he asked.

The answer came straight from my heart, making me feel the strongest wave of relief in my life. "I'm dreaming," I replied.

"You're dreaming?"

"I'm dreaming," I repeated, "This isn't real." When I said those words, a warm feeling had flooded my heart. It was as if I had uttered a great truth.

"This isn't real?" he asked.

"No."

"What is real, then?"

I took a deep breath, and through that tingling point on my forehead, I saw everyone here as unaware dreamers, or shadows, of their real selves, like avatars in a video game. I seemed to be the only one, except for Coach King, who *wasn't* a shadow. In fact, there was something very different about him, but I couldn't pinpoint it yet.

I answered, "Me. And You. You're real too."

"Do you know who I am?"

I took another deep breath. An immense, almost incomprehensible level of powerful joy surged through me, emanating from that soul calling himself Coach King. I had to close it off, or else, I felt my body would literally explode from overcharging. He was the mastermind behind all this reality, creating it just for me so that I could have that little ball of pain.

"Open your eyes," he instructed.

When I did, I saw myself looking through Coach King's own eyes, beholding a truly magnificent, self-actualized part of Himself. As King, I embodied not only that of the wonderful soul in front of me named Scott, but also as Jack, as Ty, as Jaden, as Billy, as Calvin – as all the boys on the football team. All of these individual energies culminated into this infinitely powerful, immortal, internal creator being that was literally playing with Himself, allowing these different autonomous parts to interact, create, and have fun with each other. Above all, to remember to love one another. He was the flipside of the oneness meditation.

When I, as King, beheld Scott again, my entire being burst with love and gratitude. I felt such honor to be able to help him return home.

"Are you ready, little one?" I said to myself.

As Scott, the energy from King manifested as warmth from all of the kids on the team, as if the energy had been shot through a prism. Simultaneously, I felt energy coming from an entirely different Being, carrying with it the love of my mom, Veronica, and even, surprisingly, from Stephanie Williams. All of these souls were cheering for me, hugging me, filling me with their incredible love, acceptance, and gratitude. An irresistible urge to merge with my teammates came over me, a pull so fierce that any resistance had the power of a single human against that of the entire sun.

I nodded, tears gushing out of my eyes as I answered, "Yes, I'm ready."

With that, I, as King, snapped my own fingers.

chapter forty-three

I awoke, every single cell in my body pulsating with some kind of current that flowed through my being, making me aware of the entirety of my body. It felt as if I was a battery that had just been fully charged.

"Oh, wow," I said to myself out of complete awe.

The current ebbed, and I opened my eyes. I found myself wearing my football uniform, lying in what felt like the mattress of the capsule I had tried out that first morning of over-night football camp. A cylindrical dome, just about a foot above me, covered the entire capsule, separating me from the outside world. To my right, a soft, green glow emanated from a button labeled 'Canopy'.

Before I could press it, the canopy retracted, and Billy's face peered in. "For fuck's sake, Weston," he said, "Are you going to sleep all morning?"

I exhaled, feeling as if I had been holding my breath for hours – even days – and then, I laughed out of pure joy.

"Yeah, you laugh now," said Billy, "But you're on my revenge list for what you did to me last night."

"Hahaha!" came Jack's chuckle, before he appeared on the other side. "You got him good, Scott!" he began, "Billy should have known not to underestimate you!"

Jack held out his hand, and when I took it, he pulled me out of bed and patted me on the back. I hugged him, relishing his smell and the feel of his energy, it felt familiar again; and he hugged me back. *This* was the Jack I knew.

"You're awesome!" he said to me.

Those words filled me with such elation.

"So, you know what happened between Billy and me, then?" I asked Jack, ready to put that other nightmarish experience behind me.

"Calvin told Billy and me this morning," he replied, pointing over to my team captain standing next to Billy. Calvin gave me a wide smile, walked over to me, and tousled my hair. I felt so exhilarated from all this positive attention that my arms reflexively gave him an overwhelming hug. He promptly hugged back.

"You're incredible, Scott," said Calvin, staring me in the eyes, "Way to take advantage of Billy's... opening..." Calvin began laughing at his joke, which made Billy grumble and Jack laugh even harder. I joined in as well, and then, I walked over to Billy and pulled him in an embrace.

"No, no," said Billy, "You can't hug your way out of this one." However, he did let me embrace him until I finally let go. Ty and Jaden walked over to us, followed by the other team captains and a bunch of other guys, including Jacob Gatton, the Jets' kid I went round and round with at last night's game.

"What's with the hug fest?" asked Jaden. I hugged him too, feeling absolutely no animosity toward him or him toward me.

"Well, okay then," Jaden responded with a smirk, giving me a noogie in return, "That's how *I* return hugs around here."

Then, it was Ty's turn for a hug. "Urk!" said Ty, "What's this for, buddy?" He returned the hug, and I held on to him for almost a full minute, taking in his energy and giving him mine.

"Wow. Really happy to see your boyfriend today, huh Weston?" asked Billy.

"Jealous, huh?" jeered Calvin.

Billy cracked his knuckles. "Fuck you, Williams." Calvin chuckled and winked at me.

Ty stared into my eyes, looking concerned. "You okay?" he asked, "You act like you haven't seen me in forever."

"Not the real you," I replied, leaving him confused.

"You *really* must have had an incredible night last night, according to Calvin," said Billy, folding his arms.

"A very long one, actually," I replied, the smile leaving my face.

"What happened?" he asked.

I told them about the hellish other reality that I had experienced last night – the fights we got into, the punishments, the way I was hurt, and the way I hurt other people. Worst of all, I told them of the separation I felt from everyone, including myself, not to mention the fact it all lasted for four days.

"Holy shit!" exclaimed Jack, "I didn't have that at all. I just woke up in my bed. No dreams or anything."

"Dude, that sucks," Ty said to me, with Jaden nodding in agreement.

Mason approached me, and proceeded to give me a hug, squeezing me tight and ruffling my hair. He pulled me as close to him as our pads would allow. I felt the same pain and suffering from him that I had earlier experienced, and then, it quickly faded away, replaced by an amazing sense of power, love, and confidence.

"My hell lasted five," he said to me.

My mouth dropped open, and I stared at the Jets' leader. "You went through this last night *too*?" I asked.

"Different hellish experience, and it was actually a while ago, but yes," he said.

Damian sighed. "Mine was *six*," he declared.

"Mine too," admitted Billy.

"Three," Calvin joined in, holding up three fingers.

I couldn't believe any of what I was hearing. "Are you saying *all* of you have gone through this?" I asked the four team captains. They all nodded.

"Again, all at different times," Mason clarified, "but yes."

I looked around at my other teammates.

"Anyone else?" I asked, without an answer.

Billy gave me a hug as well. I couldn't help but reel back at the shock of him showing me affection, but I welcomed it. "Welcome to the club, Weston," he said.

"What club is that?" I asked.

"You'll find out," Damian said with a grin, giving me a quick hug too, "Calvin's fucking lucky he has you on his team now."

"Wait, so Scott going through this hell was a good thing?" asked Jaden.

"Depends on your perspective," said Damian.

Jacob rubbed my hair. "You come get me if you go through that again," he said, poking himself in the chest and looking into my eyes as his face turned serious, "Whatever reality you're in, I got your back."

I couldn't help but smile at his support. I said, "Thanks, Jacob."

"How do you feel about it now?" Calvin asked me.

"Relief that the worst is behind me," I replied, looking back at the team captains, "But, I also feel what I went through will be worth it, somehow."

"I hope I don't have to go through that," added Ryder Banks, "Fuck that." Many of the other boys agreed.

"I hope you don't either," I said.

"Some might, some might not," said Calvin, but he wouldn't say anything further on why he said that.

"Well, what the *fuck* happened last night then, Scott?" Ty asked, "Calvin came up to Jaden, Travis, and me and said you, Billy, and Jack had been knocked out for the night, and he needed help carrying you guys to your beds."

"Yeah, how did you know, Calvin?" I asked.

"Veronica called me and told me what happened," he replied.

I gulped.

"Everything?" I squeaked.

Calvin winked at me. "Only the important bits."

I felt a twinge of embarrassment.

Mason and Damian grinned, with Damian giving me a thumbs up, and Mason slapping and shaking my hand.

"They know too?" I asked.

"No secrets between team captains," said Mason, raising his eyebrows at Billy, who gave a grunt in return.

"Oh, tell us, Calvin!" demanded Ty.

Billy cut in, "You aren't a team captain, Green."

Ty frowned.

"Without having to go into too much detail," began Calvin, "Billy owned Jack, thought he'd own Scott, but got schooled instead."

Damian added with a grin, "Then, Scott became the luckiest guy here."

"How so?" asked Jaden.

"Yeah, what do you mean?" joined Ryder.

"You'll have to ask him," said the Rams' team captain.

All of the guys looked at me again. I blushed.

"But not now," said Calvin, "It's breakfast time and then our morning meetings. Let's go."

"Oh, what-the-fuck ever!" grumbled Ty.

Warmth spread from my heart as I gazed at my fellow football players, feeling the connection with each one of them, something I had missed so terribly.

"You *will* have to tell us *all* the details, Weston," said Billy before he walked off with the other team captains, "You owe it to me."

"Yeah, me too!" said Jack before catching up with Billy.

Ty placed a hand on my shoulder pads as we walked out of the gymnasium. "No secrets between Colt teammates, either!" he insisted.

"Yeah!" said Ryder, trailing behind us with Jimmy and Nicholas in tow.

"Or Warriors!" added Jaden, "You were one of us too, you know."

"I still am one of you," I corrected, "Just a different sub-team, is all."

I grabbed Ty's arm and slowed down, motioning for Jaden to do the same. We let the other guys go past us.

"Ty, you haven't told us what happened with you and Veronica," I said.

Ty grinned and fist bumped Jaden. "Dude, you missed it!" he began, "While you and Jack were out for the night, Jaden and I watched everything on my phone!"

I frowned. I wanted to see Ty get gassed.

"Did Veronica gas you?" I asked.

He nodded. "When I first walked into the room, yeah."

"She gassed you *before*?"

"Yup!"

"What happened then?"

"Woke up tied to the bed. Veronica had her way with me, like she did with Jaden." Ty closed his eyes, and his face beamed. "It felt *sooo* good."

"I bet," I grinned, "Then what?"

"Then she told me to go eat dinner. It zapped nearly all the energy from me, though. That's why I was so loopy in the cafeteria."

"Oh."

"Now it's your turn to spill the beans, Scott," said Jaden.

I winked at them, then started walking away, waving my hand. "See you around, Salario," I said.

"Huh?" exclaimed Jaden, but Ty caught on immediately.

"Asshole!" Ty called after me, "You think you can just walk away from me?"

"Ty..." whispered Jaden, but Ty just about screamed as he shouted out, "No one just 'walks away' from Scottie Salario! You hear me? You hear me, Cain? I'LL BE BACK!"

I stopped in my tracks and turned around to face him. In a macho, middle-eastern accent, I replied, "And Ih'll be waiting." Then, I gave him the finger and finished our little re-enactment. "Ahhshole."

"Oh, I get it now," said Jaden, chuckling.

Ty and I burst out laughing, and it took a few seconds before he was able to speak again. "You are so good at that accent!" he said.

"Thanks."

Our safety then shook a finger at me. "But you still owe us that story."

"After lunch, guys. I promise," I assured them. "Right now, I want to go see Coach King, to thank him for something. I'll catch up with you guys at the cafeteria."

Jaden and Ty waved, and I headed towards King's office. As I passed the nurse's office, I heard the coach's voice. The door was cracked open, and I decided to peek in. My jaw dropped; there wasn't only Coach King and Nurse Veronica in there, but Stephanie too.

"Well, speak of the devil," Coach King said as the three of them faced me. "Come on in, Scott."

Stephanie blushed.

chapter forty-four

Stephanie wore a turquoise, short-sleeved shirt and a pair of denim shorts. My heart began to pound as she glanced at me. She rubbed her forearm up and down, let out a small grin, and looked away as she said, "Hi, Scott."

I clasped a wrist, rubbing it with my thumb, and rested my arms below my belly. "Hi," I managed to say.

Coach King, who was sitting on a bed, and Nurse Veronica exchanged a glance and smiled. "Come on in, he said.

I stepped slowly into the room.

"Stephanie said she ran into you and your friends at the mall on Friday," said Veronica.

"Yeah," I nodded and looked over at Coach King.

"Did you need something?" he asked, tapping on his knees. His eyes had the same twinkle. I hoped he would know, or at least remember, the exchange between us in my dream. Having Nurse Veronica, and especially Stephanie, here made me pause. I thought I might come off as crazy to them.

"I heard you had an interesting dream last night," he prompted. I furrowed my brow. Did that mean he didn't remember?

"You *heard*?" I asked.

He nodded, still tapping lightly on his knees.

"From whom?"

"Calvin Williams," he replied. "He was just in here. I'm surprised you didn't pass him in the hall."

Veronica must have seen the confusion on my face, because she placed both her hands on Stephanie's shoulders and said, "Stephanie was kind enough to drop off some of Calvin's things he had forgotten at home. When Calvin came in to pick them up, I invited them to stay for a chat."

Coach King stood up and added, "The conversation turned to you."

I felt my cheeks turning hot.

"Aw, he's blushing!" teased Veronica.

Coach King placed his hand on my shoulder pads. I relaxed, sensing a calming energy flow from him. I turned my head and looked up into his eyes, and I could immediately feel his love for me, which swelled in my heart. My gratitude flowed back to him. He responded by turning me around and hugging me, using one hand to tousle my hair. I wrapped my arms around him and closed my eyes. At that moment, I felt myself become Coach King again, and I pulled the boy's head to my chest; I was on the verge of tears for what this kid went through. I had such gratitude and pride for him. As I stepped back, I found myself back as Scott, looking up at King's smiling face.

Maybe I was feeling the effects of being one with Coach King, but when I turned around to face the girls, I sensed a oneness enveloping the two of them as well, carrying a loving energy exactly like the one I felt at the end of my long dream last night. Was the Oneness from that experience the same as the one now surrounding Veronica and Stephanie? The nurse still had her

hands on the girl's shoulders, and both were smiling at us. I wondered if they were they aware of their connection with each other.

"Coach King and Calvin hugged too," said Stephanie. "I didn't realize you boys were so close to your coach."

"And each other as well," I said. "We Panther football players are as one soul." I thumbed over to King. "With him," I added. I waited for Stephanie's reaction.

She raised an eyebrow. "What?" she said. "You can't be saying all of you are really Coach King. You're separate people, Scott."

So much more for Stephanie's awareness. I sighed, "No, what I mean is-"

Veronica and the coach broke into a laugh.

"Let's not confuse her, okay?" King suggested.

"Sorry, I'm not good at explaining this," I admitted with a shrug.

"You look really strong, Scott," Stephanie said suddenly, staring at my arms, "much stronger than last week."

That comment made the reservations I had about being here with her melt away. I trotted over to her with a grin and flexed my biceps.

She reached out and felt them, giving them a squeeze. My eyes widened at her touch, my heart began to pound again, and my palms started to sweat. I relished the scent of her apple body wash, a welcomed break from the stench of boy body odor I'd been around the last day or so.

"My brother's look much bigger, though."

I grumbled. Talk about ruining the mood.

Then, she added, taunting me, "Almost twice as yours."

I heaved a sigh. "Calvin is *not* twice my size!"

Coach King stifled a laugh.

Stephanie looked over my body and crinkled her nose. "But I will say you both look just as filthy, and smell just as bad," she continued. "I couldn't stand being close to Calvin." Stephanie, however, made no effort to step away from *me*.

"You're lucky," I replied, folding my arms. "We haven't even been outside in the heat today yet."

I expected an 'ew!' from her, but instead, she continued scanning my body. "Calvin said you guys sleep in your football uniforms."

"Yep," I confirmed.

"I'll never understand boys," she moaned. Stephanie looked up at my face. Without a word, she reached up and ran her fingers down my cheek, and then, looked at the dirt that had rubbed off. My arms dropped to my side. Something came over me, and I found myself leaning close to her face. I closed my eyes and gave her a soft, light kiss on her lips. I backed away and opened my eyes to find her staring back at me.

"Oh, that's so adorable," squealed Veronica.

The realization of what I just did struck me, along with the thought of the pounding Calvin would give me if he were to find out. I figured I should probably leave before anything else happened. I rubbed the back of my neck and stammered, "I uh... I think I need to go eat breakfast before it's too late."

Stephanie looked away, her cheeks turning red. When I turned to leave, Coach King gave me a soft clap and a thumbs up.

"Why don't you invite her to watch your game tonight, Scott?" suggested Veronica.

I gave a quick, worried glance at Veronica before looking over at Coach.

"I thought games at camp were for football players only," I replied, thankfully remembering a rule I had read in our camp handout.

"Not games between different schools," said Coach with a shake of his head. "You'll see. They draw a *lot* of spectators."

"Maybe... Maybe Calvin should invite her." I knew I sounded like a complete weenie.

Veronica confirmed exactly that. "Stop being such a weenie," she said with a slight grin.

Stephanie folded her arms. "I don't need my brother's permission to go," she said, frowning.

Coach motioned with his hands for me to invite her. I sighed – Calvin's beating be damned then. I looked at Stephanie and asked, "Would you like to go to the game?"

"I'd actually love to," she said, the excitement evident in her voice. "And don't worry, Scott. I'll invite Jean to distract Calvin." The two adults shared another laugh.

"Calvin likes Jean back?" I asked.

"Calvin doesn't notice girls, but that doesn't mean he can't be bothered by them." She winked at me. King nearly busted a gut with a howling cackle.

I smiled, feeling warmth in my heart for her. "Okay, then. See you tonight. Cheer us on!"

"I will!" she said.

Veronica hugged me, and I started getting hard. At least my protective cup would hide it from Stephanie and Coach King.

"Bye, Sweetie!" said the nurse.

I high-fived Coach on my way out. "Way go to, buddy," he whispered to me.

chapter forty-five

At the cafeteria, my fellow Colts kept congratulating me on besting Billy, even though most of them didn't exactly know what had actually happened. When asked about being 'the luckiest guy here', I repeated what I had told Ty and Jaden - I'd spill everything after lunch.

Toward the end of breakfast, Calvin said to me, "Ty said you met with Coach King."

"Um, yes," I replied, feeling my chest tense up.

"Was he still in the nurse's office?"

I nodded.

Then, his eyes narrowed. "Was my sister still there?"

Ty glanced over at me, a big grin on his face. "Yes, was she?" the fucker asked. I gave him the evil eye, which only made him chuckle more.

Calvin would find out if I lied, and then, the lap-running and ass-kicking would commence. Holding my breath, keeping eye contact to avoid seeming guilty of something, I replied, "Yes." I couldn't leave it at that, though; I had to give him something else, so he wouldn't suspect what might have happened. As always, I

could count on my brain to provide me with just the perfect follow-up. "I invited her to our game," I added.

"Good," he nodded. "I actually forgot to do that."

Calvin then started talking to our squad leaders about something, and I was able to breathe again. Ty elbowed me in the ribs and whispered. "You are a fucking master," he said. "But you can't fool me. Fess up after lunch."

I grinned at him.

The teamboys showed up in time for our meeting, full of excitement and energy, ready to spend the day with us. Calvin reviewed the Riverwood plays at our meeting and said that we were to practice them all morning and afternoon.

The morning practice flew past, and I found myself back in my game. Calvin first put me on offense, as halfback, against the defense scout team. After that, he had me on defense against the scout offense. I loved every minute of all of it, lapping it all up. *This* was what being a football player was all about. The bond that I felt with my teammates strengthened, as did the energy I had gathered over the past few days. It wasn't just me either; our entire sub-team, the Colts, came together like never before.

I hit the restroom during break, and on my way back, I passed the door to the locker rooms; a sudden urge to go in seized me. Memories of the altercations that had occurred in the other reality came flooding back as I entered. I glanced at Jack's and Jaden's lockers, where we had our fight. I sighed in relief, for that fight had happened in the other dreadful reality. Nevertheless, the pain from those experiences kept coming back. When I looked over at my own locker, images of me crying out on the floor in front of it flitted through my mind.

My heart burst open, pouring out love to this desolate self of mine in front of me. I closed my eyes and connected my heart with

his. I told this other self that it would be okay – that he was in a dream; that it would soon be over.

I opened my eyes and walked over to a mirror. I gazed at the muddy, handsome boy smiling back at me from behind his facemask; I resembled an ancient warrior, armor and body covered in dirt, grass stains, and perspiration. A wave of joy spread through me, and I passed it on to that hurt self of mine, cocooning his entire being. *"We're home,"* I told him. I felt a wave of gratitude flow back from him, and he gave himself over to me, resting within my heart and taking that ball of pain with him. He placed it within us, and we both became as one. His pains became my pains; my joy became his joy.

I took one last look at myself before turning to leave, just as the door swung open. Billy stepped inside. "There you are," he said, removing his helmet. "Been looking for you."

He wiped the sweat pouring from his head and face. He closed his eyes as the cool air hit him. "Ah, yeah," he murmured, "this is nice."

I smiled as he walked over to me. "Hey, Billy," I said, "What's up?"

He smiled back. "Whatcha doing in here?"

"Just taking care of something."

He stared at me for a few seconds before he laughed. "Jerking off in front of a mirror?"

I raised my eyebrows, in shock at the new depths of his vulgarity. I decided to run with it. Pointing to my crotch, I asked him, "Do you see my dick out?"

He shrugged and replied, "Maybe you've just finished."

After he looked around where I was standing, he concluded, "But I don't see your cum anywhere, or in your hands, so maybe not."

"You seem to know an awful lot about this," I taunted back.

He pointed to me, saying, "You'd be jerking off in front of a mirror too if you looked as good as I do." Billy ended his sentence by thumbing to himself.

"You kiss your mother with that mouth?" I jeered.

"No, just yours," he snapped back.

We shared a laugh, and Billy rubbed my hair. Then, he sat down on the bench and motioned for me to join him. "Take off your helmet, so I can see your face better," he requested.

Strange request, I thought. I removed my helmet and wiped my head, face, and neck with my towel.

When I sat down, Billy looked at me and said, "I spoke to Calvin, and he agreed that I should be the one to mentor you."

I grunted. Seriously? He had already traded me, and I really didn't want to go back to the Warriors, even though Jack and Jaden were still on his team.

"What do you mean?" I asked, "I'm already on the Colts! Calvin, Bryce, and Derek already-"

"No, no, no... shut up for a second, will you?"

I frowned.

"I should probably start over."

He looked away and closed his eyes. Then, he took a deep breath, turned to me, and opened them again. "When a piece of Ourself – known here as Coach King – goes through an awakening experience like you did last night, he's then assigned a mentor, another awakened boy to guide him. And no, it doesn't matter what sub-team they're on. Middle Schools. Football. Sub-teams. They're all just a part of this grand illusion. Everything here is for nurturing our individual selves and the love and bond we souls, as football players, have for one another. All of this, in turn, strengthens Ourself. You're with me so far?"

I couldn't help raising my eyebrows at this conversation. I still never expected Billy, of all people, to have gone through an awakening experience and talk about spiritual connections, of all things, at such a deep level. Less than thirty seconds ago, he was talking about masturbating in front of a mirror.

Billy waved a hand in front of my face. "As awakened as I am, Weston," he said, "I'm still not telepathic."

I blinked a few times and replied, "Oh, sorry. Yeah, I'm pretty much with you, for the most part."

"Okay, good. As your mentor, I will help you through any more rough patches that you go through and will help you find answers to all those questions. I'm sure you'll have a zillion of them."

That 'rough patch' part didn't sound good, and I frowned. I felt my good mood taking a dive. "You mean, I'm gonna go through shit worse than what I've just been through?" I asked in exasperation.

"No," Billy shook his head, "I firmly believe that was the worst of it all, at least the worst of it you'll have to face by yourself."

That was a relief. I rubbed my forehead and asked, "Well, what kind of 'rough patches' then?"

He placed a hand on my shoulder. "You just came out of a bad one," he continued, "So I'm not going to speculate, okay? Just know that I'm here for you, as are the other team captains. So, you aren't alone in this."

"But why you as a mentor then?"

He grinned and said, "You can figure that one out yourself, Weston."

I rolled my eyes at his blatant disregard for what he had just said about being there for me.

"I never said I'd answer the questions *for* you!" he blurted out, "I said I'm a mentor who'll *guide* you."

"So, guide me!"

Billy cracked his knuckles, then replied, "Well, you've already started kind of doing this on your own, it seems. But I'll tell you Rule Number One anyway – always take a trip inside your heart first, before asking me or the other team captains for help, okay? Learn to trust your heart."

I nodded, and he said, "If that doesn't work, we'll *tackle* it together." He winked as he said that. I laughed at his football pun, and a warm, joyful feeling flowed from my heart. I felt grateful for him.

"Thanks, Billy," I said.

"Yup," he said, standing up.

"So, we're all still middle school player boys though, right?"

As he fastened his helmet, he said, "Really? You have to ask *that*? Look around you! Smell yourself."

"I mean, I know we are now... but can this awakening change that in any way? I don't really know what to trust anymore."

Billy looked down at me, impatience on his face. "What the fuck did I *just* tell you was Rule Number One, Weston?" he asked, "I know you are *not* that slow a learner."

"I guess patience isn't a virtue mentors require," I grunted back.

"No," he quickly replied, "it isn't." The Warriors leader then thumbed toward the exit. "Now let's go. We're going to have a quick off-rails scrimmage, with one team acting as the Riverwood Wolves. You're up against the Rams."

There was something I wanted to ask him, so I called out, "Billy?"

"What?" he sighed.

"You had sex with Veronica, right?"

Billy looked surprised at my question, but answered simply, "Yup."

"Did you, by any chance, feel at one with yourself during that?"

He gave me the classic Billy Smirk and rubbed my hair. "Oh, like never before, my good man."

"Yeah, me, too," I admitted, and he nodded.

"Billy?"

"*What*, Weston?" he grunted, slamming a fist into his other hand. "We have a game to get to!"

"Right before I awoke from that hellish reality, I felt Nurse Veronica, my mom, and even Stephanie Williams as a sort of separate soul from all of us boys." I pointed between Billy and myself. "And yet, that soul seemed really close to us. I saw it again today when I ran into Nurse Veronica and Stephanie in the nurse's office."

That made him raise his eyebrows. "What was Calvin's sister doing there?" he asked before pointing to me. "And what were *you* doing in the nurse's office with them?"

Oh, shit. Me and my big mouth. I held my palms up and shook my head, saying, "Nothing!"

He banked his head and squinted his eyes. After peering at me for a few seconds, the Warriors' team captain scratched his neck and asked, "Are you lying to me?"

I let out a frustrated sigh and exclaimed, "Come on, Billy!"

"Sounds like words from a guilty boy to me," he said with a smirk. "But don't worry, being your mentor, I won't push it."

"Thanks, Billy," I said, a sigh of relief escaping me.

"Uh-huh." Billy pointed to the exit. "Now move it!"

I grinned as I put on my helmet, mumbling, "I'll... I'll be right out. I promise."